Changing Paths

Yvonne Aburrow

First Printing, 2023

Book design by keifel a. agostini

Cover design by keifel a. agostini

ISBN: 978-1-7347422-6-8

1000voltpress.com
changingpathsresources.ca

Disclaimer

This publication is meant as a source of valuable information for the reader, however it is not meant as a substitute for direct expert assistance for issues arising from religious trauma or spiritual abuse. If such a level of assistance is required, the services of a competent professional should be sought.

This book is dedicated, with love, to my parents,
Joyce and Keith.

"Changing Paths by Yvonne Aburrow is an incredibly helpful guide for anyone unhappy in their current religious or faith tradition. In their introduction, the author states that, 'The goal of the book is to help you decide your own path by guiding you through the perils and pitfalls of the terrain, and asking questions to help you deepen your understanding of the reasons for your desire to change paths.'

This promise is fulfilled.

The section on Leaving Your Current Tradition covers many of the common reasons for dissatisfaction with or unhappiness about your current tradition and takes the reader through the process of sitting with their discomfort, so that they are ready to leave.

The second section is Joining Paganism, in which Aburrow describes the slow process of identifying your new spiritual home and gradually settling into it. The process could equally be applied to other faith traditions. The book also brings together several testimonies from people who have found a home in Paganism after leaving other traditions. Each chapter includes some questions for journaling with, and a short meditation. If I were on this path, I would have found this book most reassuring and helpful. It fulfills its stated aim 'as a guide through the difficult terrain of changing paths' and I would recommend it to anyone in this situation."

—Sue Woolley,
Author and Unitarian minister (UK)
forloveofwords.com

"Changing Paths fills an important need in the Pagan community: a guidebook for how, when, and why to change your path, whether that's within or outside Paganism. Compassionate and personal, this guide offers helpful journaling prompts and meditations for the reader to find the path that is right for them based on where they are in their own spiritual journey, as well as a handy list of red flags to watch out for when considering joining a spiritual community."

—Enfys J. Book, author of *Queer Qabala:*
Nonbinary, Genderfluid, Omnisexual Mysticism & Magick
majorarqueerna.com

"Changing Paths by Yvonne Aburrow is a down to earth and extremely practical book on the complexities and intricacies of switching belief systems. Yvonne's words will leave you feeling deeply seen, especially if changing religions is something you have already encountered in your life. If you have not yet made the switch, it will provide you with the framework and steps necessary to make those changes for your future if need be.

Yvonne's tone is gentle, understanding and to the point which makes this book a refreshing change to others that try to tackle the dense topic of personal religion. Yvonne's words are kind and accepting of all beliefs making this a book that is truly for everyone. I especially love how they sum up the best way to know if your chosen religion is beneficial to you or not: "If religion or spirituality makes us more disconnected from other people, less compassionate, less rational, then it is harmful. If on the other hand, it enables us to feel more love and compassion for others, and be better able to cope with the sorrowful aspects of life, then it is helpful."

Covering topics such as religious trauma, gender and sexuality acceptance within various religions, the religious issues with patriarchy and opposite issues associated with a matriarchy and following it all up with a rich guide on joining or converting to paganism in any of its many forms. Changing Paths is a well-researched and easy to absorb book filled with wisdom and practical advice on what can often be a difficult and confusing topic for many people.

I truly wish I had a copy of this book during my own transition from evangelical Christianity to Witchcraft. It would have saved me a lot of frustration, confusion and ill-informed anger by providing the guidance and prompts required of a shift that big."

—Hana the Suburban Witch,
host of the *Witch Talks Podcast*.
www.suburbanwitchery.com

"The Greek pre-Socratic philosopher Heraclitus of Ephesus once insisted that 'panta rhei' (everything flows) and many centuries later the Roman poet Lucretius, echoing this insight, wrote that 'omnia migrant' (everything moves). Both of them in their very different ways understood something that contemporary physics in our own age is also now fully recognizing, namely, that all things are always-already flowing and fluxing and, therefore, always-already 'becoming.' In other words, each of them is reminding us that what it is for anything to be the thing it is is to be something in motion. But so much of religion—especially the prevalent kinds found within British and North American culture—finds movement, flow, flux and becoming frightening because it cuts against the idea that that which is of ultimate value is something which, as the writer of the Letter of James once put it, must be without 'alternation or shadow of change' (1:17).

In thoughtfully and insightfully tracing their own moving, flowing and fluxing movements of becoming the kind of religious person they are today, Yvonne Aburrow offers us a helpful book which opens up to the sympathetic reader many practical ways by which they, too, might come to understand and gently embody the truth that all paths are always-already changing paths, and that changing paths may well turn out to be the most fundamental and authentic way of being religious in our own, or any, age."

—Andrew James Brown, Minister
Cambridge Unitarian Church (UK)
www.cambridgeunitarian.org
andrewjbrown.blogspot.com

TABLE OF CONTENTS

Foreword

It was R.E.M. who gave us the enigmatic song "Losing My Religion" and, while it's using the word religion as a metaphor, it does speak to me of my own spiritual journey. "Losing my religion" is a Southern expression meaning "losing my sh*t" and, you could say, becoming disconnected from oneself.

The journey from one religion to another (or not) can be a disorientating process. I am qualified to say that because I still feel a deep sense of disconnection and disorientation. I trained for five years to follow my calling/dream to become an Anglican (Episcopalian) priest. It was blood, sweat, and tears, but was also the most exciting and rewarding experience. I ended up serving the Church of England for a little over a decade in two different priestly roles.

In many ways, however, I was a square peg in a round hole. It's not the place to describe my departure, suffice to say that around 15 years ago I quit!

Experiencing, on the one hand, the shell-shockingly frightening feeling of loss, as well as, on the other hand, an immense freedom, I quickly found myself jumping headfirst into raw and wild British Paganism. I had long been fascinated with the world of earth-based paths but had never really had the permission to explore them in an open and public way.

Since those days I have tried to find my place, sometimes moving further into Paganism, other times moving back toward Christianity, and more often, trying to harmonize them. I have not managed to yet!

Looking back at this destructive/constructive process, I can say that Yvonne's book would have been an immense comfort and soul guide were it around back then. It describes and illuminates many (most) of the feelings and experiences that we "spiritual travelers" go through when our paths take us onto new highways.

This book is beautifully written, expertly researched and wisdom-filled.

With much personal honesty and many helpful anecdotes, Yvonne takes you on an exciting journey that cannot fail to offer some sense of guidance and companionship.

They go "back to basics" with an exploration into the original meaning of the word religion. And they touch on all of the most important current issues that hundreds of thousands of spiritual seekers face, to do with abuse etc.

They also speak to the LGBTQ2SIA world, which is currently under newer and crueler forms of attacks from various kinds of religious adherents.

You will find many helpful resources here, for your devotional and spiritual life too.

In short, this book is a treasure trove for the spiritual wanderer and the religious troubadour.

Mark Townsend

Mark is an author, priest, stage magician, celebrant, Dudeist, Christian, Druid, and author of several books, including *The Path of The Blue Raven, Jesus Through Pagan Eyes: Bridging Neopagan Perspectives with a Progressive Vision of Christ,* and *Diary of a Heretic: The Pagan Adventures of a Christian Priest.*

www.marktownsendministry.co.uk

Introduction

> I will not follow where the path may lead, but I will
> go where there is no path, and I will leave a trail.
>
> —Muriel Strode, *Wind-Wafted Wild Flowers.*[1]

Are you entering Paganism, leaving Paganism, or changing traditions within it? How do you explain your new path[2] to friends, family, former co-religionists, and yourself? How do you extricate yourself from your previous tradition and its associated ideas? How do you unpack your complex feelings about your path and why you are changing direction?

If you have ever changed paths or considered changing paths, this book is for you. It is a guide for people who have entered Paganism from another tradition, people leaving Paganism for another tradition or none, and people changing from one tradition to another within Paganism.

Most Pagans were not born and brought up as Pagans but joined from another tradition, whether that was atheism or another religion. Many people see Paganism through the lens of the mainstream view of what religion is, much of which does not apply to Paganism. Many of us have lingering trauma from our previous religious traditions because of unethical behaviors or beliefs espoused by those traditions.

Some people encounter similar structures and beliefs within Pagan traditions and are disappointed. Some people re-evaluate their original tradition and seek to return to it. Some people are afraid that the fundamentalist beliefs that they were taught might be true.

---

1 Strode, Muriel (1903) "Wind-Wafted Wild Flowers," *The Open Court*: Vol. 1903 : Issue 8, Article 5. Available at: https://opensiuc.lib.siu.edu/ocj/vol1903/iss8/5 The quote is widely misattributed to Ralph Waldo Emerson, but it was first written by Muriel Strode (see www.quotegarden.com/blog-who-is-muriel-strode.html)
2 Pagans tend to refer to religions as "paths" or "traditions," rather than as "faiths" or "religions." I have used the terms interchangeably in this book.

I have written this book because I have lived through the experience of changing paths. I was brought up in the exclusive Plymouth Brethren (a more extreme version of the sect that Aleister Crowley was raised in). My parents left the Plymouth Brethren when I was nine years old, and initially got involved in something similar, then in a more mainstream evangelical church, and then in a charismatic church for a while. When I was about fourteen, I joined a local church that had a charismatic group within it. I left both that church and the charismatic group when one of my best friends came out as gay and the people in the group said that God would reject him if he was actively gay. I had been having doubts before that, but it was the catalyst that finally propelled me out of that group and out of Christianity. I became a Pagan in 1985 and got initiated into Gardnerian Wicca in 1991. At this point, I was an atheist Pagan with occasional forays into polytheism. However, I still had an underlying fear that the fundamentalist beliefs that I had been taught were true. I buried this fear beneath a volcano of anger, which would occasionally erupt when Christianity was mentioned. Then, in 2006, I decided to do a master's degree in contemporary religions and spiritualities. While I was studying that, I became interested in forms of Christianity that embraced and welcomed LGBTQ+ people. I was also attending interfaith events, where a lot of people had embraced the view that all religions are different perspectives on the same mountain. At the same time, I had become disgruntled with several aspects of Paganism, and thought that perhaps Christianity would be better. Initially I joined an Orthodox church but the church's attitudes and many of the congregation were homophobic (though the leaders of that particular church were not), and I lasted two months before trying Unitarianism,[3] which is LGBTQ-inclusive and where it is acceptable to be Pagan and have an interest in mystical Christianity. My Unitarian phase lasted for three years, but eventually I realized that I personally found it too difficult to follow

---

3   This was while I was still living in the UK, where the religion is called Unitarianism (not Unitarian Universalism as in the USA) because of its unique history.

two different traditions. I decided to focus exclusively on Wicca, and push for making Wiccan ritual more LGBTQ-inclusive. Although my temporary change of paths was painful, at least it cleared out and dealt with the lurking fear at the bottom of my psyche. Since returning full-time to Wicca, I have been deepening my personal practice of Wicca and have written three books on making Wicca more inclusive.

While I was going through this period of upheaval, it was hard for others to imagine my mental state, as they were not in the same headspace as I was, and there did not seem to be any books that helped me to navigate the tidal wave of emotions and fears involved in the process. There were people (Pagan and Christian) who helped me by asking questions and trying to help me to remain open to all possibilities. But it was hard for the Christians to understand the Pagan worldview; and it was hard for people (either Pagans or Christians) who were not brought up in a fundamentalist or evangelical church to understand the issues experienced by someone with residual trauma from fundamentalism. My parents did their best to shield me from the worst effects of the Plymouth Brethren; however, I absorbed a lot of bad ideas from the charismatic Christian group that I joined as a teenager.

This book is intended as a guide through the difficult terrain of changing paths. Whether you decide to stay on the path you are on, or switch to a different one, is up to you. The goal of the book is to help you decide your own path by guiding you through the perils and pitfalls of the terrain, and by asking questions to help you deepen your understanding of the reasons for your desire to change paths.

I found it difficult to write publicly about my experience of changing paths for a long time, because I needed to get some perspective on it. I think this is also true for other people. Several people whom I asked for contributions to the personal stories section of the book said that their experience was still too new and too raw for them to write about it for others to read. I was telling my friend

3

Karl Stewart about this, and he commented, "In order to understand your pain, you have to understand your healing." In other words, you need to have found your way out of the labyrinth before you can get enough perspective to write about it. I hope that this book will make the process of healing and understanding your pain easier by acting as a companion on the path.

Each section of the book explores a different aspect of changing paths: leaving a religion, evaluating your reasons for leaving, the conversion process, deciding which tradition is right for you, arriving in a new tradition, dealing with unexamined baggage, changing traditions within Paganism, understanding the shadow side of a community, returning to a spiritual community, and what makes people stay, and it includes questions, reflections, and exercises, and it also offers firsthand accounts from people who have changed paths.

This book will help you to navigate all the issues that arise from changing paths. It will help you to evaluate whether you want to stay in or leave your current tradition. It explores what religions are and how to evaluate and compare them. It will also be of interest to people seeking to understand the process of changing from one tradition to another because they have a friend going through that process. Although this book is mainly aimed at people entering or leaving Paganism or switching to another Pagan tradition, it is also relevant to people switching between other traditions.

Each chapter includes journal prompts, questions for reflection, and exercises to help you navigate the terrain. There is also a list of further reading and a bibliography for any issues you want to follow up on. I hope that your journey will be less bumpy, and your landing softer, as a result of the signposts offered here.

Before we can explore the various paths on offer, it helps to figure out what religion is. A religion is not just a set of beliefs, it is a lifestyle, a culture, a set of values, a discourse, and a group of people.

4

The word religion comes either from the Latin word religio, meaning to connect or to bind, or from the Latin word relego, meaning to re-read. All of these possible meanings are relevant, as in many ways, religions both connect us to the Divine (however we conceive of that concept) and bind us to a community, a set of values, and a worldview. Many religious traditions like to claim that they are not a religion, seeing the concept of religion as excessively legalistic or bound by tradition; but at its best, religion can be a joyful sense of connection with like-minded people who share a set of symbols and an encounter with the mysteries.

Leaving a religion or worldview rarely happens all at once. It happens gradually, rather like the unraveling of a knitted garment. There are many reasons for leaving a religion, and while there may be one reason that stands out above all the rest or a defining moment when you decided to quit, there are usually multiple reasons for leaving. Often it is because its worldview does not work for you any more. What does it mean to leave a religion? How do you remain friends with people in the religion you are leaving behind? What if you are changing paths but your spouse and family are not?

Often, the pathfinder is asking themselves the question, "Should I stay or should I go?" for quite a while before they actually leave. This book will show you how to evaluate your reasons for leaving. Can you change the community from within, or are the obstacles you face unmovable? Are you lending legitimacy to an oppressive system by staying? What helpful features exist in the tradition you are leaving? Can you find replacements for them after you leave?

The process of changing your beliefs, values, and religious community can be a process of huge upheaval and turmoil. The experience of arriving in the Pagan community, however, is often referred to as a homecoming and rarely as a conversion. This is because of the sense of having found a community of shared values and practices that feels like a good fit. But this feeling might not happen straight away—you might need to explore a bit before finding a part of the Pagan community (which is really more than one community, these days) that feels like home to you.

It takes time to decide which tradition is right for you. Many people explore a variety of paths before settling in to follow one path. There may be a period of pursuing two paths in parallel. Selecting the path that is right for you may involve a fair amount of reading and research. One of the great things about the Pagan community is that people are used to the idea of people practicing more than one tradition or a syncretized version of two or more traditions.

On arriving in a new community, people often want to see it as ideal, but every community has its shadow side. The new spiritual community has its own worldview, values, culture, and beliefs (some of which may be unwritten or unconscious). Learning to navigate in a strange new community can be difficult—even in the "honeymoon" phase when it all seems ideal.

Changing your religious or spiritual path can result in unexamined spiritual, emotional, and intellectual baggage from your previous tradition, which can cause all sorts of issues from depression to anger. We all need to unpack and deal with our unexamined baggage. The Tarot card of the fool traditionally depicts a small dog leaping up and biting the Fool's butt. The dog can be seen as representing material from the unconscious trying to attract the attention of the conscious mind.

It can also be problematic when we bring this unexamined baggage to the Pagan community and expect Pagan traditions to look like the ones that we left. Many people, unless they have engaged in a very thorough deconstruction and reconstruction of their beliefs and attitudes, bring some of their views and expectations from their previous tradition into their new one.

Changing paths within Paganism can also be tricky. It may not be as dramatic as switching between two completely different traditions, but it shares some of the same features: a change of worldview, a sense of disenchantment with the tradition that you are leaving, and a negotiation between the old paradigm and the new one.

We all have different perspectives on the divine and/or deities, and everyone's journey is different. My mountain is not your mountain, and that is okay.[4] Interfaith dialogue can have the result that participants see all religions as different perspectives on the same mountain and become attracted to a more universalist or perennialist view of religious traditions. However, different religions do have distinct perspectives and are particular to the culture from which they emerged. Although there are shared features among many spiritual traditions, it helps to be grounded in the particularities of one tradition. When a religion is exclusivist in its world view, this is sometimes called the scandal of particularity, because in that situation, the particularity can be weaponized to disparage other religions. But particularity can just mean adhering to one particular mythology or set of symbols while respecting other mythologies and symbol systems as equally valid.

Returning to a spiritual community that you left can be a time of readjustment. Sometimes people leave a spiritual tradition and return to it, usually because they had a spiritual wobble. That is why I always say, don't bang the door on your way out—because you might want to come back.

Once you have settled on a chosen community, staying in it can also be a challenge. Once the honeymoon period has worn off, what makes us stay in a new religious tradition? How do we resolve the conflicts we had with it in the first place? How do we get to grips with the fact that all religious communities have their internal divisions, and often contain people whose values are diametrically opposed to our own? Even if you leave religion altogether, you will encounter these difficulties in every community, whether it is your local pub or a roomful of atheists.

---

4   Yvonne Aburrow (2014), "Your mountain is not my mountain and that's just fine." *Dowsing for Divinity.* https://dowsingfordivinity. com/2014/03/11/mountains/

In the end, after all this upheaval, we have to get on with the business of living. We cannot live on the rarefied heights of spiritual experience all the time; other less intense experiences are available. Sometimes we need the steadying experience of being in community with others and doing comforting everyday things. Those are also true and real and valuable. We do not always need to hack our own path up the mountain; we can grasp the handholds left by others along the way.

Part One:
Leaving Your Current Tradition

Woman walking away from the camera down a snowy sidewalk.
Undated negative scan. (Simple Insomnia/Flickr)

Chapter 1.
What is religion?

Religion is not something separate and apart from
ordinary life. It is life—life of every kind viewed
from the standpoint of meaning and purpose: life
lived in the fuller awareness of its human quality
and spiritual significance.

—Arthur Powell Davies

Some of my favorite religious experiences relate to darkness and
candlelight. In the 1980s, I attended a midnight church service on
Christmas Eve. The church was dark and hushed, and the only
light came from the candles. I recall a sense of peace, and wonder,
and deep joy (not so much from the theme of the service as from
the candlelight in the darkness, glinting off the polished wood of the
pews and the brass fittings in the church).

I have been practicing Wicca since 1991, and now candlelight
in the darkness is a regular part of my religious experience, but it
never fails to create that sense of wonder. I have also always been
drawn to the Moon and the stars. I remember once, as a child,
standing outside in the street looking up at the stars and seeing the
constellation of Orion and looking at the Moon gazing down on the
Earth.

Darkness is not a negative thing in Pagan religions, nor in other
mystical traditions. Darkness is the source of dreams and mysteries,
the deep well of the unconscious. It is also a symbol of the Divine
Feminine. There are very few experiences of darkness and the Divine
Feminine available in Protestant Christianity, which is one of the
reasons I found it disappointing.

When we seek out new religious experiences, or find that there is something missing in our spiritual lives, it is because the discourse we inhabit (the system of connotations and denotations, and the experiences that are permissible in a framework) places restrictions on what we can do, think, and feel.

❀⊱•°•❀•°•⊰❀

A religion is a set of shared practices, values, and narratives that make the world meaningful for its adherents.[5] Religions usually have a set of practices that are designed to facilitate a sense of connection with the numinous (the mysterious other that some call the divine) and with fellow adherents of the religion. Most of the world's religions are not focused on shared beliefs in the same way as Christianity, but on a shared set of practices, and more esoteric religions are gathered around a shared experience of the numinous, or of mystery. Even those religions that have a foundational text are in dialogue around their traditions and beliefs. A religion is also the community of people who adhere to it, however tenuously. Some writers have asserted that since it is hard to define religion in such a way as to include all the different versions of it, the word is essentially meaningless; but since people know what they mean when they say the word, even if they do not all agree on which traditions count as religion and which do not, we can probably say with some certainty that if it looks like a religion, smells like a religion, and sounds like a religion, it probably is a religion.

The word religion may be derived from the Latin word religare, to reconnect, or to bind; or it may be derived from relego, to re-read. I like the connotations of reconnection, as it implies compassion and connection—both to other people and to the divine. Binding can be seen as a negative connotation, but it can also be seen as providing security and safety (as in a safety harness or the joining of hands in a circle). The connotation of re-reading implies living an examined

---

5   Yvonne Aburrow (2010), "What is liberal religion?" *The Stroppy Rabbit.* https://stroppyrabbit.blogspot.com/2010/07/what-is-liberal-religion.html

life, the interpretation of experience, and the pursuit of knowledge. It also relates to one particular person's conversion experience. He saw a Bible and heard the words, Tolle et lego (Take it and read). This implies that revelation can only happen through reading, and not from experience. The experience of reading can be powerful and revelatory, but we often respond to the contents of a book because they resonate with our experience of the world. Many people like to contrast religion with spirituality, implying that spirituality is freer and easier, but there are many issues with spirituality. Many opportunities for spiritual abuse occur in spiritual settings, so let the buyer beware. Groups that use the word spiritual instead of religious to describe themselves also have a discourse within which certain things are not permissible to think or do.

Melissa and James Griffith[6] characterize spirituality as "a commitment to choose, as the primary context for understanding and acting, one's relatedness with all that is." They note that spirituality places relationships at the center of awareness, whether those are interpersonal relationships with other people or intrapersonal relationships with the Divine or other spiritual beings. They contrast spirituality with the psychological domain, which is about how the self is organized in terms of intentions, choices, plans, desires, and behaviors, and the physiological domain, which is focused on a person's relationship with their body. They describe religion as "a cultural codification of important spiritual metaphors, narratives, beliefs, rituals, social practices and forms of community among a particular people that provides methods for attaining spirituality." The Griffiths' definition of spirituality as primarily about relationships feeds into their view of religion as something that happens in a community, where shared meanings emerge from a community of practice.

---

6   James L. Griffith and Melissa Elliott Griffith (2002), *Encountering the Sacred in Psychotherapy: How to Talk with People about their Spiritual Lives.* New York: Guilford Press.

In evaluating a particular person's relationship with religion and spirituality, James and Melissa Griffith ask whether it is helpful or harmful. Does it expand the person's sense of connection with all that is, their circle of love and compassion? Does it provide reassurance and a sense of meaning? Or does it close down the possibility of love and connectedness, estrange the person from people outside their religious or spiritual circles, and make them fearful and bigoted?

Variations within religions

Even in traditions that have codified beliefs that their adherents are supposed to subscribe to, individual interpretations of their creeds can and do vary considerably. If you start an interfaith dialogue with any type of Christian, you are likely to encounter many interpretations of their tradition, even within the same denomination. For example, there are seventeen different views of the doctrine of atonement, and many other doctrines have other variations. The notion of a single unified "truth" that all Christians adhere to starts to look pretty shaky, once you look at the history of theological disputes within Christianity.[7] In practice, individual believers do not all believe the same things, even if they pay lip service to the idea that they should. Even in evangelical Christianity, there is a variety of opinions about being gay,[8] for example.

The traditions of Jewish interpretation and exegesis[9] (whether Orthodox, Liberal, or Reform) say that there are many interpretations of the Torah, and they really enjoy debating them.

Even though Islam is often thought of as having a fixed set of beliefs, there is room for interpretation of the Quran and a tradition of interpreting it in the light of the hadith (sayings of the Prophet) and Islamic tradition. The word fatwa means an interpretation or an opinion. So if you are unsure about what to do about a particular

---

7 Diarmaid MacCulloch (2011), *Christianity: The First Three Thousand Years*. Penguin Publishing Group.
8 Kristin Aune (2009), "Between Subordination and Sympathy: Evangelical Christians, Masculinity and Gay Sexuality," in *Contemporary Christianity and LGBT Sexualities*, 1st Edition, Routledge
9 Exegesis is the formal analysis of scripture.

thing, you go and ask a mullah or a qadi for an interpretation of the Quran. So it is not assumed by most Muslims (except Wahhabis) that there is only one possible interpretation of the Quran.

There is religion as it is officially supposed to be according to its doctrine; and then there is the reassuringly messy, fuzzy, and human way that people actually do it.

In religions where the divine is usually viewed as immanent in the world, or as so diffuse that it is not a person, the source of authority is viewed as the self (as in one's conscience) and not a "higher power." Fundamentalists usually believe that God is the source of moral commandments. An excellent book by Richard Holloway called *Godless Morality*[10] explains exactly why God's being the source of moral commandments cannot possibly work—even if you actually believe in God (which Holloway does not). His reason is this: Because we cannot be sure what "God" wants, or even if She/He/They exists, we cannot claim in our moral pronouncements to speak for God. If two people both claim to be doing what God wants, but do exactly the opposite, how do we decide between them? By using ordinary evidence, reason and compassion to decide.

For myself, I see religion as spirituality practiced in community. Spirituality is another concept that is difficult to define, but I regard it as a sense of mystical connection with the universe and all beings within it. In feeling this sense of connection, we experience compassion for the sufferings of other beings, and we have empathy with their joys. We can enhance this sense of connection by finding a community where we can be ourselves and practice compassion and connection; if we do not engage in spirituality in a community setting, it can become self-centered and shallow, disconnected from everyday reality. It is the experience of actually living and sharing with others that enables us to grow and become our authentic selves. This can be done by the creation of a community of shared values and shared experience of mystery, which models in microcosm the

---

10   Richard Holloway (2013), *Godless Morality: Keeping Religion out of Ethics*. Canongate Books.

desired qualities of community. Of course there will be conflicts and tensions, but it is in how these are resolved that the real values of the community will be tested and refined.

I believe that the religious life is a shared spiritual journey toward greater communion with the cosmos, where Spirit descends into matter rather than escaping from it—but this communion does not involve erasing individuality. Rather, it is the celebration of diversity and the quest for authenticity, because the divine, the numinous, or the vision of ultimate worth is the potentiality of all life to share in mystical communion. But we must expand our compassion to all beings, not just to those whose beliefs we share, and we do this by engaging in social action—caring for the marginalized and the oppressed, protecting the environment, standing up for human rights, and promoting freedom, peace, and justice.

We cannot really expect others to be convinced that we are "mystical" or "spiritual" unless we put compassion into practice by helping others. The two aspects of religion go hand in hand: Without a sense of connection there is no basis for compassion, and without the expression of compassion in the form of caring, the life of a mystic can be barren and unproductive.

People become disenchanted with a spiritual tradition or religious community when its values and beliefs and attitudes come into conflict with their own, when they perceive an internal inconsistency within those values or beliefs, or when their tradition fails them at an important juncture in life. When a religion that preaches compassion and tolerance is intolerant and harsh toward a specific group of people, its lived values are in conflict with its professed values. This often creates cognitive dissonance for its adherents. There are two possible responses to that cognitive dissonance: to adhere more strongly to the religion and suppress the source of difficulty or to seek another religious community that displays more congruence between its professed values and its lived praxis.

Griffith and Griffith[11] distinguish between two types of belief: conviction and assumption. A conviction is a core belief that is tightly held and hard to shift. Sometimes convictions are not even verbally articulated; they are lodged quite deep in the psyche. An assumption is a more loosely held belief, a working hypothesis about something, that can be changed when new evidence comes to light. I think this is a very helpful distinction, because it enables us to think about our beliefs, articulate them, and let go of or adjust the ones that do not serve us or that are incompatible with health and well-being (our own and that of others around us).

Sociologists of religion Paul Heelas and Linda Woodhead[12] have identified four main categories of religious groups (mainly with reference to types of Christianity, though these may also be useful for categorizing other religions). The categories are:

- Congregations of difference, which emphasize the distance between God and humanity, creator and created, and stress that the created should be subordinate to the creator.
- Congregations of experiential difference, which still emphasize the gulf between God and humanity but focus on intense experiences (such as the conversion experience) as a way of bridging the gap.
- Congregations of humanity, which emphasize that humanity shares in the nature of the divine, and the divine shares in the nature of humanity. They tend to emphasize the value of service to humanity as a way of serving God.
- Congregations of experiential humanity diminish the gap between the divine and the human still further and tend to emphasize inner experience of the divine through connection with community and individual mystical experiences.

11   James L. Griffith and Melissa Elliott Griffith (2002), *Encountering the Sacred in Psychotherapy: How to Talk with People about their Spiritual Lives.* New York: Guilford Press.
12   Paul Heelas and Linda Woodhead (2005), *The Spiritual Revolution: Why Religion is Giving Way to Spirituality.* Wiley.

Heelas and Woodhead also identify two main ways of engaging with spirituality: subjective-life, in which the individual spiritual life is paramount; and life-as, in which individuality becomes subsumed to the collective identity. The expression "life-as" refers to the emphasis placed upon the role of the individual in relation to others (parent, spouse, child, sibling, etc). In the past, adherents of subjective-life spirituality were often regarded as heretics and often killed or persecuted. These two approaches to spiritual life attract different types of people and have very different results.

When evaluating your own approach to religion and spirituality, it can be useful to assess which of these models is most or least attractive to you—and which one resembles the tradition you are leaving or the tradition you are joining.

Religions also have different approaches to ritual and liturgy; some do not even refer to what they do as ritual or liturgy (often preferring the word "service" to describe their rituals). These different approaches can often confuse people, especially if they vary greatly from the style of ritual they grew up with. Modes of ritual have been described by Ronald L. Grimes,[13] and are very useful for understanding the different styles of ritual and worship in different traditions.

The word liturgy means "the work of the people," and Grimes describes it as a collective waiting for power to manifest. The congregation creates an atmosphere of reverence that is conducive to the manifestation of the divine, and then it waits for it to manifest among them. Liturgical rituals tend to be formal, structured, and planned and to avoid outbursts of emotion or spontaneity.

Another mode is the celebratory mode, in which power is released or unleashed. There is a sense of wildness and anarchy, a reversal of the normal order of things. Celebratory rituals can include fireworks, bonfires, and the lighting of candles. Celebratory rituals tend to be

---

13   Ronald L. Grimes (1982), *Beginnings in Ritual Studies*. University Press of America.

informal and have moments of spontaneity.

Magical rituals involve wielding power; they regard the magical practitioner as a conduit of power that can be directed to specific ends. Western religion has traditionally frowned upon magic as the usurpation of divine powers.

Ceremonial rituals are those in which power is honored. These are typically aimed at reinforcing existing power structures, and examples include things like the state opening of a parliament or congress.

It may be possible to map these different types of ritual onto Heelas and Woodhead's model of different types of religion. Congregations of humanity (such as Methodists and Anglicans) generally tend to be more formal and liturgical in their approach; congregations of difference and experiential difference often avoid elaborate liturgy and focus on what they regard as authentic, sometimes spontaneous manifestations of divine power. Congregations of experiential humanity (such as Unitarians, Unitarian Universalists, the Religious Society of Friends,[14] and Spiritualists) can vary tremendously, and often mix and match ritual styles.

There are also different styles of ritual in Paganism and other religions, and you may find yourself drawn to, or repelled by, a tradition, community, or group because of its ritual style as well as because of its values, beliefs, and attitudes.

It may be possible to apply the Heelas and Woodhead model to Pagan and occult traditions.[15] Some Vodouisants (practitioners of Voodoo) stress the all-powerfulness of the loa and the relative powerlessness of humans—could this be an example of a religion of difference? And when the participants really focus on an experience of the loa during possession, could that be an example of a religion

---

14   The Quakers
15   Yvonne Aburrow (2008), "Theoretical models of Paganism." *The Stroppy Rabbit*. https://stroppyrabbit.blogspot.com/2008/12/theoretical-models-of-paganism.html

of experiential difference? Some Pagans and polytheists speak of being chosen by a deity, and having had little choice about which deity picked them. This also seems to stress the relative powerlessness of humans in the face of divine prerogatives. Fortunately, there has been considerable pushback against this notion of being chosen by a deity in recent years, as it goes against consent culture and personal autonomy. Some reconstructionists stress the similarity of deities to humanity, do not practice magic, and stress the importance of tradition—could this be an example of a religion of humanity? Many other Pagans stress the importance of inner experience and cultivate individuality—could this be an example of a religion of experiential humanity? It is certainly an example of subjective-life spirituality.

When you are exploring traditions or paths within your new religious paradigm, you may like to compare them to this model and see if they fit, and how you feel about that.

Comparing religions

The way I like to evaluate religions is by the effects of their beliefs, values, and traditions. Are they life-affirming? Do they bring joy and peace to their adherents? How do their adherents treat other people—especially marginalized people? What is their attitude toward other religions? Are they hierarchical and rule-bound or egalitarian and creative? Do they regard tradition as something that evolves, changes, grows, and expands, or do they regard it as set in stone, unchanging, and rigid? People's wellbeing should always be more important than tradition, and we should be in creative dialogue with tradition, not subjected to it.

If you want to evaluate a belief or concept, one way to do so is to find out how many different religions agree on it. For example, numerous religions believe in reincarnation (and they are not all derived from each other), and there are people from numerous cultures and traditions who have had flashbacks to their previous lives. Therefore, this would seem like a reasonable thing to believe in.

On the other hand, there is only one religion that believes in a savior sacrificing himself to save people from his vengeful father (and not all of them interpret it like that), so that does not seem like a particularly reasonable idea.

Another idea that appears in every religion in one form or another is the idea of personal transformation. This may be called initiation, baptism, or by some other name, but it occurs in almost every religion and has three distinct phases: an encounter with the divine, a descent into the depths of the psyche (also known as the dark night of the soul), and an inner transformation or sacred marriage within the psyche. Sometimes people discover it for themselves, even if their religious tradition does not explicitly discuss it.

It can also be useful to evaluate scriptures that are apparently oppressive or exclusive in the light of other religious traditions and concepts. For example, Jesus is reported to have said, "I am the way, the truth, and the life, and there is no way to the Father except through me." If we examine this in the light of other spiritual perspectives, it seems that what he was really saying was, the self (the psyche) is the way, the truth, and the life, and there is no way to the divine source except through the self—in other words, you can connect to the divine through the depths of your own psyche. Or, as Doreen Valiente wrote in The Charge of the Goddess, "if that which thou seekest thou findest not within thee, thou wilt never find it without thee." (In this sentence, "without thee" means outside of the self.) This, it seems to me, is a much more promising way of relating to the divine. Since we are all part of the universe from which everything is born, and in which the divine is immanent, we must all carry the divine spark within us. Many religious traditions teach this in a variety of ways.

"Comparative religion" used to mean comparing Christianity with other world religions in an attempt to demonstrate that Christianity was the best. Maybe it still does mean that in some places. In Western discourse about religion, there is a general tendency of viewing everything through the lens of Protestant Christianity. (For example, Christians have asked me things like "How does salvation work in Paganism?" The answer is that the concept of salvation has no place in Paganism.) Even atheists tend to view other religions through the lens of Protestant Christianity because most of them are ex-Christians. But if you start comparing religions with each other, without any attempt to view them through the distorting lens of a completely different religion, you will see that there are common ideas across religions, although each religious tradition is unique and particular to the region and culture from which it emerged. This exercise of comparing religions' ideas on various aspects of the spiritual journey can be very useful to correct any oppressive ideas you have absorbed from the tradition you were brought up in.

Exercises, journal prompts, and reflections

- Make a list of the pros and cons of your current religion—values, attitudes, beliefs, styles of ritual, and what type of religion it is according to the Heelas and Woodhead model.
- Does your religion successfully facilitate an encounter with the Divine for you? If yes, can that be replicated elsewhere?
- Does your religion expand your sense of connection with all that is, your circle of love and compassion? Or does it seek to restrict that circle to the adherents of the religion?
- If you are considering joining another religion, or have changed your religion at some point, do the same for that religion.
- Meditate on your current or chosen tradition in the form of a tree. Where are its roots? How has it grown? What are its fruits? Does it need pruning?
- What type of ritual do you prefer? Formal or informal, structured or spontaneous? Are you drawn to liturgical, celebratory, or magical styles of ritual?
- Do you find that you connect better with the Divine (however you see that concept) on your own, or in a group; in Nature, or in a building?
- What other religions do you feel drawn to? What attracts you to them?
- What experiences, values, or traditions do you hold sacred?
- What songs or poetry do you find spiritually uplifting?
- Make a scrapbook or an online collection of artwork, poetry, and songs that you find helpful or uplifting.
- Which of your beliefs would you describe as convictions, and which are assumptions?

- Which of the types of religion identified by Heelas and Woodhead did you find most or least attractive? Which of them resembled the tradition you grew up in or the tradition that you are exploring?
- Make a list of the key ideas from a selection of religions. Identify which religions hold these ideas (or have embraced them in the past). Do you find these ideas helpful or harmful?

Meditation: The trees and the forest

As you sit in a quiet place, breathing softly, with your own particular concerns, be aware of our common humanity. Each of us has our own hidden wellspring of joy, our own experience of sorrow, our unique perspective on the Divine and its relationship with the world.

Let us celebrate the diversity of dreams and visions.

Think of the trees in the woods: Each grows into its individual shape to fit its particular place and the events that have shaped its growth, but each is recognizable as one of a species: oak, birch, holly, maple, yew, beech, hawthorn.

Religions are like that: Each has its own unique characteristics, shaped by place, culture and history; but all of them have their roots in the fertile soil of human experience, and all seek the living waters of the Divine presence.

Let us honor the beauty and diversity of religions in the world while loving and cherishing our own particular visions and traditions, recognizing that we too are rooted in our common humanity. We are all seeking the nourishment of the endless outpouring of love and wisdom that we call by many names—all of them holy.[16]

---

16   Yvonne Aburrow (2014), "Your mountain is not my mountain and that's just fine." *Dowsing for Divinity*. https://dowsingfordivinity. com/2014/03/11/mountains/

Chapter 2.
Leaving your religion

"Should I stay or should I go now?"

—The Clash (1982)

Have you ever experienced a moment of profound discomfort with your religion? A moment when you look around you and wonder what you are doing in this setting, with these people?

Someone says or does something that is profoundly at odds with your values, and you wonder if they are expressing the mainstream view of the religion. Are you on the margins of the tradition, or are they?

Or you experience something that makes you aware that your religious tradition is deeply wrong about something.

I experienced this disconnect when I saw the film *Gandhi* in the cinema, when it first came out.[17] For the first time, I entered into the feelings of people from another religious tradition, and I saw their devotion. According to evangelical Christians, only Christians are going to heaven. I could not believe that Gandhi was not going to heaven (nor the millions of devout Hindus, Muslims, Sikhs, and so on). This was a profoundly consciousness-expanding experience.

❀⊱•°•⊰❀⊱•°•⊰❀

There are many reasons for leaving a religion. Often it is because its worldview does not work for you any more, or because your values are no longer aligned with it.

There are numerous issues with the idea of an all-powerful creator deity. If God is all-powerful, why doesn't he[18] prevent suffering?

---

17   *Gandhi* was released in December 1982 in the UK. https://en.wikipedia.org/wiki/Gandhi_(film)
18   Or she, or they. There are numerous hints that God either has no gender, or encompasses all genders, in monotheist traditions.

One argument in response to this is that he gives us free will, and our choices lead to suffering—but that does not explain cancer, earthquakes, and other natural disasters. Another argument offered by fundamentalists is that the world is controlled by the devil—an argument that leads to extreme paranoia.

Another problem is that if God is love, why would he condemn anyone to hell for all eternity for not believing in him? Many people come to the conclusion that the only valid response to this question is to believe in universal salvation (also known as apocatastasis,[19] which was espoused by some early Christian thinkers but was declared heretical by the church in the fourth century CE).

In response to these questions, many people stop believing in an all-powerful creator deity. I believe in an underlying energy in all things (which theologian Paul Tillich called the ground of all being) but not that it is the creator of the universe, nor that it is all-powerful, and I do not think it has a personality. I also experience this energy as more female than male. Perhaps it is really genderless, but I like the Hindu idea of the goddess Shakti as the underlying energy of all things.

If you are interested in these theological questions, I recommend reading Karen Armstrong's book *A History of God*,[20] where she discusses the different ideas of God that have existed throughout history, and the issues with them. Another great read is *36 Arguments for the Existence of God* by Rebecca Goldstein.[21] It is a novel that examines the conflict between science and religion, and that between living for yourself and living for your community. But in the appendices, she goes through all thirty-six arguments and demolishes them one by one: except for one, the idea of God as Nature (Deus sive Natura), put forward by Baruch Spinoza, which in and of itself negates the other thirty-five arguments.

19   Apocatastasis and universal salvation are not exactly the same concept, but they are similar. Apocatastasis is the belief that God will reconcile all things to himself. Universal salvation is the belief that the salvation brought by Jesus applies to all humanity and does not require us to believe in it for it to apply to us.
20   Karen Armstrong (1994), *A History of God: The 4,000-Year Quest of Judaism, Christianity and Islam*. Random House Publishing.
21   Rebecca Goldstein (2011), *36 Arguments for the Existence of God: A Work of Fiction*. Vintage.

What does it mean to leave a religion? How do you extricate yourself from its beliefs and values? How do you remain friends with people in the religion you are leaving behind? What if you are changing paths but your spouse and family are not?

The decision to leave a religion is often a lengthy process of indecision and can be painful and scary. It can be triggered by a series of clashes between your values and beliefs and those of your religious tradition, or by one big thing (for example, being LGBTQIA in a religion that rejects variance in gender and sexual orientation).

When you experience a clash of beliefs or values with your current religion, there are several things to consider. Is the clash just with specific people within your religious community who hold these views, with the local community, your denomination, or the whole faith tradition? Are you clashing over a core tenet of the religion, or a peripheral one? Is there just one issue that you have with the tradition, or are there multiple issues?

A belief is backed up in a person's mind by stories that reflect or uphold it. If a person receives an answer to prayer or conducts a successful magical working, the story of that success reinforces their belief in the power of prayer or magic. For example, if a person does magic to get some money, and receives an unexpected check in the mail, they are likely to attribute it to the magic that they performed.

Beliefs can also be undermined by stories that contradict them or that open a person to new perspectives. If you hold beliefs that are easily contradicted by science or by experience, it is likely that your religious convictions will be unraveled. I was already uncomfortable with the idea that only Christians go to heaven, and the story of Mahatma Gandhi further undermined that belief, because he was clearly a holy person, and the faith I had grown up in claimed that he would not get to heaven.

Can it be changed from within?

Are there other people in your religious community with views
that are similar to yours? Is it possible to band together with them to
try to change things from within, or are you upholding a powerful
retrogressive institution by your continued presence within it? This
depends on how much institutional power is vested in the tradition,
and how receptive it is likely to be to being changed from within it is
likely to be. In the 1950s, several Unitarians[22] asked Harry Emerson
Fosdick, a liberal Christian, to leave mainstream Christianity
and join their church. He pointed out that by remaining within
mainstream Christianity, he retained the institutional power of that
tradition.[23] He was a strong anti-racist who went on to become a
co-founder of a liberal and ecumenical church in New York that still
exists today—and which is now LGBTQ-inclusive. He was also a
popular broadcaster on liberal Christianity.

In 2014, when my book about making initiatory Wicca less
heterocentric was published,[24] several people suggested that I leave
Gardnerian Wicca and found my own tradition. Inspired by Fosdick,
and by the many people who supported the idea of inclusive Wicca,
I decided to stay put and help to transform the tradition from within.
Many people were pushing for greater inclusion of LGBTQIA
people in Wicca, and the people who oppose these changes are now
in a minority.

What made these shifts possible was that there was already a
group of people who supported these ideas. Fosdick had the backing
of the Rockefeller dynasty and the many progressive and liberal
Christians of his day. People interested in making Wicca more
inclusive started our own Facebook group, and developed our ideas
in a safe space away from the naysayers. This is a classic tactic of
social justice movements: Feminism did it by creating women-only

---

22 The American Unitarian Association merged with the Universalist Church of America in 1961. See https://www.uua.org/beliefs/who-we-are/history

23 Harry Emerson Fosdick (1956), *The Living of These Days; An Autobiography*

24 Yvonne Aburrow (2014), *All acts of love and pleasure: inclusive Wicca*. Avalonia Books.

spaces, LGBTQIA people did it by creating queer-only spaces; and BIPOC people have done it by creating BIPOC-only spaces.

If you belong to a tradition that is too rigid and entrenched in its views to be changed from within, and/or you do not have a group of like-minded others with whom you can develop an alternative, it may be better to leave. You may find that it is too difficult to adjust your own beliefs to a less rigid perspective, and you need to abandon them altogether. This happened to me when I left Christianity in 1985. I did not know about progressive groups within Christianity, and even if I had known about them, I would have found it difficult to shift from the fundamentalist views that I held back then to a more nuanced view. As far as I was concerned, it was all or nothing. This happened before the inclusive church movement or the deconstructionist movement gained strength and popularity, although there were progressive Christians at the time. I had multiple issues with the only type of Christianity that I was familiar with: the idea of an all-powerful Creator, the idea that other religions were not valid, the idea of the Bible as inerrant, the attitudes toward sexuality and the body, the concepts of sinfulness and salvation, and the anti-gay attitudes. I was unaware of the extent of alternatives to these ideas. There was no internet back then to help me find different types of Christianity or to rectify the fundamentalist ideas that I had been taught. I did not, however, believe in really bizarre ideas like young-Earth creationism, and I am fairly sure that I didn't really believe in the Devil.

On the other hand, you may find that your views have diverged significantly from those of the tradition and that you can no longer find common ground with them on any issue. At that point, it is best to leave the tradition or denomination.

When I was considering leaving Paganism in 2007, a number of things had occurred that I found really frustrating. There was the reburial controversy, which was a debate over whether archeologists should rebury human remains that they have excavated (I believe that archeological evidence is an important and valuable source of what we know about our ancient polytheist and animist ancestors). I started to realize that there was a significant amount of heterocentric and homophobic attitudes within Pagan traditions. I began to see considerable value in Christian spirituality, mysticism, and discursive theology, especially queer theology, liberation theology, and process theology. I was frustrated by the way that Pagans frequently dismiss theology as a Christian concept, when in fact the word theology was coined by the ancient pagan author Cicero in 45 CE, in his book *De Natura Deorum* ("On the Nature of the Gods"). Pagans often say that we do not need theology because it would make our tradition too rigid, whereas I believe that if you do not have a theory underpinning your practice, you are likely to replicate all sorts of retrogressive ideas.

As the saying goes, you can take the girl out of Paganism, but you can't take Paganism out of the girl. Fortunately the people I approached with a view to joining their religion were very open-minded. To start with, I investigated Orthodox Christianity, which has very different theological perspectives than Western Christianity, as well as very beautiful music and liturgy. An exploration of Orthodox Christianity can be a helpful change of perspective, especially if you were brought up in a fundamentalist version of Christianity. Several Orthodox Christians were keen to help me find the right religion for me, rather than trying to sell me their religion. I discovered, however, that I could not believe in all the tenets of their faith. After that, I attended Unitarian churches for a few years, which I could do in parallel with running a Wiccan coven, and I found their liberal approach to religion very helpful and refreshing. In the end, I found that I did not fit in Unitarianism either, so I returned to Wicca and Paganism full time.

I gained several things from my wanderings. One was the insight that all religions and communities contain reasonable and unreasonable people and ideas (one would think that would be

obvious, but one does not necessarily think clearly when one is in
the midst of a crisis). Another gain was that I finally got rid of my
simmering volcano of anger at Christianity and, more importantly,
the fear that lurked beneath it. There is plenty to be justifiably
angry about with Christianity, but it helps if that anger is focused
on specific issues and not concealing a big lump of fear that the
fundamentalist version of it might be true.

Reasons for leaving

If you are considering leaving your religion, make a list of the
reasons. This will make it easier to explain your change of heart to
others. Leaving a religion is very much like getting divorced, and it
may involve similar amounts of upheaval. If you belong to a closed
or fundamentalist community that will ostracize you when you leave,
then leaving is an excellent idea. But it can be very hard to leave your
family and friends behind. This type of community is often referred
to as "high control"—they want a lot of control over all areas of
your life, which may include your clothing, sexuality, finances,
employment, and/or living arrangements.

If you are leaving a group whose members will still talk to you
afterwards, your worldview and theirs are very likely to diverge.
You will no longer have a shared set of practices, values, and beliefs
that are part of belonging to a community. You may find a new
community that will share your values and beliefs, and that can be
really fulfilling, but they will also be less-than-perfect, like any group
of people. Do not let the perfect be the enemy of the good; you will
probably find a community that is good enough. It is also important
that your new community be relaxed and open enough that you
can get a sense of connection with others as well as with your new
community.

Not all reasons for leaving are hugely traumatic or revelatory;
sometimes people just drift away from a religion because it ceases
to have meaning in their life. Sometimes they become preoccupied

with some other aspect of life, like bringing up their kids. I saw some statistics about church attendance compiled by the Methodists a few years ago, and it was very noticeable that the missing age group in their attendees was people between the ages of about eighteen and thirty. I quipped at the time that it is because that age cohort is too busy having sex on Sunday mornings to go to church, and therefore churches should provide a service on a weekday evening—but it may also be because that age group is busy having kids and bringing them up. It is also often the case that people drift away from the religion they were brought up in because it was taught to them at a child's level of understanding. Because they never graduate to the adult level of understanding it, it fails to address for them the issues that affect adults.

Though I have seen people move from one religious community to another (within Paganism and within Christianity) because they were looking for a more intense or powerful spiritual experience, I do not believe that this is the right reason to look for a new spiritual community. It is better to look for a spiritual community that is congruent with your values, not one that provides more intense experiences, but might not share your values. A less intense group will be continually nourishing, and not just create a series of peaks and troughs in your spiritual life.

It is hard to leave a religion if your spouse, other members of your family, or friends, still adhere to that religion—especially if you have children and your spouse still wants them to be involved in your former religious community. This may require negotiation and compromise. One source of difficulty is expectations around the celebration of religious holidays, especially if a more secular version of the holiday is part of mainstream culture as well. Another source of difficulty and potential conflict is whether your children will be brought up in the religion that you are leaving. Most online resources on this issue are aimed at parents who are parting ways and who have different ideas about whether their children should be brought up in their religious tradition. But this can be difficult even if you are not splitting up, and many of these resources are also applicable to continuing relationships. Those that are aimed at parents with different religious views who are continuing their relationship assume that it is possible to compromise and negotiate.[25]

Things that you will need to consider and negotiate include the ethical values that you and your partner want your children to learn, and to what extent these are informed by your partner's religion, your new set of values, or your new religion.[26] You will need to think about how your religious or secular ethical values will impact choices around education or medical procedures. Are you willing for your children to participate in activities with your former religious community? Does your partner want this to happen? Does your partner want to retain or impose religious restrictions on diet or clothing or medical interventions on your children? What holidays or religious traditions does your partner want the children to be involved in? If you are parting ways, will the holidays impact your access to the children, or that of other family members such as grandparents?

There are several ways in which these negotiations can be managed. You may want to introduce a neutral mediator who can hear your partner's concerns and yours—and take the heat out of the discussion when explaining your respective positions to the other party. If this is not possible, perhaps you and your partner could each make a list of what you consider to be negotiable and non-negotiable. Then start the discussion with the negotiable items, working your way up to the more difficult and non-negotiable items.

It is possible that the relationship with your partner, as with your religious tradition, has broken down irretrievably and your only option is to get out. This happens a lot with people leaving high-control religious traditions. In this situation, professional marriage

25   Carvell Wallace (2018), "Should I Let My Husband Drag My Kids to Church?" *Slate*. https://slate.com/human-interest/2018/04/parenting-advice-on-a-family-with-one-churchgoing-parent-and-one-who-dislikes-organized-religion.html
26   Porchlight Law (undated), *Co-Parenting with Religious Differences*. https://porchlight.law/co-parenting-with-religious-differences/

counseling may be necessary, or if the marriage has broken down irretrievably, there are organizations who will help you to get away.

Discussions about these matters can be especially difficult if your partner has any sort of power over you (physical, psychological, or financial), and they may require intervention from professionals. Even if your partner is willing to negotiate, it can still be a painful process, particularly if your partner believes that nonbelievers are damned. The main thing to hold onto in these discussions is that your children have a right to be free from oppressive religious systems, and it should be their choice as to whether they continue to be involved in your former religious community.

However, even if all your current friends and family are members of the religion that you are leaving, there are many ways to make friends that do not involve them being from the same religion as you, such as getting involved in conservation work, short study courses,[27] handicraft courses and clubs, hiking, and other hobbies. Many of these have been unavailable during times of pandemic and physical distancing, but there are still ways of finding community through the internet, and social events hosted online.

You may be very angry with the tradition that you are leaving over the harms that it inflicts on marginalized people (this can include BIPOC people, women, disabled people, and LGBTQIA people) and the harms it has inflicted on you. Your concerns and your anger are valid. Sometimes people from your former tradition will try to gaslight you into believing that you are in the wrong for being angry. But anger is a useful emotion because it propels us out of harmful situations. Once we are out of danger, though, it is good to critically analyze the helpful and harmful aspects of the situation we have left (even if the helpful aspect was only teaching you how not to live your life).

---

27   In the United Kingdom, the University of the Third Age is a good option for older people. In the United States, there are the Osher Lifelong Learning Institutes.

If you are leaving a fundamentalist tradition, be aware that its tentacles will be hard to extract from your psyche. You may need therapy to help you extricate yourself from any fear that remains within you. This is because fundamentalism preys upon some of our most deep-seated psychological fears: fears of abandonment, uncertainty, insecurity. It creates a false and rigid structure that is opposed to the perceived moral laxity of the rest of the world, and it creates a persecution complex in its adherents, so that they regard themselves as in opposition to the rest of the world. It also seeks to drain you of autonomy and agency so that you are controlled by the charismatic or authoritarian leader of the group. It can take many years to deconstruct the structures and blockages that this creates in the psyche. It is also necessary to avoid falling into the same type of trap in your new community. Even ex-fundamentalists who become atheists sometimes fall into this trap and go looking for a similarly rigid construct, in the same way that abused people often end up in another abusive relationship, because predators can manipulate them more easily. It is important to recognize spiritual abuse and the patterns associated with it, and get help with whatever causes you to end up experiencing the pattern again.

Spiritual abuse

If you are leaving a fundamentalist group and planning to sever all ties with them (or if they are likely to sever all ties with you), there are organizations that will help you to get away, and provide support while you regain your balance. One example is Spiritual Abuse Resources,[28] a program of the International Cultic Studies Association, which provides information and assistance to victims of spiritual abuse, clergy and other religious professionals, mental health professionals, families, and anyone concerned about spiritual abuse.

---

28   Spiritual Abuse Resources (SAR), www.spiritualabuseresources.com

There are many patterns and types of spiritual abuse. One of the most common is gaslighting.[29] People engaging in gaslighting will behave abusively toward you, and then deny that they behaved that way, or they will say that your justified anger in response to their behavior is because you are dysfunctional. In religious settings, this often takes the form of telling you that your behavior is contrary to the rules of the religion or is displeasing to God.

Another form of spiritual abuse is known as religious abuse. This is characterized by the use of religious authority to engage in abusive behaviors. These can include using the beliefs or scriptures of your tradition to embarrass or humiliate you; forcing you to give money or other resources; forcing you to engage in unwanted intimacy or sexual acts; and making you feel obliged, coerced, or pressured into any action that you do not want to do. This includes coercing people into praying in public settings, such as schools, sporting events, and so on.

Religious and spiritual abuse can also happen as a component of domestic violence. In this context, it can take the form of shaming or ridiculing you for your religious beliefs, forcing you to practice your religion differently than you would prefer, demanding that your children be raised with a particular set of beliefs, using scriptures and beliefs to bully or shame you, or to justify other kinds of abuse (which could involve physical violence or withholding the use of contraception). Major feelings experienced by victims of spiritual abuse are shame, guilt, and fear. This can happen if you have different beliefs from your partner about the religion or its values, or if your behavior transgresses a rule that your partner believes to be important.

I read an account of a woman who escaped from a very controlling husband who was a fundamentalist pastor. The first time she stood up to him, he "rebuked Satan" for speaking through her.

---

29   The behavior known as gaslighting is named after the film *Gaslight*, directed by George Cukor, where the villain convinced his wife that she was going mad by varying the brightness of the gaslights in the house, and then telling her that there was no variation in brightness and she was imagining it.

We were driving through the part of Arkansas
where bluegrass runs through the hills like blood in
the veins. It was dusky dark. And you could cut the
tension with a knife. We'd just come from a visit
with a "church mediator." I asked a few questions
about our family finances, and the man accused
me of "usurping my husband's authority." My
husband was a meek man. But I guess the meeting
had given him courage, because on the way home
he said: "Detra, you need to get back on my side."
Right then something snapped. I hadn't said a cuss
word since the age of ten, when I got a whipping
for saying "gosh." But I called my husband a son
of a bitch, right there in that burgundy suburban.
He pulled over to the side of the road. He got right
in my face with his finger, and said: "Satan! Don't
speak through my wife anymore!" For the first time
I didn't cower. I didn't grovel. I grabbed my purse,
opened the door, and stepped out onto the side of
Interstate 40. I knew I was crossing a line of no
return.[30]

Spiritual abuse may also involve either a religious leader, a
religious organization, or your partner controlling your finances,
what you wear,[31] how you style your hair, your decisions, your
behavior, your sexuality, and other aspects of your life. You do not
deserve to be treated this way, and help is available from domestic
abuse helplines and shelters and from organizations that assist
victims of spiritual abuse.[32]

Spiritual abuse can have devastating effects on one's ability to
form friendships, enjoy relationships, and many other aspects of
life. It can affect self-confidence and self-esteem. It can also be

30 Detra Thomas (2022), post 1 of 15 on Humans of New York @humansofny, Instagram. www.instagram.com/p/Cclco-vuteS/
31 Many people choose to wear head-coverings or other religious clothing; this is not abusive if they have chosen it freely.
32 *Signs of Spiritual Abuse*, by WebMD Editorial Contributors. Medically Reviewed by Dan Brennan, MD on December 01, 2020. www.webmd.com/mental-health/signs-spiritual-abuse

perpetrated by parents upon their children. Spiritual abuse is distinct from merely bringing a child up within a specific religion; it usually involves coercing the child to believe and behave in a certain way, along with restricting or prescribing their choices of friends, clothing, entertainment, and exploration of other religions. Spiritual abuse is very sneaky, because if you have doubts or criticisms of the religious leader or beliefs, you are told that it is sinful to doubt, or that you are being "tempted" to believe differently.[33]

Spiritual abuse can also take the form of sexual abuse of community members by clergy or other spiritual leaders. Even if both parties in this situation are adults, this is still abuse because there is a power differential between the spiritual leader and the community member. Sexual abuse of minors and vulnerable adults is obviously abuse. All forms of sexual abuse can cause significant psychological harm. This situation can be made significantly worse if there is shame and silence around sexual matters in the religious tradition concerned. If you are in this situation, there are organizations that can help you (see the Further Reading section at the back of this book).

Another significant issue in confronting spiritual abuse is that no religious community wants to admit that its adherents might be perpetrators of such behavior.[34] This is especially true if the community is marginalized or widely misunderstood by mainstream society. During the COVID-19 pandemic, many religious traditions have become aware of the extent of abuse within their communities, as this has been thrown into sharp relief by the fact that victims of domestic abuse were isolated with their abusers and, tragically, there was an exponential increase in cases of abuse.

There are also numerous cases of religious abuse in institutional settings. Residential schools run by churches in Canada abused

33   *Shame and Silence: Recognizing Spiritual Abuse.* February 1, 2017 • Contributed by Mackenzi Kingdon, MA, LMHCA www. goodtherapy.org/blog/shame-and-silence-recognizing-spiritual-abuse-0201175
34   "Breaking the silence: Awareness of spiritual abuse in UK religious communities." January 29, 2021. European Academy on Religion and Society. https://europeanacademyofreligionandsociety.com/news/awareness-of-spiritual-abuse-in-uk-religious-communities/

Indigenous children for decades with impunity, punishing them for speaking Indigenous languages, indoctrinating them with Christianity, feeding and clothing them inadequately, sexually abusing them, starving them, and inflicting extreme punishments on them. These abuses were cataloged in great detail by the Truth and Reconciliation Commission's report in 2015, and more recently, thousands of unmarked graves of children who died or were killed at these schools have been found.[35]

Abuse has also occurred in other Christian schools, involving beatings, exorcisms, forced "conversion therapy" (also known as "pray away the gay"), isolation, and other physical and psychological abuse.[36]

It is not only Christian schools that perpetrate these kinds of abuse. Many private schools that are not subject to the same level of inspection as other schools have been found to be abusive; this sort of thing has also happened with extreme Jewish schools.[37] Similar abuses have occurred in extreme Islamic schools, but there has recently been a program of reform for those schools.[38]

The main thing to remember is that the abuse is not your fault. Abusers will try to make you believe that everything is your fault, including the abuse. It is easy to feel that you could have prevented the abuse somehow, or to accept the negative view of you that the abusers try to impress upon you. However, abusers are very manipulative and seem to know that abuse is a vicious downward spiral. You feel vulnerable, so they are able to abuse you, which makes you feel more vulnerable, which makes you more prone to abuse, and so on. It is frequently hard even to see that what has been done to you is abuse. Erika Bornman, who escaped a cult in South Africa, says that:

35   The Final Report of the Truth and Reconciliation Commission of Canada (2015). https://nctr.ca/records/reports/
36   Jason Warick (2022), "Exorcisms, violent discipline and other abuse alleged by former students of private Sask. Christian school." *CBC Investigates.*

www.cbc.ca/news/canada/saskatoon/abuse-alleged-former-students-of-private-christian-school-1.6532329 (extremely disturbing article)
37   Kim Willsher (2022), "Pupils at Jewish school in France taken into care after abuse allegations." *The Guardian*. www.theguardian.com/world/2022/feb/02/pupils-ultra-orthodox-jewish-beth-yossef-school-france-taken-into-care-after-abuse-allegations

Harriet Sherwood (2022), "A 'tumultuous journey' from ultra-Orthodox school to physics degree." *The Guardian*. www.theguardian.com/world/2022/jul/22/a-tumultuous-journey-from-ultra-orthodox-school-to-physics-degree
38   Diaa Hadid, Abdul Sattar (2019), "Pakistan Wants To Reform Madrassas. Experts Advise Fixing Public Education First." *NPR*. www.npr.org/2019/01/10/682917845/pakistan-wants-to-reform-madrassas-experts-advise-fixing-public-education-first

It took me almost three years to realise fully
that what I had experienced and witnessed was
abuse. Then, the more I became myself, the
easier it became to go up into that dusty attic and
occasionally open a box. To write this book, I had
to march up the stairs into that attic, bring down
every damn box to the lounge and open them one
by one, delving into their decades-old content.
And I asked other survivors to do the same with
their own attics full of boxes. For two years, I
sat and wept in my lounge for myself and for all
the others who shared their stories with me. I'm
surprised I still have any tears left. Something I
realised in therapy that helped me tremendously
is that the shame I had owned for close to four
decades belonged to them, not me. The shame
of wetting my bed as a 10-year-old. The shame
of being defiled by my religious counsellor. The
shame of my mother disowning me. The shame of
never being good enough. And now I can tell the
stories with empathy for the little girl I was, but
without the accompanying shame I felt for so many
decades. That makes it a lot easier.[39]

Whatever form of spiritual abuse you are experiencing, do not
suffer in silence. Recognize it for what it is, and get help. It may
take several attempts to find a therapist who can deal with religious
trauma, and this kind of therapy is often more expensive because it
requires a therapist with experience in this area and one who can
deal with the complex compound issues resulting from spiritual
abuse. But it is worth it.

---

39   Erika Bornman (2022), *Mission of Malice: My Exodus from KwaSizabantu*. Penguin Random House. https://www.litnet.co.za/major-
international-award-for-erika-bornman-author-of-mission-of-malice/

Religious trauma

Spiritual abuse can (and usually does) cause religious trauma. Religious Trauma Syndrome is a collection of symptoms that occur in response to stressful, traumatic experiences with religion. Religious Trauma Syndrome is often experienced by people who have escaped fundamentalist religions, cults, or abusive religious organizations. These symptoms are similar to the symptoms of complex post-traumatic stress disorder.[40]

The symptoms of RTS can include having confusing thoughts; a reduced ability to think critically; having negative beliefs about yourself, other people, and the world; having trouble making decisions; feeling depressed, anxious, grieving, angry, or lethargic; feeling isolated or that you have lost your way in life; losing interest or pleasure in things or activities you used to enjoy; experiencing a loss or disconnect from your community (family, friends, romantic relationships); feeling isolated or that you do not belong (especially if there is some aspect of yourself that your religious community rejects); feeling out of the loop with regard to mainstream culture; experiencing symptoms of PTSD such as flashbacks, nightmares, dissociation, and having difficulty dealing with your emotions.

Therapy can help with these symptoms and get you thinking in a different way about your life and experiences. Some cultures and age-groups view therapy with suspicion, but it can offer a set of tools that can enable you to take a different perspective on things.

---

40   Mackenzi Kingdon, MA, LMH. "Religious Trauma Syndrome and Faith Transitions," Restoration Counseling. www. restorationcounselingseattle.com/religious-trauma-transitions

'Exvangelicals' and deconstruction

Deconstruction is a method or process for breaking down the toxic and harmful ideas of evangelical and fundamentalist Christianity—usually the North American forms of that tradition. It can involve re-examining Christian tradition and history to find out how ideas developed, or it can mean looking at other Christian traditions to see how they view the concepts being examined. Some people who engage in the process of deconstruction remain Christian; others do not.

'Exvangelicals' are people who have left evangelical Christianity, especially white evangelical churches in the United States, and have become atheists, agnostics, progressive Christians, or joined other religious traditions. The triggering incident that causes them to leave is often the treatment of women and LGBTQIA people in evangelical churches, and/or the right-wing attitudes espoused by many evangelicals. The hashtag #exvangelical was coined by Blake Chastain in 2016 to enable people to find solidarity with others who have experienced similar situations.[41] You can find posts with this hashtag on Twitter and Instagram. Similar movements include #EmptyThePews, which was prompted by the large number of evangelicals who supported Donald Trump. The #EmptyThePews hashtag was started on Twitter by exvangelical Chrissy Stroop. Another important hashtag is #ChurchToo (based on the hashtag #MeToo) which was created to draw attention to sexual abuse in churches. *(Be warned that this hashtag will bring up posts that have harrowing details of sexual, physical, and psychological abuse.)* You can also find advice by searching the Instagram hashtags #ReligiousTrauma and #SpiritualAbuse.

---

41   Chastain also started a podcast called *Exvangelical*, and there are other popular exvangelical podcasts such as *Almost Heretical* and *Straight White American Jesus.*
https://en.wikipedia.org/wiki/Exvangelical
https://www.instagram.com/explore/tags/exvangelical/
https://twitter.com/search?q=%23exvangelical

John Beckett has written some very helpful articles on recovering from Christian fundamentalism.[42] He breaks down the process, starting from what you were taught as a child and working through realizing something is wrong, doubting what you were taught, trying a nicer form of Christianity (which often does not help because its outer trappings are insufficiently different from fundamentalism), going through a vaguely deistic outlook on life, and then realizing that you may need to fill the vacuum left by your previous tradition with a more definite system (whether that is atheism, Paganism, or something else). He also points out that although reason and evidence can help remove residual fundamentalism, religious and spiritual ideas are embedded in the emotions:

> Don't expect a purely intellectual approach to
> succeed. Fundamentalism is intellectually flawed
> and exploring those flaws will build a good
> foundation for your escape. But ultimately, religion
> is a spiritual and emotional matter. It's not enough
> to know the lie, you have to feel the lie… and feel
> the truth of something better to replace it.[43]

One of the most important recommendations from John Beckett is not to argue from within the paradigm of your former tradition. Their scriptures are not authoritative, and you no longer wish to give them control over your life; so do not use them in arguments, otherwise you are treating them as authoritative and normative.

It is important to read widely around the subject. Read the history of Christianity, Judaism, Islam, Biblical criticism; replace the simplified and biased history that you were taught with an external perspective. I especially recommend the books of Karen Armstrong, Diarmaid MacCulloch, and Richard Holloway. Read about science and evolution. Read about other religions and appreciate that they

---

42   John Beckett (2020), "Exorcising Fundamentalism: The Steps on My Journey." *Under the Ancient Oaks.* www.patheos.com/blogs/johnbeckett/2020/04/exorcising-fundamentalism-the-steps-on-my-journey.html
43   John Beckett (2015), "Escaping Fundamentalism." *Under the Ancient Oaks.* www.patheos.com/blogs/johnbeckett/2015/09/escaping-fundamentalism.html

have very different perspectives and values. Enjoy the power of humor poking fun at fundamentalist worldviews.

Leaving a liberal religious tradition is usually not a problem. You can just stop going to their events and cease to participate in the community. This also applies to leaving a Pagan tradition. It might be a bit difficult if all your friends are Pagans, but you can still be friends with them. Most Pagans are very accepting of people changing to a different religion, taking the view that people should follow whatever spiritual path is right for them. It is a good idea not to slam the door on your way out, however, because many people decide to return to Paganism.

Sadly, just like in every other religion, there are abusive groups and individuals within the Pagan movement. That's why there are numerous articles about evaluating any group that you are planning to join. The warning signs of an abusive Pagan group are exactly the same as the warning signs of other groups: overly powerful leaders, discouraging people from having different opinions or making friends outside of the group, demanding excessive amounts of money from adherents, sexual manipulation and abuse, gaslighting—all the usual coercive and controlling behavior. In 2018, several people left a group because of the alleged abusive behavior of one of its leaders, and the alleged abuse was very similar to that found in other manipulative and abusive groups and cults.[44]

When religion turns bad

Sometimes religion can be harmful even at moments when it seems most likely to be helpful. This is especially true of religions that believe in miracles occurring without the assistance of science and medicine. They can hold out false hope of a miraculous divine intervention in the midst of some of life's most traumatic events. Melissa and James Griffith discuss several tragic outcomes of such

---

44   Thora Drakos (2018), "On my years in CAYA Coven." *Dreams from the West Wind*
https://tadrakos.wordpress.com/2018/03/23/on-my-years-in-caya-coven/

beliefs. In one instance, a family attended a faith healing service, and believed that God had healed their diabetic son. He stopped taking insulin, and the family believed that the return of his symptoms was a test of their faith. Sadly, the boy died from a lack of insulin in his system three days later. The authors discuss this situation compassionately while looking at the implications for how churches that host faith healing services need to ensure that this sort of thing does not happen. Many religions take the view that medicines are a gift from the Divine, and can be taken in tandem with efforts at spiritual healing or faith healing.[45] There have been numerous other cases of deaths resulting from situations where parents believed that their child had been miraculously healed and threw away necessary medication.[46]

The problem with believing in miracles is that, when they do not happen (which is most of the time), the believer is likely to be very disappointed, and believe that God does not care about them, or that they have done something that means they do not deserve divine intervention. They think that if only they could just pray harder, or believe more fervently, they think, then the miracle would happen. When it does not happen, they often regard God as harsh and judgmental as a result.

Believing in the power of prayer or magic to give comfort, relieve pain, or similar, is different from a belief in miracles, because prayer and magic work within the laws of nature, whether by some "quantum woo" means that we do not understand, by giving comfort to the person suffering, or by the belief of the person that they will get well, which works in tandem with the medical intervention. A miracle, by definition, is an event that is outside the laws of nature.

It is more helpful to believe that the Divine (however you view the Divine) accompanies us through the painful situations of life, such as

45   Griffith, James L., and Griffith, Melissa Elliott (2002), "When Spirituality Turns Destructive" chapter 9 in *Encountering the Sacred in Psychotherapy: How to Talk with People about their Spiritual Lives*. New York: Guilford Press.
46   Nancy Mills (1988), "The Promise of a 'Miracle,' a Tragic Tale of Faith Healing." *Los Angeles Times*. https://www.latimes.com/archives/la-xpm-1988-05-17-ca-2829-story.html

disease, death, and disaster, and to draw comfort from a sense of the Divine presence.

Griffith and Griffith discuss other ways in which religion can be destructive. One situation is when an overly rigid adherence to a particular faith position can get in the way of healing and relationships. One example they give is that of a gay man who believed that being gay was sinful; he broke off his relationship with his boyfriend because of this belief. His view of God was as a judgmental and harsh deity, rather than as a loving one. Another example is of a woman who found more fulfillment in her relationship with Jesus than she did in her marriage, and she ended up refusing to work on her marriage as a result.

I have occasionally been told by "spiritual" people that anger is a bad emotion to have. I disagree, as I believe that anger is the way that our brains warn us of abusive or harmful situations. If we push our anger down and do not act upon it, it becomes depression— sometimes severe depression. Prolonged anger that is deliberately stoked by continual reopening of the wounds inflicted might be harmful, but the original impulse to anger in the face of abusive behavior is a good thing.

Sometimes spiritual or New Age people will be suspicious of allopathic medicine. They may believe that physical symptoms (such as headaches) are the result of spiritual phenomena rather than physical ones, or believe that they can heal themselves through "mind over matter" or the power of positive thinking. These views can also be dangerous. It is best to allow medicine (whether allopathic or homeopathic) to work in tandem with spiritual practices, not to substitute spirituality or religion for medical intervention.

The goal of religion and spirituality should be to confer an ability to cope with all the vicissitudes that life throws at us—and to be more loving and inclusive. If religion or spirituality makes us more disconnected from other people, less compassionate, and less rational, then it is harmful. If on the other hand, it enables us to feel more love and compassion for others, and to be better able to cope with the sorrowful aspects of life, then it is helpful.

Therapy, support groups, and spiritual guidance from experienced practitioners can help you to gain perspective on difficult situations and create a healthier view of the Divine. They will generally try to work within your chosen religious paradigm.

Warning signs

You may be looking back over your time with the group or religion you are involved in, and wondering how you got to where you are now. Perhaps it started out seeming reasonable and helpful, and only later became more demanding of your time, money, and attention.

I have been temporarily involved with several online groups where people were drawn in because they wanted to change the world, but then the group became hung-up on language. They started policing how other people in the group expressed themselves. Participants had to use a certain set of terminology in the right way, otherwise they were obviously not thinking like the group. In Cultish: The Language of Fanaticism by Amanda Montell,[47] the author explores the excessive amounts of in-group jargon that cults create and impress upon their followers. The author gives several examples of the intensity and impenetrability of cultish language (the jargon used by Scientology, Heaven's Gate, and Jim Jones) and they're quite alarming. These sociolects (a term for a dialect espoused by a particular group) have the effect of isolating the members of the group from the rest of society, because the in-group becomes completely unintelligible to the out-group. All groups have their own terminology, but the more extreme groups take this to a whole new level, using acronyms and abbreviations, twisting the meaning of words and phrases, and so on.

---

47   Amanda Montell (2021), *Cultish: The Language of Fanaticism*. Harper Wave.

Another manipulative trope described in Cultish is the thought-terminating cliché. This tactic was first named by Robert Jay Lifton,[48] and it describes how people end a conversation by implying that the line of inquiry is heretical, forbidden, ridiculous, undecidable, or just not a fruitful question. For example, I have observed an online Catholic forum where people would shut down conversations by dismissing the other person's position as heresy. Pagans and Wiccans sometimes dismiss certain ideas as "fluffy"[49] or "not traditional".

The book also examines the phenomena of cult fitness studios, wellness culture, Instagram influencers, multi-level marketing, conspirituality, and QAnon. It posits that social media and its algorithms are responsible for the intensification of subcultures.

I also appreciated that the book debunked some of the myths about "brainwashing." Popular culture likes to believe that the victims of cults are uniquely vulnerable, desperately sad, and not very bright. However, the book points out that many of the people who join cults are highly idealistic, fairly intelligent, and looking for something that will make the world a better place. In that sense, anyone who is looking for a cause or seeking to find meaning is potentially vulnerable, so it behooves us all to be on our guard.

Breaking free

If you are hesitant about your decision to leave your current tradition, a helpful tool that a friend of mine shared with me many years ago was first to imagine yourself staying in your current situation, and fully inhabiting that choice. Do you feel trapped, relieved, sad, happy, safe, unsafe? Fully experience all the emotions involved in that choice. Now imagine yourself leaving your current situation, and fully experience what that choice will be like. What feelings arise from that choice? I found that this really helped me

48   Robert Jay Lifton (1961), *Thought Reform and the Psychology of Totalism: A Study of 'brainwashing' in China*. Norton.
49   Angela Coco and Ian Woodward (2007), "Discourses of Authenticity Within a Pagan Community: The Emergence of the "Fluffy Bunny" Sanction." *Journal of Contemporary Ethnography*, Volume 36, Issue 5. https://doi.org/10.1177/0891241606293160

to make the decision (in this instance, leaving a verbally abusive relationship, so it was definitely the right choice). Ask yourself whether your current religious tradition is helping, healing, and nurturing, or whether it is harmful, corrosive, and traumatizing.

Griffith and Griffith[50] identify a collection of internal states that can be listed under two headings: vulnerability and resilience. They list despair, helplessness, meaninglessness, isolation, resentment, and sorrow as states that make you vulnerable to exploitation, abuse, depression, and mental illness. They contrast these with states of resilience, which they label hope, agency, purpose, communion, gratitude, and joy. If your religion inflicts an inner state of vulnerability on you and does not create an inner state of resilience, then it is harming you far more than it is helping. If you frequently feel any of the states listed as states of vulnerability (especially in connection with thinking about your religion), then it is better to leave it and find a religion that cultivates resilience by offering joy, purpose, and community.

Once you have left the tradition, take a deep breath, and rest in your new-found freedom for a while. Take your time exploring new friendships, new hobbies, and other activities before taking the plunge into other spiritual communities. This is a bit like that necessary breathing-space between romantic relationships—when you are single and enjoying some time as an autonomous individual. Go paint the town red!

If and when you are ready to join a new spiritual community (which may be never, and that is totally fine), take your time to read multiple perspectives on it, attend several events (start with day events, not a whole week, or even a weekend, just yet). Read blogs, articles, and books by different members of the tradition, or group of traditions. Attend rituals or services run by different groups within the broader tradition. You probably want to get a broad perspective

---

50   Griffith, James L., and Griffith, Melissa Elliott (2002), *Encountering the Sacred in Psychotherapy: How to Talk with People about their Spiritual Lives*. New York: Guilford Press.

on it before diving deep and getting involved. We will look at the process of joining a new spiritual tradition in a later chapter.

Exercises, journal prompts, and reflections

- Imagine yourself staying in your current situation, and fully inhabiting that choice. Fully experience all the emotions involved in that choice. Now imagine yourself leaving your current situation, and fully experience what that choice will be like. What feelings arise from that choice?

- Make a list of all the feelings, negative and positive, that are aroused by your current situation, and the causes of those feelings.

- Evaluate the religion or group that you are leaving against the Advanced Bonewits' Cult Danger Evaluation Frame (ABCDEF).[51] This is a framework devised in the 1970s for evaluating how controlling, manipulative, or dangerous a religious or political group is.

- Read some broader perspectives on the religion you are leaving; these will help you to get some much-needed objectivity about it, which will be beneficial whether you stay or leave.

- If you are leaving fundamentalist or evangelical Christianity, there are two major hashtags on Twitter and Instagram that people use to share resources about leaving evangelical churches and deconstructing the harmful ideas peddled by these groups: #exvangelical and #deconstruction. There is also the #hexvangelical hashtag for ex-evangelicals who are exploring witchcraft.

- Do things that you find comforting and nurturing, such as walking outside in nature, reading books that you enjoyed as a child (preferably ones that have nothing to do with the religion you are leaving), talking with friends, pampering yourself, having a bath or a shower, or preparing nourishing food.

---

51   The original Advanced Bonewits' Cult Danger Evaluation Frame is at www.neopagan.net/ABCDEF.html. It has been used by the FBI and by the South African government (and helped to bring about the legalization of same-sex marriage in that country).

Meditation: Grounding and centering

Begin by focusing on your breathing. Don't breathe in any special way, just notice how your breath comes in and out of your nostrils and how your belly rises and falls.

As you breathe in and out, feel your feet planted firmly on the ground. Relax your hips and your knees and imagine a thread extending from the top of your head to the center of the sky (this helps to align your spine with the axis of the Earth).

Imagine that your feet are tree roots, and extend your roots deep into the earth. Your roots push down into the earth, through the rich soil, finding their way among rocks, and down deep into the molten core of the Earth. As you breathe out, extend your roots; as you breathe in, draw up energy from deep within the Earth.

As the energy makes its way into your body, draw it up through your legs and feel it gathering and pooling in your solar plexus. Note the color of the energy.

Now extend a tendril of energy up your spine. Imagine that your spine is the trunk of a tree, and extend your aura at the top of your head, growing branches. Extend your branches up into the sky, beyond the atmosphere, and reach for the energy of the starlight. As you breathe out, extend your branches; as you breathe in, draw the energy down from above. Feel it gathering and pooling in your solar plexus, mingling with the energy from below.

Now draw energy from above and below at the same time, and let the energies mingle in your solar plexus. As you breathe in, draw in the energy from above and below; as you breathe out, feel it spiraling and swirling.

Now allow the energy to fill your whole body, extending out to your feet, your fingertips, the top of your head. Feel how you are aligned with the cosmic axis.

Now acknowledge the four directions: North for Earth, representing the body, sensation, physicality, and structure; East for Air, representing intellect, thought, inspiration and breath; South for Fire, representing passion, intuition, and spirit; and West for Water, representing emotion, the Moon, dreams, and the blood that flows in your veins.[52]

52   Yvonne Aburrow (2016), "Embodied Spirituality: Grounding and Centering." *Dowsing for Divinity.* https://dowsingfordivinity. com/2016/01/06/embodied-spirituality-grounding-and-centering/

Chapter 3.
Religion and sexuality

The Lord is my Shepherd and he knows I'm gay.

—Troy Perry,
founder of the Metropolitan Community Church

I will never forget the day that one of my closest friends came out to me as gay. It was a moment of truth.[53] We were both volunteer ushers at a local theater, and it was the interval of the play. We were standing in the corridor between the bar and the lobby. My friend told me that he was gay and I said that was fine. I had known my friend since he was five years old, and he was one of the kindest people I had ever met.[54]

When I told the charismatic Christian group that I belonged to at the time that my friend had come out to me as gay, they told me that God would be angry if he acted on it, and that if he wanted to be "saved" he would have to be celibate. It was the 1980s, so there was no internet where I could find progressive or inclusive Christians. I was also worried about other aspects of evangelical Christianity, such as their belief that they are the only ones who are going to get to heaven, but this idea that my friend would be condemned for an intrinsic aspect of his personality—my friend who is such a good person—I could not accept it. I left Christianity and became an atheist soon afterwards.

Many years later, in 2015, I went to a Pride march in London, UK, and there were Unitarians, Quakers, and Christians marching at Pride. The Quakers had a big banner that said "Queer Quakers"; the Unitarians had a rainbow banner, and the Christians had signs

---

53 Yvonne Aburrow (2018), "Coming out: an act of truth." *Dowsing for Divinity.* https://dowsingfordivinity.com/2018/10/26/coming-out-an-act-of-truth/
54 He is a therapist these days, so he is still a very kind person.

such as "Let's put the Bi back in the Bible" and "Maybe Jesus was actually saying 'Ah! Men."

In 2011, I conducted a service at New Unity Church, Islington, for the Rainbow Unitarians.[55] I included a reading from an article about Christian de la Huerta's ten queer spiritual roles; carols and readings for Yule, Hanukkah and Christmas; a poem by Ursula Fanthorpe (a lesbian poet); and an article by a gay Anglican priest. We also had a reading from the Polari Bible: the Gospel according to Lucille, chapter 2, verses 1 to 18. It was so moving to hear a gay man read from the Bible in Polari. It was as if we had been given our language back.

Even though I am not a Christian, I regard the Bible as a significant part of our culture, and to hear it in Polari gives it a whole new sparkle. And being able to hear the Polari version in a church was very healing.

❀⤚•°•⤜❀⤚•°•⤜❀

Many religions, especially high-control conservative ones, seek to impose norms around sexuality and gender. Some valorize celibacy and frown upon all sex except procreative sex within marriage, which generally involves imposing heterosexual sex and the gender that is associated with your biology. Others are not bothered about celibacy but do tend to impose compulsory heterosexuality, monogamy, and binary gender norms. This is especially difficult if you are lesbian, gay, bisexual, pansexual, polyamorous, intersex, asexual, nonbinary, transgender, queer, and/or two-spirit (an identity that is unique to Indigenous people in North America), as many conservative religions seek to suppress these orientations. For example, through the practice of sending their queer kids to "conversion therapy" (which has rightly been made illegal in many countries, and outlawed by professional associations of psychotherapists), or to boot camps, they seek to impose heterosexuality and cisgender identity.

---

55   Yvonne Aburrow (2012), "Fabeness to Gloria in the highest, and on earth peace, bona will toward homies." *Polari Magazine*. www.polarimagazine.com/oralhistory/fabeness-gloria-highest-earth-peace-bona-homies/

"Conversion therapy" (also known as "pray away the gay," or "ex-gay therapy")[56] is a cruel and completely unscientific process whose proponents seek to change the sexual orientation or gender of queer kids. It has now been demonstrated by decades of research that it is impossible to change a person's sexual orientation or their lived sense of gender, so all that results from these efforts is to instill deeply felt guilt, shame, and severe depression into the victims of this horrific practice. Some victims have been tortured using electric shocks to the genitals, sensory deprivation, psychological torture, and other unpleasant methods. In some cases, being subjected to these methods has led to suicide by the victim. In other cases, victims have spent thousands of dollars attempting to be cured of same-sex attraction, something which is perfectly natural. Peterson Toscano, a survivor of "conversion therapy," writes:

> Fear and shame often choke the life out of ex-gays
> and people involved with conversion therapy. This
> is true of conversion therapy survivors as well. This
> toxic mix makes it hard for folks to think clearly.[57]

As a popular meme points out, homosexuality exists in thousands of species of animal; homophobia exists in only one: humans.

"Conversion therapy" is rejected by the overwhelming majority of psychiatric, psychotherapeutic, and medical associations in Australia, New Zealand, Canada, Hong Kong, the UK, and the USA, together with the World Health Organization and medical, psychiatric, and psychotherapeutic associations in Albania, Brazil, Chile, India, Ireland, Israel, Lebanon, Norway, Spain, and South Africa.[58] Some countries have criminal bans on the practice of "conversion therapy." These include Albania, Canada, France, Germany, Malta, and Mexico. In other countries, including Brazil, Ecuador, and Taiwan, medical professionals are barred from practicing "conversion

---

56 I have added quote marks around "conversion therapy" each time I have referred to it, because it is not a proper therapy technique, and it fails to achieve anything other than torture.
57 Peterson Toscano (2017), "The challenges of coming out from conversion therapy." https://petersontoscano.com/challenges-coming-conversion-therapy/
58 Wikipedia: Medical views of conversion therapy, https://en.wikipedia.org/wiki/Medical_views_of_conversion_therapy

therapy."[59] Several other states are reportedly planning to ban it in the near future.

If you have been subjected to "conversion therapy" or any other form of "pray away the gay," seek help from a queer-affirming therapist who is affiliated to an organization that rejects "conversion therapy." You may be suffering from internalized homophobia or transphobia, and this can eat away at your self-esteem and cause depression, anxiety, and post-traumatic stress. The harm caused by "conversion therapy" can include:

- emotional harm—difficulty trusting other people, forming relationships, or distrusting your own feelings;
- psychological harm—feelings of hopelessness, low self-esteem, guilt, shame, fear.
- spiritual harm—feelings of being rejected by God or your religious community, lack of trust in spiritual leaders, fear of rejection by your religious community.
- relationship harm—Many in the ex-gay "movement" are told that their family of origin was to blame for their gayness. This is harmful to the LGBTQ+ person who is told this, harmful to their relationship with their family, and harmful to their parents. In addition to this, many "ex-gay" people try to marry people of the other sex, and these marriages can cause a lot of emotional damage to both partners. Many people who leave the "ex-gay" movement also lose most of their friends in their former religious community, and they find it very hard to make new friends because of trust issues.
- financial harm—Many people spend thousands of dollars on books, tapes, CDs, DVDs, "therapy" sessions, boot camps, etc.
- career harm—Many people have been steered into a different career by the "ex-gay movement" and their career

59   Wikipedia: Conversion Therapy: Legal status https://en.wikipedia.org/wiki/Conversion_therapy#Legal_status

prospects were damaged, either because of the severe depression caused by "conversion therapy" or because they attended "ex-gay" sessions instead of pursuing higher or further education.

- sexual harm—The internalized homophobia, fear, and shame induced by the "ex-gay movement" and "conversion therapy" make it a lot harder for survivors to pursue a healthy and happy gay sex life.

- developmental harm—Because of all the energy and commitment diverted into the pursuit of being "ex-gay," and the psychological harm and post-traumatic stress inflicted by it, many survivors find that their development as a person has been thwarted by it.

Check out the accounts of survivors of the "ex-gay movement" on the Beyond Ex-Gay website.[60] They make for harrowing reading, but if you are a survivor of this "therapy," it will be helpful to recognize that you are not alone in the various sorts of harm inflicted by it.

Even if you were not subjected to "conversion therapy," the experience of being in a religious tradition that does not affirm and celebrate your sexuality and/or gender is harmful, and you may wish to consider working through issues that arise from this with a therapist or a support group.

Many religions also seek to control and limit sexual activity even between people of different genders. For example, having sex before marriage is frowned on in many religious traditions, with a high value being placed on "purity" and virginity. Women who are prevented from access to their own sexual desires and development grow up with a very thwarted and distorted view of sexuality. Groups such as "Silver Ring Thing"[61] and the "Quiverfull movement"[62] are extreme examples of a very widespread trend in American

---

60   Peterson Toscano (2013), "Ex-Gay Harm—Let Me Count the Ways." *Beyond Ex-Gay.* https://beyondexgay.com/article/harm1.html
Responses to the above: https://beyondexgay.com/article/harmstories.html
61   Wikipedia: Purity ring https://en.wikipedia.org/wiki/Purity_ring
62   Ex-Quiverfull life stories, QF & Abusive Religion Survivor resources
https://quiverfullmyblog.wordpress.com/ex-quiverfull-life-stories-survivor-resources/

evangelicalism, that seeks to ensure that girls remain virgins until marriage and then produce as many babies as possible. As Erika Bornman writes:

> Here's the thing. Parents who think they are protecting their girl children by not teaching them about sex are actually leaving them wide open to exploitation. These parents, and they're mostly super-religious people, teach their daughter that purity is the ideal state. Her understanding of what purity entails will vary depending on what they allow her to know. They also teach their daughter that she is inferior to men. They may not think that this is what they're teaching her, but they are. Trust me on this. She learns about her inferiority from watching her mother interact with her father. She learns it in their religious institution. She learns it from seeing how much more freedom boys have than girls. If she's Christian, she learns it when female characters from the Bible are decried from the pulpit. Chances are, she has no agency over her body, and she's not at liberty to decide what she wears. Her purity is the prize. This is a message she hears repeatedly.

I believe that the reason religions seek to control, limit, and even prevent sexual pleasure is because it is an independent means of accessing spiritual states such as a sense of oneness with the universe. They also fear the independence that these experiences bring because they give people direct access to the Divine. They fear women's sexuality because it is held to be polymorphous and wild. Women are associated with the body, sometimes referred to as "the flesh." This was the result of an ascetic and world-denying approach to spirituality and religion that arose in the early part of the Axial Age (the era when individual prophets founded several new religions).

The right-wing religious obsession with preventing people from getting access to abortion and contraception (and the recent reversal of Roe v. Wade) is clearly about controlling women's sexuality. They also realize that getting converts is difficult, so the only way to make more of the faithful is to make babies. So, they spread lies that contraception and abortion are the same thing, try to prevent people getting access to contraception, and seek to shut down abortion clinics and other reproductive healthcare facilities. The fact that they want to prevent people from getting access to contraception makes it obvious that anti-abortion campaigns are about controlling sexuality, not about being "pro-life."

Heterocentric traditions

Not all religions are anti-gay, but not all religions are LGBTQ2SIA-affirming or inclusive either. The warning sign of a religious tradition that is heterocentric is that even if they have no anti-gay doctrines, they will not advertise that fact because they do not want to draw attention to it; they will focus more on heterosexual stories and lives than they will on queer lives and stories; and they will not affirm specifically queer life events such as coming out and transitioning. Their symbolism and ritual will be focused on heterosexual and cisgender life events and stories. They are not necessarily against queer people, but they do not make any real effort to include them either. This may not apply to the whole of a religious tradition and can vary from one group to another within that tradition, but it is still a good idea to keep an eye out for real inclusion, as opposed to mere tolerance.

LGBTQ2SIA-affirming traditions

If you are planning to join any religious group, check that they are LGBTQ-affirming before joining. Most liberal religious groups are LGBTQ-affirming and will perform same-sex marriages. Some of the earliest groups to welcome LGBTQ+ people were the Quakers (1966), the Unitarians in the UK (1970), the Unitarian Universalists (1970), Liberal Judaism (1970s), Reform Judaism (1977), Reconstructionist Judaism (1984), Shinto, Paganism (1980s onwards), and the United Church of Canada.[63] Even within these affirming groups, however, you may still find pockets of homophobia and transphobia among the more conservative elements. There is, unsurprisingly, a church founded by and for LGBTQ+ people, the Metropolitan Community Church (founded in 1968), which has churches in many major cities in English-speaking countries. You can check the views of most religious groups on Wikipedia or on the Human Rights Campaign website, which has pages about different religions' attitudes to homosexuality.

Liberal religious groups tend to put human needs above tradition and above a narrow interpretation of their scripture. They recognize that all scriptures have been written by humans in response to some interaction with the Divine and, therefore, are subject to interpretation and debate. Judaism is especially skilled at this, as they enjoy debating the multifaceted meanings of the Tanakh (the Hebrew Bible). A Jewish man told me that in Judaism, it is a sin to refuse something that is a pleasure to you, so if you are gay, it would be sinful to refuse the pleasures of same-sex love.

If you are still hung up on homophobic interpretations of scriptures, there are numerous books and websites that show that the Jewish and Christian scriptures are not homophobic, and in any case, they should not be taken literally or regarded as divinely inspired. A great place to start working through these resources is the

---

63   The United Church of Canada. "Gender, Sexuality, and Orientation."

https://united-church.ca/community-and-faith/being-community/gender-sexuality-and-orientation

Yvonne Aburrow

Would Jesus Discriminate? website[64] (the short answer is, of course he wouldn't).

The Shinto religion seems to have always regarded sex as a natural phenomenon to be enjoyed with few inhibitions. Shinto beliefs are diverse, but Japanese Shintoism does not condemn homosexuality, and the Konkokyo sect of Shintoism is fully affirming.[65]

Liberal religions are also characterized by promoting equality and education for women and allowing women to be ministers (the Universalists in the US ordained their first woman in 1860, the Unitarians in the UK in 1904, and the Congregationalists in 1917; Quakers do not have ministers but women have been able to give ministry in their meetings from the start). They are also often involved in interfaith dialogue and regard other religions as valid paths to the Divine.

Being part of a LGBTQ2SIA-affirming religion gives LGBTQ2SIA people a sense of being appreciated, welcomed, and valued as part of the community instead of being shunned, persecuted, marginalized, and erased. It is often the case that conservative people want to reduce LGBTQ2SIA people to their sexual activities, dismissing the possibility of same-sex love and partnership; or they want to dismiss our lives as merely a "lifestyle choice." Being part of a community that affirms and celebrates LGBTQ2SIA people, and our love, is validating and important. Everyone wants to be seen as being a full member of the community and not to have to hide part of who we are. It is also important that same-sex love is reflected and included in the liturgy, which is why I and others have developed LGBTQ-inclusive Wiccan practices and liturgy.

Other mainstream Protestant denominations have become more accepting of homosexuality, but there are still holdouts, both whole denominations and individual churches, so make inquiries before

---

64   *Would Jesus Discriminate?* https://wouldjesusdiscriminate.org/
65   Wikipedia: LGBT-affirming religious groups: Shintoism https://en.wikipedia.org/wiki/LGBT-affirming_religious_groups#Shintoism

joining. Some have only recently accepted same-sex marriage, and others have explicitly rejected it and/or require gay ministers to remain celibate. Somewhat to my surprise, many evangelical Christians are cautiously accepting of LGBTQ+ people, according to research by Kristin Aune,[66] even if their churches and denominations are not. In 2013, Steve Chalke, a prominent evangelical leader in the UK, stated that he is in favor of same-sex marriage.[67]

Buddhism tends to promote celibacy (or some variation upon it) for all practitioners regardless of gender or sexual orientation, so they are not especially opposed to homosexuality, but not especially affirming of it, either. A 2017 survey of Muslims in the USA showed 52 percent support for equal treatment and legal protection of LGBTQ+ people.[68]

Pagan groups, being very decentralized, can vary a lot. The vast majority are welcoming to LGBTQ2SIA people, but they may have heterocentric and ciscentric practices and symbols. Very few are actively homophobic or transphobic, but sadly such groups do exist. I have been sharing ideas for inclusive practice in Wicca since 2014. Some groups have adopted these suggestions or developed similar inclusive practices of their own, and others have not. There was still a lot of homophobia and transphobia in Pagan and occult circles as late as the 1980s, according to Phil Hine,[69] which necessitated queer Pagans organizing their own traditions, events, and rituals. Some of these spaces and organizations still exist, such as the Minoan Tradition and the Radical Faeries. There are also witchcraft traditions that have been inclusive of queer people from the beginning, such as the Anderson Feri Tradition.[70]

Some people who are opposed to making Pagan traditions

66   Kristin Aune (2009), "Between Subordination and Sympathy: Evangelical Christians, Masculinity and Gay Sexuality." *Contemporary Christianity and LGBT Sexualities*, 1st Edition, Routledge.
67   Christopher Bunn (2013), "The radical evangelical whose support for gay marriage is rocking his field." *The Guardian*. www.theguardian.com/commentisfree/belief/2013/jan/23/evangelical-gay-marriage-steve-chalke
68   Human Rights Campaign: *Stances of Faiths on LGBTQ Issues: Islam–Sunni and Shi'a*. https://www.hrc.org/resources/stances-of-faiths-on-lgbt-issues-islam
69   Phil Hine: Queer Magic Interview. https://youtu.be/rRwIyRKqIKo
70   Yvonne Aburrow (2020), *The Night Journey: Witchcraft as Transformation*. Published by the Doreen Valiente Foundation in association with the Centre for Pagan Studies.

inclusive of queer people ask the question "But what about the tradition?" My answer is that all traditions evolve and change in response to new situations and understandings of the world, and Pagan traditions must evolve in response to new perspectives, or they will die. Ancient paganism was inclusive of same-sex attraction and gender diversity, so contemporary Paganism should also be inclusive of them. Traditions exist to serve people and facilitate spiritual growth. People do not exist to serve traditions, especially ones that are not inclusive and welcoming of their gender or sexuality.

At the time of writing this, controversy has arisen due to a handful of individuals posting a transphobic statement online. This has been harmful for many people inquiring into Wicca, especially as they are referring to themselves as "traditional" and everyone else as "reform,"[71] which could be confusing for seekers who are looking for a "traditional" practice. These individuals have based their transphobic stance on a fundamental (and fundamentalist) misunderstanding of the history and practice of Gardnerian Wicca. The majority of the initiatory Wiccan community has emphasized that they are trans-affirming. If you see someone claiming that they are "traditional," ask them what exactly they mean by that.

Given the prevalence and loudness of homophobia and transphobia spouted by many religious people, and the fact that the media tends to report on the loud homophobes and transphobes instead of the inclusive, welcoming, and affirming groups, it is probably unsurprising that many queer people assume that all religions are homophobic and transphobic. This is not the case, and religion is not inherently anti-queer. Many religions, denominations, and traditions are welcoming, affirming, and/or inclusive of LGBTQ2SIA people. You just need to shop around a bit to find them.

---

71   Jack Chanek, "'Traditional' versus 'Reform' Gardnerians" https://www.youtube.com/watch?v=6Y0_s31Dmhk

Exercises, journal prompts, and reflections

- Gather images and stories of LGBTQ2SIA people from various religions.

- Gather images and stories of sex-positive people of faith.

- Make a shrine for queer spiritual ancestors.

- Tell their stories to others.

- If you are still suffering from guilt and shame as a result of trauma inflicted on you for your sexuality by your previous religious community, seek out sex-positive and queer-affirming stories of people from that tradition. Make a list of the qualities in yourself that you have been taught to dislike, and list reasons to like them. Try to find out if the sex-positive and queer-affirming people you have found also embody these qualities.

- Make a list of heterocentric rituals, practices, and symbols in your religious tradition, and rewrite or reimagine them to be queer-affirming.

Meditation: The sacred body

Light some candles and some incense, and put some sensual music on (either in the bathroom, or in your bedroom). Lie in the bath, or on your bed, and caress your body. Affirm that your body is holy, you are holy, and your sexual desires are holy. If possible, say this out loud. You may also wish to get up and dance to the music, still caressing your body. If you have gender dysphoria or body dysmorphia, close your eyes and imagine your body as the embodiment of your most authentic self.[72]

---

72   Adryan Corcione (2022), "The FOLX Transgender Meditation Guide: How to Meditate When You Can't Sit Still." https://www.folxhealth.com/library/transgender-meditation

Point of Pride (2020), "A Trans Day of Visibility Guided Meditation." https://www.pointofpride.org/blog/a-trans-day-of-visibility-guided-meditation

Chapter 4.
Religion and gender

"Like my kith and kin before me, I swagger-
staggered in high heels, and I wore a dress and a
hat to church. But my fabulous tail often fell below
my hemline, and my ears twitched until my hat
pitched, at the very least, down over both my eyes,
and sometimes clear across the room."

—Clarissa Pinkola Estés,
Women Who Run With the Wolves.[73]

There is something profoundly affirming about seeing a person
who looks like you leading a religious service or ritual, "equal to the
others and respected for her worth."[74] It is even more empowering if
there is an image of the Divine who looks like you. These are two of
the reasons why Pagan religions are so popular with women: They
have female leaders, and goddesses, and gods, and nonbinary deities.

I remember the first time I visited a Unitarian service after
attending an Orthodox Christian church (where women are allowed
to lead certain aspects of the service but not allowed behind the
iconostasis). At the Unitarian church, a woman minister stood at
the front, talking about all religions being equally valid, and sharing
a story about Buddhism and cats. I felt at home. It was deeply
reassuring on so many levels.

73   Clarissa Pinkola Estés (1992, 1995), *Women Who Run With the Wolves*. Ballantine Books.
74   Charlie Murphy (undated), *Burning Times*. www.christymoore.com/lyrics/burning-times/ (This song has some historical inaccuracies in it, but I still find it moving.)

When I was a child and my family attended Plymouth Brethren meetings, women were only allowed to call out hymn numbers for the people to sing. They were otherwise expected to be silent in the meetings. They also had to keep their hair long and wear headscarves. I have never felt able to wear anything resembling a headscarf since.

❀ॐ•°•ॐ❀ॐ•°•ॐ❀

There are several aspects to religions' attitudes to gender: how they treat women, how they respond to gender variant people, and what their attitude to reproductive choice is.

Gender diversity

Many conservative religions and people want to enforce the gender binary and erase the possibility of gender fluidity and nonconformity, whether that is oppressing transgender and nonbinary people or seeking to force women to be subordinate to men.

People often assume that Islam and Judaism are much the same as Christianity, but they have their own distinct attitudes and values and should not be conflated with Christianity, either under the label of "monotheism," or under the label of "Abrahamic religions." [75]

The views of Islam on gender are quite complex and different from those of Christianity. For instance:

> Transgender men and women are recognized
> and accepted in many Islamic cultures around
> the world. In fact, the idea of a man or woman
> identifying as a member of the opposite gender
> is more likely to be accepted than that of a man
> or woman expressing sexual desire for someone
> of their own gender. As early as 1988, gender

---

75   Many Jewish commentators object to the use of the term Abrahamic to include Christianity and Islam as an over-simplification of the reality of these distinct traditions. Source: Jon D. Levenson (2010), "The Idea of Abrahamic Religions: A Qualified Dissent" (Originally published in Jewish Review of Books, Spring 2010.) *Tikvah*. https://tikvahfund.org/uncategorized/the-idea-of-abrahamic-religions-a-qualified-dissent/

reassignment surgery was declared acceptable
under Islamic law by scholars at Egypt's Al-Azhar,
the world's oldest Islamic university. In Iran, in
1987, Ayatollah Khomeini declared transgender
surgical operations allowable. The basis for this
attitude of acceptance is the belief that a person is
born transgender but chooses to be homosexual,
making homosexuality a sin. Nevertheless, many
transgender Muslims after reassignment surgery
suffer rejection, socially and culturally, in their own
communities due to their remaining in their place
of origin. If one is unable to relocate to another
region where they are not known, they often suffer
verbal and physical violence.[76]

It is often tempting to assume that other religions have the same
attitude as Christianity; this is known as viewing the world through
a Protestant lens. This attitude is particularly prevalent among New
Atheists, many of whom assume that all religions are equally toxic.

The Reconstructionist Movement in Judaism welcomes
transgender people, accepts transgender students to the
Reconstructionist Rabbinical College and ordains transgender
rabbis. They have developed rituals and prayers specific to events
in the lives of transgender people, and they provide support to
Reconstructionist communities working toward becoming more
inclusive of transgender people. Similarly, Reform Judaism welcomes
transgender people, allows for the ordination of transgender
rabbis, and encourages its communities to become fully inclusive of
transgender people.

76   Human Rights Campaign: *Stances of Faiths on LGBTQ Issues: Islam—Sunni and Shi'a*. www.hrc.org/resources/stances-of-faiths-on-lgbt-issues-islam

Check Christian denominations' and churches' websites for what they do and do not say about sexuality and gender. Inclusive denominations will explicitly say that they support reproductive choice for people who can get pregnant, and that they support LGBTQ2SIA equality and diversity. They usually have affinity groups for LGBTQ2SIA people.

Pagan groups are mostly affirming of gender variant people and of women, encouraging women to take up leadership positions. In many cases, they adjust ritual and liturgy to include LGBTQ2SIA people. However, just like any other grouping in society, there are transphobes and homophobes in the Pagan, Heathen, and polytheist communities. Look for evidence that the group you are looking to join is genuinely inclusive of LGBTQ2SIA people, has a healthy consent culture, and advocates for women's rights.

The position of women

In conservative Christianity, women are expected to be subservient to men and are refused education, equality, and independence. This takes the form of denying them autonomy, authority, sexual agency, financial independence, and control over their reproductive systems. This is also the case with other patriarchal religious groups, but beware of assuming that other religions have exactly the same set of behaviors toward women as conservative Christians. It is hardly surprising then, that among Generation Z (people born between 1997 and 2012), women who do not identify as a member of any religion outnumber men who do not.[77] This is a significant change, as until around 1990, female religious adherents outnumbered male ones. As Hemant Mehta writes:

> There's the inherent sexism associated with Purity Culture.
>
> There are the policy positions held by

---

77   Hemant Mehta (2022), "A Gen Z shock: Among Zoomers with no religion, women outnumber men." *Only Sky*. https://onlysky.media/hemant-mehta/a-gen-z-shock-among-zoomers-with-no-religion-women-outnumber-men/

many conservative religious leaders that disproportionately hurt women—including abortion restrictions and possible contraception bans.

There's the disrespect shown to prominent female preachers like Beth Moore when they challenge traditions.

There are the limitations on what roles women can have in church, ranging from formal bans on the priesthood down to unofficial rules saying they can't lead.

Christian denominations, churches, and individuals vary tremendously in their affirmation of gender diversity and equality. Liberal Christian denominations and churches often affirm equality and diversity, but check to see who is at the back making the tea and coffee and doing the washing up at the end of the service. Who is allowed to get married, and who is allowed to lead services? If women are allowed or encouraged to lead services, can they preach a feminist message from the pulpit? If gender-nonconforming people can lead services, are they allowed or encouraged to preach LGBTQ2SIA-inclusive sermons?

If a religious group is pro-choice, they are likely to be members of the Religious Coalition for Reproductive Choice,[78] which includes Protestant, Catholic, Unitarian Universalist, Jewish, Muslim, Hindu, Buddhist, and Pagan[79] perspectives.

Judaism takes the view that a fetus does not become a person until it has been born and taken its first breath (in other words, when it can exist independently outside the womb).[80] The organization Jews for Abortion Access campaigns for reproductive rights.[81]

---

78   Religious Coalition for Reproductive Choice. https://rcrc.org/
79   Judy Harrow (undated), "Prayers from an Earth-Centered Spirituality." Religious Coalition for Reproductive Choice. https://rcrc.org/prayer-from-earth-centered-spirituality/
80   Rabbi Danya Ruttenberg (2022), "My Religion Makes Me Pro-abortion." *The Atlantic.* www.theatlantic.com/family/archive/2022/06/judaism-abortion-rights-religious-freedom/661264/
81   Jews for Abortion Access. https://www.jewsforabortionaccess.org/

Catholics for Choice,[82] founded in 1973, is a nonprofit organization that amplifies the voices of the majority of Catholics who believe in reproductive freedom. They use their knowledge of the church to "advocate for sexual ethics that are grounded in justice and gender equity and for genuine religious freedom and access to reproductive health care."

Most Pagans are pro-choice,[83, 84] to the extent that no-one has created a Pagan pro-choice organization, and ironically a group of "pro-life" Pagans does exist. In ancient Pagan societies, as Patti Wigington points out:

> …women sought out abortions from medical men and healers. Early Egyptian papyrus records show that pregnancies were terminated via herbal prescriptions. It also wasn't uncommon in Greece and Rome.

The issue of reproductive choice is a litmus test for gender equality in religions because it is about giving people control over their own bodies, allowing them to engage in sex for pleasure and use contraception, to make their own decisions, and not to be forced to give birth. In many cases, pregnant people have died when pregnancies were not viable and they were not allowed to have abortions. This attitude that the fetus is more important than the person carrying it shows that women and nonbinary people and trans men who can get pregnant are devalued and reduced to being mere carriers. People have also been imprisoned for murder after having a miscarriage.[85]

82   Catholics for Choice. https://www.catholicsforchoice.org/
83   Star Bustamonte (2019), "Pagans react to new abortion bans." *The Wild Hunt.* https://wildhunt.org/2019/05/pagans-react-to-new-abortion-bans.html
84   Patti Wigington (2019), "How Do Pagans and Wiccans Feel About Abortion?" *Learn Religions.* https://www.learnreligions.com/abortion-in-paganism-and-wicca-2561713
85   Robin Levinson-King (2021), "US women are being jailed for having miscarriages." *BBC News.* www.bbc.com/news/world-us-canada-59214544

Various authors (2022), "El Salvador: woman sentenced to 30 years in prison for homicide after miscarriage." *The Guardian.* www.theguardian.com/world/2022/may/10/el-salvador-woman-sentenced-prison-after-miscarriage

You can be pretty sure that if a religion actively promotes anti-abortion propaganda, it is also actively opposed to equality for women and gender-variant people.

Another red flag is when religious traditions forbid women to preach, prophesy, or lead rituals and services, or they strongly discourage them from doing so. In conservative Christianity, this is based on a misinterpretation of an injunction in one of Saint Paul's letters (or a letter mistakenly attributed to him) which appears to be trying to discourage a particular group of women from teaching that they were the "originators of men." The interpretation of the passage is tricky,[86] because the Greek words used are unusual and have changed their meaning since the text was written. It is also frequently taken out of context with everything else that Paul says, which encourages women to prophesy and speak in tongues in the churches. Either way, it seems odd to base a whole religious tenet on a 2000-year-old text, even if it was not misinterpreted and taken out of context.

Other issues where religions seek to control women's behavior and sexuality include conservative dress codes for women, often referred to as "modest dress" (not to be confused with "plain dress" in Quakerism, which is about avoiding the conspicuous display of consumption). Of course, if women choose to dress in a way that conceals rather than reveals areas of the body that are considered "sexy," then that is their choice. We should also critique the near-compulsory display of those areas of the body in secular culture, not because it is "immodest," but because it deprives women of agency and choice. As Emma Jones points out,[87] if an item of clothing makes the person wearing it feel safe and comfortable, then that is good, regardless of whether some religions would classify it as "modest". If you have been subjected to attempts to control what you wear, you

---

86   John Walker (2012), "Why The Argument Against Women In Church Leadership Is Theological Rubbish." *John Walker's Electronic House.* https://botherer.org/2012/11/21/why-the-argument-against-women-in-church-leadership-is-theological-rubbish/

John Walker (2012), "The Bible On Women In Church—An Update." *John Walker's Electronic House.* https://botherer.org/2012/11/24/the-bible-on-women-in-church-an-update/

87   Emma Jones (2017), "Origins, function of modesty in fashion warrant critique." *Miscellany News.* https://miscellanynews.org/2017/04/12/opinions/origins-function-of-modesty-in-fashion-warrant-critique/

may want to experiment with various clothing styles before settling
on a wardrobe that works for you. When Karen Armstrong left the
nunnery, she went to a clothing store with some trusted friends to
buy new outfits.

> Her body gave her a great deal of trouble when
> she left the convent. Used to a Victorian design of
> habit, with a cape and small black buttons up the
> neck, her nakedness was agonising. With shorn
> head, and a body that hadn't seen the light of day
> for seven years, she was hurried into a Marks and
> Spencer mini skirt and cardigan. Friendly but
> bemused girls at the college took her out the first
> day, still in her habit, and chose her clothes for her
> with the money the convent gave her on leaving.
> She was appalled at her own nakedness.[88]

To me, the most appalling aspect of the subordination of women
in conservative religions is the requirement for them to obey men.
This is often based on the idea that Eve was the first sinner because
the serpent tempted her to eat the apple. I prefer the Gnostic
interpretation of the Garden of Eden story, that the serpent was the
bringer of wisdom, and the prohibition of eating the apples on the
Tree of Life was the edict of a patriarchal entity. There is absolutely
no good reason why women should obey men. The patriarchal
system has messed up the world with wars, industry, pollution,
habitat destruction, and species extinction. There have been women
who have collaborated with the patriarchy, but there is no doubt that
it is a system of oppression.

Various other religious traditions also oppress women, including
Hinduism, Islam, Judaism, and Buddhism. Their patriarchal ideas
arise out of their particular cultural contexts and values. These are

88   Polly Toynbee (1983), "Interview with former nun Karen Armstrong." *The Guardian*. www.theguardian.com/world/2015/sep/12/karen-armstrong-nun-interview-polly-toynbee-1983
Karen Armstrong's own account of this momentous change from a nun's habit to secular clothing can be found in Chapter 11 of her memoir, *Through The Narrow Gate: A Nun's Story*.

different from those of cultures where Christianity is the hegemonic religion. Patriarchal ideas can be found in all religious traditions. Much of the Pagan Revival has sought to root out patriarchal notions, but as we are part of mainstream society, people still bring patriarchal ideas and behaviors into Pagan, Heathen, and polytheist communities.

Two-spirit people

Two Spirit is a modern, pan-Indigenous, umbrella term used by some Indigenous North Americans to describe people in their communities who fulfill a traditional gender-variant ceremonial and social role in their cultures. The term Two Spirit was created in 1990 at the Indigenous lesbian and gay international gathering in Winnipeg, Canada. The term Two Spirit does not diminish the tribal-specific names, roles and traditions that nations have for their own Two Spirit people. Examples of such names are Nádleehí (one who is transformed) among the Diné (Navajo) people, Winkté (indicative of a man who behaves as a woman) among the Lakota, Niizh Manidoowag (two spirit) in Ojibwe, and Hemaneh (half man, half woman) in Cheyenne. Two Spirit is a role that exists in a Native American/First Nations/Indigenous tribe for gender queer, gender fluid, and gender nonconforming tribal members. If you do not have a tribe/nation, you cannot claim that role.[89] Two Spirit people are seen as having both a male and a female spirit within them. Being Two Spirit is not the same as loving members of the same sex; Two Spirit people may be gay, but not all gay people are Two Spirit.

Two Spirit people have been adversely affected by colonization, forced conversion, and Christian supremacist suppression of traditional gender-variant roles in Indigenous cultures. When Two Spirit people were forced to attend residential schools, they were stripped of their lived experience of gender as well as their language, culture, and community. Christians sought to suppress gender

---

89   Tony Enos (2018), "8 Things You Should Know About Two Spirit People." *Indian Country Today*. https://indiancountrytoday.com/archive/8-misconceptions-things-know-two-spirit-people

variance among the Indigenous Peoples of North and South America beginning in the 1500s. In some cases, they destroyed the records of Indigenous Peoples, such as the Aztec codices, which contained valuable stories of these gender roles.[90] Christian preachers and missionaries preached against Two Spirit people, and Indian agents tried to force them to perform binary gender roles and dress as the gender they were assigned at birth. Among the Crow people, gender variant people were called Badé, and a famous Badé in the late nineteenth century was called Osh-Tisch. The local Indian agent made the Badé cut their hair, wear men's clothing, and perform manual labor—planting trees. In 1903, a Baptist minister arrived on the reservation and preached against Osh-Tisch. After Osh-Tisch died, no-one else among the Crow people became a Badé.[91]

In the twentieth century, prejudices spread among Indigenous people, instigated by Christianity, and acceptance of gender diversity and androgynous people declined sharply. Two Spirit people were often forced by government officials, Christians, and even their Indigenous communities to conform to binary gender roles. Those who could not conform went underground or committed suicide. The imposition of Euro-American marriage laws prevented the same-gender marriages that were once widespread among Indigenous peoples across North America. The revival of Indigenous cultural pride that began in the 1960s ushered in a new awareness of Two Spirit people and has since brought about a gradual increase of acceptance and respect for gender variance within Indigenous communities.

Other cultures that had gender variant social roles experienced oppression under colonialism. They are only just beginning to recover from this oppression in some cases, and are perpetuating it in others. The history of oppression of gender-variant people and same-sex love varies from one context to another, but in most cases,

---

90 Duane Brayboy (2016), "Two Spirits, One Heart, Five Genders." *Indian Country Today*. https://indiancountrytoday.com/archive/two-spirits-one-heart-five-genders
91 *Ibid.*

the oppression was spread by Western Christian interference in the norms of their cultures.

It is vital that religions do not become fixated on one particular understanding of gender and sexuality, which may have seemed progressive when it was first established but gradually becomes retrogressive and often oppressive. For example, the Christian insistence on monogamy was once necessitated by the tendency of patriarchy to treat women as property and to have multiple wives. Monogamy was then progressive in that women began to be seen as human beings with rights and feelings, but later it was used to impose unrealistic expectations upon marriages.

The Pagan insistence that there is at least one feminine divine principle—the Goddess—was radical and liberatory until people started conflating different goddesses from different cultures, insisting on biologically essentialist views of what it means to be a woman, and using the idea of the Divine Feminine as a way to prescribe gender roles.

One particular version of this is "the Triple Goddess,"[92] often described as a Maiden, Mother, Crone archetype. This archetype can be very limiting, and there are many other triple goddesses who are worth exploring: goddesses of the land and sovereignty, goddesses with many skills and roles, goddesses who are women in their own right—not just performing roles in relation to a man.

I find the archetype of the Maiden, Mother, Crone unhelpful for several reasons. One is that it is biologically essentialist. In its most basic sense, it refers to a virgin, a woman who has given birth, and a postmenopausal woman. Biology is important, as it is how we are embodied; but culture and personality and creativity and spirit are also important, and biology is a lot more varied than most people think.

---

92   Yvonne Aburrow (2017), "Triple Goddesses." *Dowsing for Divinity.* https://dowsingfordivinity.com/2017/02/05/triple-goddesses/

Biologically essentialist views of goddesses exclude trans and nonbinary people, people who have never given birth, and people who do not identify as motherly types. It can be profoundly upsetting for people who cannot give birth or who have had an abortion. I once attended an event where two fairly prominent Pagan women were holding forth about the profoundly mistaken notion that "you are not a real woman until you have given birth." This really upset two other women, and it annoyed me. Many people do give birth, and that is a beautiful thing. But it is not the only archetype of an adult woman available, and not everyone who gives birth is a woman, as trans men and nonbinary people can also give birth.

People can often get confused by the archetype of the Maiden. According to some interpretations, a maiden or a virgin is actually a sexually independent woman (not a woman whose hymen remains intact). For feminists, the idea of a sexually independent woman is much more empowering than the idea of a woman whose hymen remains intact. The idea of a woman who "belongs to" her father and will be "given away" to her husband is utterly patriarchal and oppressive and has no place in Paganism—sorry (not sorry) to be dogmatic here, but I really believe that. The notion that a virgin is a woman who has not been penetrated by a penis is hopelessly patriarchal, and it overly privileges penetrative sex. People of all genders can be virgins in a variety of ways.

The notion that a sexually active woman must also be a mother also seems patriarchal to me. It implies that the ultimate role of an adult woman is to be a mother and that all sexual activity leads to parenthood. Some people have claimed that the idea of Maiden, Mother, and Crone is matriarchal, but I do not want to live in a matriarchy any more than I want to live in a patriarchy. The idea of a matriarchy is gender-essentialist, and potentially oppressive for those of us who do not fit in the gender binary model.

The Crone archetype is perhaps a bit more empowering, as it involves facing up to death and embracing the wisdom of old age.

But why does the dividing line between mother and crone have to be the menopause? This once again excludes trans women, nonbinary people, and so on, and is also biologically essentialist. Menopause can be a profound and powerful experience for many people—and that is awesome—but we are more than just our biology.

The idea of Maiden, Mother, Crone also leaves out lots of other archetypes, such as the priestess, the hag (Dark Moon), the warrior, the poet, the architect, the writer, and many more.

Even Robert Graves, who more or less invented the Maiden, Mother, Crone archetype, described the Triple Goddess in other ways, such as Mother, Bride, Layer-out and Maiden, Nymph, Hag. Graves seems to have still seen these as her roles in relation to a man, but at least they are different archetypes.

There are plenty of other triple goddesses who are depicted as independent beings in their own right. One very powerful triple goddess is Brighid, who has three roles: smith, healer, poet. At first glance these roles seem unrelated, but the smith reforges and transforms metal, the healer transforms flesh and spirit, and the poet transforms words. All three are aspects of the creative impulse.

Another really important Celtic triplicity was the Matronae, who are frequently depicted in Romano-British statuary. I have seen an example of these in the Corinium Museum at Cirencester, in the UK. They are three women, sometimes depicted as married, sometimes as unmarried, with bouquets of flowers, fruit, or wheat. They are the same age. They are sometimes given the name of local goddesses; the depiction at Cirencester was dedicated to the Suleviae, which was probably their local name.

Most examples of triple goddesses from actual mythology are either sisters or a single woman with three different roles.

Other mythologies also had triple goddesses who were not Maiden, Mother, Crone archetypes. Hekate, a very complex ancient

83

Greek goddess, was sometimes depicted as threefold, but she had several epithets and roles. The earliest depictions of her were not three-formed. The threefold imagery (Trimorphe, three-formed; Triodia or Trioditis, the one who frequents crossroads; and Trivia, three ways, a Roman form) came later. Pausanias wrote that Hekate was first depicted as threefold by the sculptor Alkamenes in the Greek Classical period of the late 5th century BCE.[93]

There are many goddesses in Pagan mythology. Most are singular in form, and some are triple. The threefold goddesses of antiquity were generally three sisters, three mothers, or three queens and were goddesses of the land, associated with grain, flowers, and fruits. Some were a single goddess with three different roles, like Hekate and Brighid. Some were responsible for weaving fate, like the Norns, the Sulevice, the Parcae, and the Moirai; others were responsible for creating joy, like the Three Graces.

People like to oversimplify and conflate these entities when, in reality, their diversity and complexity is important.

The vast majority of Pagans believe in equality, but we still need to deconstruct some patriarchal, heterocentric, and ciscentric concepts. Some years ago, a Pagan woman pointed out that a particular meme celebrating the trope of the Horned God pursuing the maiden Goddess in spring was an instance of rape culture, and I agreed with her. We need to examine which ancient myths are helpful and life-affirming and which are not, and we should not be afraid to create new twists and perspectives on these old stories.

Culture and traditions can change and evolve, and we can embrace new understandings of gender and sexuality—and reflect these in our rituals and our values.

93   Danielle Mackay (2021), "Everything You Need To Know About Hecate (Maiden, Mother, Crone)." *The Collector.* https://www.thecollector.com/hecate-goddess-magic-witchcraft/

Exercises, journal prompts, and reflections

- Gather images and stories of gender-variant people and women from different religions.

- Make a shrine for gender-variant and female spiritual ancestors.

- Tell their stories to others.

- If you are still suffering from guilt and shame as a result of trauma inflicted on you for your gender by your previous religious community, seek out stories of gender-variant people and women from that tradition who resisted patriarchy. Make a list of the qualities in yourself that you have been taught to dislike, and list reasons to like them. Try to find out if the gender-variant people and women you have found also embody these qualities.

- Make a list of ciscentric[94] and patriarchal rituals, practices, stories, and symbols in your religious tradition, and rewrite or reimagine them to be affirming of gender equality and diversity.

---

94   Ciscentric: Centering on or overemphasizing cisgender people and identity.

Cisgender: Identifying with the gender you were assigned at birth.

Meditation: You are divine

Sit, lie down, or stand (whichever is most comfortable for you). As you breathe in and out, become aware of your connection to the Divine. Notice where you feel that connection in your body. Now let it expand and imagine the Divine presence filling your whole body. Do you experience it as light, or darkness, or something else? Let the presence fill you. You are one with that presence, and you have always been part of it. You are divine. Whatever your gender is, the Divine contains that gender, and is expressing it through you. Visualize the Divine as being the same gender as you. Affirm (out loud if possible) that you are divine, in whatever words feel right to you.

Chapter 5.
At the crossroads

"Only one heart had to find its true position and
travel on from there and all the rest would follow,
for no matter how isolated the one felt itself to
be, in the deeps of all life all were united and no
one could move accurately without all ultimately
moving with it…"

—Laurens van der Post, *A Far-Off Place*.[95]

I was fifteen years old. The tension had been building for months
as I began to become aware that Christianity was the wrong religion
for me. A good friend had come out to me as gay. Another dear
friend had pointed out that, if you take the view that only Christians
can get to heaven, but you get in on a technicality if you never
heard the gospel, then if a missionary goes to the Amazon jungle
and preaches Christianity to an uncontacted tribe, and only half
of them become Christians, then he has done the unconverted half
considerable harm, because previously they would have got into
heaven on a technicality, but now they won't. I had seen the film
Gandhi and concluded that it was wrong to think that devout people
from other religions would not get into heaven. I felt myself to be at
the crossroads, sitting on the fence between Christianity and atheism.
At the moment of transition from one to the other, I was standing in
the front garden of my parents' house in Southampton, UK, near the
birch tree they had rescued from the path of a motorway when it was
a sapling. The change-over from Christian to atheist was very quick,
as I could not sit on the fence for long. It was all or nothing. I felt a
huge sense of relief as I jumped off the (metaphorical) fence.

---

95   Laurens van der Post (1978), *A Far-Off Place*, p.304. Mariner Books.

❀⤸•°•⤻❀⤸•°•⤻❀

The crossroads is a liminal place, an in-between place. It is often seen as uncanny, the place where criminals and suicides were buried, a place that might sweep you off your feet and carry you to some unknown destination, a place where you went to sell your soul to the Devil in exchange for some great talent. The crossroads is a profoundly uncomfortable place to be. So is sitting on the fence between two positions. But the ambiguity of the crossroads gives you freedom. You have at least four paths to choose from, plus the option of staying where you are.

The time when you are in-between paths and exploring your options is a great place to be. As I said in the previous chapter, enjoy your newfound freedom, and explore different options. Thankfully, you do not need to sell your soul to any dubious supernatural entities to gain new wisdom, insight, or skills while you are down at the crossroads.

Some people who have left very rigid religious traditions report feeling that they no longer know what is right or wrong, and making dubious ethical choices that hurt other people. So take your time to examine your personal ethics, and what you consider to be right and wrong, separate from the morality imposed on you by your former religious tradition. Ethics are found in every religious tradition and are a human construct intended to establish a system that guarantees the maximum amount of human flourishing; they are not a divinely-imposed mandate. If you feel confused about ethics, read widely on other traditions' approach to ethics, including atheism and humanism. I found Richard Holloway's reflections on morality without God to be particularly helpful; he talks about ethical decisions as balancing competing understandings of what is good.[96]

If you are considering getting involved with a new religious tradition, read as much as you can about various religious traditions,

---

96   Richard Holloway (2013), *Godless Morality: Keeping Religion out of Ethics*. Canongate Books.

whether you feel drawn to them or not. It is also a good idea to evaluate any religious tradition that you may feel drawn to against the Advanced Bonewits Cult Danger Evaluation Frame.[97]

While you are in this exploratory phase, take the time to examine whether and how your new self is different from the persona you built while you were part of your former religious community. Your values, interests, activities, and friendship group may change, either suddenly or gradually, depending on how separated your former community is from the rest of society.

You may find it helpful to find other people who are going through the process of extricating themselves from your former community, as you can compare notes about what was wrong with it.[98]

Therapists are not always trained in dealing with religious trauma and spiritual abuse survivors, so a support group may be your best option (and is often free or low-cost).

Gillie Jenkinson, an expert on recovering from cults, recommends a four-phase recovery model:

- Phase 1: leave physically and psychologically
- Phase 2: cognitively understand
- Phase 3: emotionally heal the trauma, loss, and pre-cult vulnerabilities where relevant
- Phase 4: recognize recovery and post-traumatic growth[99]

The first phase may involve moving to another house, or even another town, to get away; but equally important are challenging the norms and assumptions of the group, developing your critical thinking skills and your own opinions, and recognizing the coercive and controlling nature of the group that you have left.

97   The original *Advanced Bonewits' Cult Danger Evaluation Frame* is at http://www.neopagan.net/ABCDEF.html and there is a list of cultlike groups at https://rationalwiki.org/wiki/Cult
98   Gillie Jenkinson (2019), "Out in the World: Post-Cult Recovery." *Therapy Today*. https://www.academia.edu/38689948/Out_in_the_World_Post-Cult_Recovery
99   *Ibid.*

The second phase involves understanding the mechanisms and techniques of brainwashing, and even of ordinary conversion experiences, so you can unpack them and understand how you (or your parents) became involved in the group. It is also necessary to identify aspects of your personality that are present because they reflect the norms or expectations or assumptions of the group (such as assuming that you are sinful or bad or unlikeable). This can sometimes take the form of a whole pseudo-personality.

The third phase is to process the emotions resulting from being in the group. This can be very painful, and is slightly different for people who were born into a cult and people who joined a cult as an adult, because people who joined as an adult can remember what they were like before they joined, and they can examine the reasons they joined the cult at that stage in their life. This is also the stage at which it may be appropriate to look at whether you have developed a tendency to be drawn to other cultlike groups to replace the feeling of security or belonging that you may have gained from the group that you are leaving.

The fourth phase is to recognize that healing has occurred, to integrate the personality around new values and experiences, and to start the process of growing beyond the painful experiences, and evening regarding them as opportunities for learning.

All of this is why I think it is important to process and deal with the experience of your former religious tradition (even if it was not technically a cult) before getting involved in a new path or tradition. The definition of a cult is multifaceted,[100] and many groups exhibit at least some of the characteristics of a cult. Even philosophical groups, discussion groups, psychotherapy groups, sales and marketing groups, political and social movements, psychic or occult groups, can exhibit the characteristics of cults.[101] Cultlike characteristics

---

100   Michael D. Langone (2015), "Characteristics Associated with Cultic Groups—Revised." *ICSA Today*, Vol. 6, No. 3, 2015, 10. https://www.icsahome.com/articles/characteristics
101   Richard Turner (2022), "Identifying abusive cults." *To think again.* https://www.tothinkagain.co.uk/identifying-a-cult

have also been observed in some Pagan groups,[102] so even they are not immune from this behavior. Much as we would like to think that Pagan traditions are decentralized and that it is easy for people to walk away from them, the decentralized nature of these groups makes it easier to behave in this way, because there is no oversight from outside the group. Be very wary of becoming dependent on any group for housing, employment, or financial remuneration (this applies to even the most liberal-minded groups).

One of the most insidious cult behaviors is subtly discouraging people from having friends who are not members of the group. This can occur because people in a group develop a particular way of speaking based on their worldview, and it can be hard for outsiders to understand the jargon. It is natural for people to hang out with like-minded others, and if you are involved with the group to the exclusion of other social activities, it is very easy to lose interest in friends who do not share your worldview or your obsession.

I have been involved in online discussion groups that started to develop cultlike characteristics as the terminology became more abstruse and people started to be ever more critical of those who do not share the insights and terminology of the group. I was fortunate that someone I trusted drew my attention to the cultlike characteristics of the group, or that I started to become aware of it myself.

One of the characteristics of cults and cultlike groups is the requirement to hold opinions rigidly and not to diverge from the views of the charismatic group leader. This is why having an evidence-based approach to opinions is important. It is good to test an opinion against all the evidence, evaluate what the consequences of the opinion might be, look at who else holds the opinion, and hold it lightly, so that if new evidence emerges to refute the opinion, you can relinquish or modify it in the light of that new evidence.

---

102   Tadrakos (2018), *On my years in CAYA Coven*. https://tadrakos.wordpress.com/2018/03/23/on-my-years-in-caya-coven/
See also https://rabbittestimony.blogspot.com/

That does not mean having an opinion vacuum into which any fashionable new idea can float; it means basing your opinions on evidence—and modifying them in the light of new evidence (rather like the process known as the scientific method).

You do not need to have an opinion about absolutely everything, but it is important to understand the political issues of the day (social and environmental justice, climate change, gender and sexual orientation, and the effects of systemic racism and inequality). If someone's rights or existence is threatened by the status quo or by a group seeking to take away their rights, then not having an opinion on that topic is an expression of privilege (the privilege of being personally unaffected by that issue).

If you are traumatized by your previous religion, make sure to get some help (therapy if you can afford it or your insurance covers it, or a support group if not). This is especially important if you are suffering from religious trauma, post-traumatic stress disorder, internalized homophobia, internalized ableism, internalized misogyny, internalized transphobia, low self-esteem, depression, suicidal ideation, flashbacks, stress, or any other serious symptoms.

It is important to ensure that you are not going to replace the issues you were having with your previous group with a similar set of issues with any new group that you join. That is why it is important to develop your own personality and preferences independently of the group you left, before getting involved with another group. You need to linger at the crossroads, looking around at the landscape. Society at large is always trying to compel us to make a choice, have an opinion, choose a road or a path. But we can linger in the twilight zone of agnosticism if we so choose, while building up new values and interests and developing resilience to people who want to control or dominate others.

You may have noticed that there are a lot of metaphors in this chapter. I started with a metaphor of being at the crossroads. In ancient times, a statue of Hekate Triformis stood at the crossroads. The name triformis means "three paths." In medieval times, the crossroads was a liminal and uncanny place, because it was where people were hanged, and so it was on the threshold of death (the ultimate change of paths).

The inner life, religion, and spirituality make extensive use of metaphors. By describing our experiences using a metaphor, we are using a familiar physical experience to attempt to describe something intangible and inchoate.

When we become disenchanted with our existing spiritual community, it is partly because its metaphors cease to sustain us and, in some cases, are actually harming us. For example, many people report being disturbed by the phrase "sinners in the hands of an angry God." To me, that metaphor conjures up an image of a large threatening male entity, throwing tiny people around.

Other, much more nurturing, metaphors for the Divine are available, such as a mother hen sheltering her chicks under her wings[103] but these more nurturing images are not widely used, and they tend to be marginalized—especially in fundamentalist groups.

Only certain metaphors are permissible in each religious tradition,[104] and often they do not make sense to someone from a different culture or tradition. On a transatlantic flight, I got chatting to a Muslim man next to me. First we were discussing food, and then he turned the conversation to religion. In his view, those who reject Islam will be rejected by Allah. He used the metaphor of a child becoming estranged from its mother, and he said that the mother would then be justified in hating the child. I disagreed, thinking of the story of Emeth the faithful Calormene in CS Lewis's The Last Battle, and of the biblical story of the Prodigal Son.[105] It is easy to see in this example how each of us had ideas about how Allah might

---

103   Psalm 91:4, New Living Translation. *Bible Gateway.* www.biblegateway.com/passage/?search=Psalm+91%3A1-4&version=NLT
104   Griffith, James L., and Griffith, Melissa Elliott (2002), *Encountering the Sacred in Psychotherapy: How to Talk with People about their Spiritual Lives.* New York: Guilford Press. Chapter 3: Metaphor and spirituality.
105   Luke 15:11-32, New Living Translation. *Bible Gateway.* https://www.biblegateway.com/passage/?search=Luke%2015%3A11-32&version=NLT

react that were conditioned by the stories that are prevalent in our cultures. It was also of great interest to me that I could listen to his theological ideas without much emotion being aroused (whereas if I heard a Christian expressing similar ideas, it would be very likely to reopen old wounds). I think my emotions were not aroused because his metaphor for, and idea of, God did not chime with any cultural tropes that I am familiar with.

When someone changes from one religious tradition to another, they are changing not only their values and beliefs, but also their metaphors. Metaphors are a powerful aspect of people's inner lives, and they are immensely important in how people relate to the Divine. It can take a long time to shift metaphors for that relationship, even if they have changed paths to a radically different religion. I have frequently heard people bringing ideas from their previous tradition into their new one. There is more detail on that in the chapter on unexamined baggage.

Frequently, changing your religion also frequently involves learning to live with uncertainty. The fundamentalist traditions peddle the notion of certainty, but that sense of certainty is bound to be shattered by facts that contradict it. People who cling to fundamentalism have to defend the concept of inerrant scriptures, conservative views of sexuality, and the improbable concept of a creator deity. These doctrines are shattered when they discover a contradiction in the scriptures, or a real-world fact that contradicts their view of scripture (such as evolution); or they discover that their best friend is gay and have to choose between their conservative views and their friend; or a family member is not involved in their religion and the religion holds the view that nonbelievers are going to hell. Some people react to these contradictions by clinging even more fervently to their fundamentalist worldview. Others react by flipping over to another equally rigid set of views, such as New Atheism or "Hard Gard" Wicca.[106] Others learn to live with uncertainty and

---

106   Gardnerian Wiccans who hold rigid views on tradition are often referred to as "Hard Gards" (and sometimes self-identify as such).

ambiguity as a kinder, gentler alternative, relying on their feelings instead of holding to creeds that can easily be refuted. Some succeed in reconciling their views with science in various ways.

Living with uncertainty is entirely possible if you are deeply connected to your spiritual tradition through feelings of joy, fulfillment, and community. If you can replace the fears implanted in you by fundamentalism with a joyful experience of divinity, it provides assurance and reassurance that "all shall be well, and all shall be well, and all manner of thing shall be well."[107]

For now, I just want to take a moment to appreciate the huge paradigm shift that leaving a religion involves. It may be because your old set of metaphors no longer serves you or is actively hurting you; nonetheless, it is hard to let go of those metaphors. It sometimes feels like they are "just how things are," and it can take considerable insight to even realize that they are metaphors, and adjust them to something healthier.

In the chapel of Manchester College, Oxford, England, there is a beautiful set of nineteenth century stained glass windows with images of angelic wings and the Earth in the depths of space. They are Unitarian windows, and the text in them reads "Élargissez Dieu"—in other words, enlarge your understanding of God.[108] It's a beautiful metaphor for changing your relationship with the Divine.

107   Julian of Norwich (1373), *Revelations of Divine Love*.
108   "Elargissez Dieu! - a quotation from Diderot, roughly translated as Set God free! or Broaden your concept of God!" Manchester College Oxford Chapel Society (2022), *The Chapel*. https://www.ukunitarians.org.uk/oxford/chapel.htm

Exercises, journal prompts, and reflections

- Develop your own personal code of ethics, without reference to any higher power or deity. Examine your personal ethics and what you consider to be right and wrong, separate from the morality imposed on you by your former religious tradition.

- Read widely on other traditions' approach to ethics, including atheism and humanism.

- Identify which of the phases described by Gillie Jenkinson best describes your current state of mind. Have you left your former religion both physically and psychologically? Do you have an understanding of the processes they used to manipulate you? Have you recovered from the trauma inflicted by the group? Are you starting to develop your own personality, values, ethics, and worldview?

- If you were going to design a religion from scratch, what elements would it include?

- Make a list of features that any religion or philosophical system that you would consider getting involved in should have. Your list could include beliefs, values, rituals, practices, and metaphors. You may want to divide your list into "must have" and "nice to have" features.

- Make a list of features that any religion or philosophical system that you would consider getting involved in should not have. Your list could include beliefs, values, rituals, metaphors, and practices.

- Make a list of the key features of different religions and philosophical systems. Can you group them into families of similar traditions?

- What metaphors do you have for the Divine or other powerful spiritual forces? Are they helpful or harmful? If they are harmful, can you shift them to something more

helpful? If they are helpful, can you imagine any situation
where they might not sustain you? How can they be
adjusted to sustain you in that situation? Or can you think
of a different metaphor that would help in that eventuality?

- Do you feel the presence of the Divine? Where in your body
  does this feeling manifest itself?
- If you do not feel the presence of the Divine, try relaxing
  and breathing, and maybe using a technique like centering
  prayer,[109] to open yourself up to the Divine (however you
  perceive the Divine).

109   Yvonne Aburrow (2014), "Pagan Prayer'. *Dowsing for Divinity*. https://dowsingfordivinity.com/2014/03/12/pagan-prayer/

Meditation: Centering prayer

Centering prayer was developed by a group of Trappist monks
(Thomas Keating, William Meninger, and Basil Pennington), based
on the contemplative practices of the Desert Fathers, and in response
to a burgeoning interest in Buddhism in the 1970s.[110]
Choose a word that you find positive and uplifting to focus on during
the prayer. The technique is similar to that of meditation, in that you
relax your breathing and focus on the body, but you hold the concept
you wish to focus on in your heart for the duration of the prayer,
perhaps repeating the chosen word.

110   Rose, Phil Fox. "Meditation for Christians." *Patheos.* http://www.patheos.com/blogs/philfoxrose/meditation-for-christians/

Chapter 6.
The conversion process

摸着石头过河

Mōzhe shítou guòhé.

Cross the river by feeling the stones.

– Dèng Xiǎopíng

My realization that I am a Pagan was a gradual process. I had always been drawn to stars, standing stones, trees, and the Moon. As a child, I remember feeling thrilled when my parents told me about Pagan solstice celebrations where people would light bonfires on the tops of hills to make the Sun come back after the longest night. I remember when I was about twelve years old, talking to the trees and hoping they would talk back, like they did for Lucy in Prince Caspian.[111] Later, I read Puck of Pook's Hill by Rudyard Kipling, and I loved the Pagan rituals of Parnesius and Pertinax. After I ceased to be a Christian, I began to wish that there were other Pagans in the world (I thought I was the only one, although I had heard rumors of the revival of Heathenry).

I can remember exactly where I was when I decided that I am a Pagan. It was 1985, and I was in the middle of a huge roundabout called Charlotte Place in Southampton, England, which had a pedestrian walkway through it.[112] I was thinking about how I love Nature and the pleasure of being alive, and that essentially, that meant that I am a Pagan. Although I had a "moment of truth," the buildup to this realization was a gradual one, informed by many different experiences, feelings, and thoughts. It is worth noting that

---

111   "Lucy's eyes began to grow accustomed to the light, and she saw the trees that were nearest her more distinctly. A great longing for the old days when the trees could talk in Narnia came over her."

– C.S. Lewis, *Prince Caspian.* https://www.goodreads.com/work/quotes/3348636-prince-caspian?page=5
112   Weirdly, there is now a hotel in the middle of the roundabout but it was just a large flat space at the time. The whole area has changed massively, with different buildings around it. https://goo.gl/maps/kUqqJPSGpcBXqspL7

I had been walking and thinking when I came to this realization. Walking is a great way to process one's emotions.

❀౿•°•౾❀౿•°•౾❀

When most people think about conversion, they think of a "road to Damascus" experience:[113] a sudden flash of revelation or a vision leading to instantaneous conversion. However, conversion is a process, not a moment in time. First the old worldview comes unraveled, perhaps by some triggering event or insight; then the new worldview begins to form.

Conversion literally means "turning around". Before about 1400 C.E., it meant "turning away from sin and toward God" (which we would now describe by the word "repentance"). After that time, it came to mean changing from one religion to another.[114] A related word is metanoia, which means "changing your mind."[115] It is more useful to think of the process of turning around as a large ship turning around, and taking some time to do so, rather than as the quick and simple process of a person changing direction.

Lewis Rambo, a sociologist of religion, describes a seven-phase model of the conversion process (context, crisis, quest, encounter, interaction, commitment, and outcomes).[116] The first phase is the context: how the person was brought up, their culture, their previous religious experiences. People can only start from their current position, so it is important to understand where they came from. If you have left a religion with a complex set of beliefs, setting out on your new path might involve a lot of negation of those original beliefs before you can start affirming your new beliefs and experiences. For example, people who have left Christianity spend a lot of time processing how they feel about the divinity of Christ and its related theological concepts. For people leaving other religions, the question

---

113   The "road to Damascus" refers to when Paul (formerly known as Saul) had a vision of Christ on the road to Damascus, and became a Christian as a result. (Acts 9: 1-7)

114   https://www.etymonline.com/word/conversion

115   https://www.etymonline.com/word/metanoia

116   Religion & Ethics News Weekly (2000), *Lewis Rambo Extended Interview*, www.pbs.org/wnet/religionandethics/2000/11/10/november-10-2000-lewis-rambo-extended-interview/13744/

of the divinity of Christ is usually meaningless and irrelevant (unless they are in the process of becoming a Christian).

Friends of mine who have left Judaism or Islam have told me that they deliberately violated a well-known taboo from those traditions as a way of emphasizing that they have left: They eat a bacon sandwich (which violates the taboo against eating pork). Similarly, it is said that, in the medieval period, people who became witches would trample on a crucifix (this would be hard for many ex-Christians to do, because it is an act of blasphemy rather than taboo-breaking).

In the second phase, people go through some kind of crisis. This could be dissatisfaction with their current belief system, a trauma or shock of some kind, or a mystical experience. The crisis can be deeply painful and frightening and may involve considerable emotional upheaval. Even if they have had some kind of mystical experience, which sounds like a pleasant thing to happen, it can be worrying or disturbing, especially if it challenges their existing worldview. Dissatisfaction with your current religion can also be shocking and unpleasant, as it often happens because there is a conflict between your sexual orientation or lived experience of gender (or that of someone you know) and your conservative religion. If it is a choice between your religion and your gender or sexuality, the discovery that your religion is hostile to something so intrinsic to your nature can be deeply unpleasant. In many cases, people have undergone so-called "conversion therapy" (also known as "pray away the gay"), which is a deeply violent, damaging, and traumatizing process, as previously discussed in Chapter 3: Religion and Sexuality.

In the third phase, people go on a quest to find something that fits their new model of the world. This might be a different religious tradition altogether, or a more progressive version of their current tradition. The quest phase can last for a very long time, and it may involve trying multiple religious traditions before finding one that fits. It can also happen more than once.

People may also encounter someone in a tradition that they are exploring who is deeply inspiring and spiritual, and it may be this encounter that leads them to decide to commit to this tradition. Meeting someone from a spiritual tradition is frequently the way people become aware of it. Rambo also said, in an interview with PBS, that "One of the best secular analogies to conversion is falling in love, because falling in love is such a wonderful experience. It is dramatic; it is intense. The world looks different; you feel different." However, he also points out that after the honeymoon phase, the convert needs to get to grips with the reality that not everyone in their new community is nice, and to internalize and deepen their engagement with the new religious tradition that they have joined.[117]

The next phase involves interaction: attending rituals, often as a guest or observer, and learning how to do their chosen religious practice. At first, any problems that may exist within the community are obscured by everyone being on their best behavior around the newcomer and by the rosy glow of being in love with the new tradition. The interaction phase should last a reasonable length of time. In Wicca, we recommend that seekers get to know the coven they want to join for at least a year and a day before deciding to commit. Making the interaction phase last for a least a year means that you get to experience all of the seasonal rituals of your chosen path, and you get to see the community you are planning to join for a reasonable length of time and in a variety of different moods and settings.

The next stage is commitment. There is often a ritual, such as initiation or baptism, to enter fully into membership of the new community. Such rituals forge a new identity, a new sense of meaning, and a new way of interacting with life and other people. Examples of initiation rituals include baptism, being given a new name, or a commitment ceremony. There is often an element of ordeal in initiation ceremonies. This ordeal is intended to bring

117   Religion & Ethics News Weekly (2000), *Lewis Rambo Extended Interview*, www.pbs.org/wnet/religionandethics/2000/11/10/november-10-2000-lewis-rambo-extended-interview/13744/

about change in the candidate's psyche. While the candidate is undergoing the initiation, they are in a liminal state, on the threshold, neither one thing nor the other. The state of liminality is a powerful experience. Once the candidate has crossed the threshold, they are a fully fledged member of the group, albeit a very new and inexperienced one.

The final phase is consequences or outcomes—the transformation brought about by the commitment. This could be lifelong development in the chosen faith, or it could be disillusionment and going back to the quest phase. The outcome phase is just as significant as the other phases and also has its own ups and downs, periods of drama and crisis, doubt and faith, commitment and apathy.

Sometimes people have a profound mystical experience that leads them to completely reorient their feeling and thinking, but even after such a numinous encounter, there is still the process of joining a new community, learning the traditions of the community, meeting new people, and understanding the concepts of the tradition. This multiphase model is still a useful way of understanding the process of conversion because, as soon as the process involves other people, it gets more complicated.

Finding a group

One of the reasons for having a long exploratory phase when you are trying to find a new spiritual path and a religious community to practice it with, is that groups can be problematic.[118]

The benefits of being in a group include having people to celebrate festivals with, sharing ideas, having people to learn from, having conversations about issues that never normally get discussed, and experiencing those moments when all the energies of the group flow together and become something greater.

118   Yvonne Aburrow (2015), "Paganism for Beginners: Finding a group." *Dowsing for Divinity.* https://dowsingfordivinity. com/2015/07/30/finding-a-group/

Groups can be awesome if you find the right people to celebrate with; they can also be dysfunctional. The trick is to stay alert. If you experience warning signs and feel that the group you are considering joining does not fit your needs, proceed with caution. Finding the right group can be tricky. Most people are either incredibly cautious about approaching groups or over-enthusiastic and, therefore, vulnerable.

It is very tempting to ignore the warning signs and assume that the group you have found was somehow meant for you. If the group you are considering joining tries to tell you that they are the One True Way and that all the other groups have got it wrong, then run away. Even if the group does not exhibit the classic warning signs, but their approach and philosophy is just not a good fit with yours, then maybe they are not the right group for you—and you are not the right new member for them.

One of the ways to identify a "high control" group (one that wants to control all aspects of your life) is to look at whether it distinguishes between "sacred time" and "ordinary time." Unethical religions never let you leave "sacred time": You always have to be thinking the way they think, dressing the way they dress, using their language, focusing on their goals.[119] Ethical religions have a clear boundary marking the end of a service or ritual, and a process to help you transition back into a normal mode of consciousness. The more intense the religious experience, the more important this transition is. For example, Unitarians and Unitarian Universalists start with a chalice-lighting and finish with closing words, then gather in a separate room for tea, coffee, and snacks. Quakers start by sitting in a circle or square and gradually create their gathered silence; then at the end, people get up and move about. They also have tea, coffee, and snacks. Wiccans and Druids start by casting a circle, calling the quarters; then at the end, there's a feast (which helps participants to ground), we say farewell to the quarters, and un-cast the circle. This

---

119   Amanda Montell (2021), *Cultish: The Language of Fanaticism*. Harper Wave.

provides a clearly delineated start and end to sacred time, and the social chat at the end forms a liminal space to help with the return to everyday living.

I often come across people who prefer to avoid groups altogether. Some of them have had a bad experience of being in a group that has put them off. That is understandable, but not every group is the same. Others say that they need to do more work on themselves before joining a group. But a group is a great place to work on yourself, because social interaction is where personal change and growth usually happens. I would add the caveat that a prerequisite for seeking to join a group is being comfortable in your own skin; you need to like yourself and have some confidence and self-esteem.

Another reason that I sometimes hear for not wanting to join a group is being an introvert. That seems like a valid reason, but joining a group does not necessarily mean you have to reveal your deepest secrets or spend vast amounts of time with others; it does mean engaging with them on a quest for meaning and connection.

When you are approaching a group, ask lots of questions.

- Does the group have ground rules?
- How often do they meet?
- What are their expectations about members' commitment and attendance?
- What is their attitude to theological, magical, or political disagreement?
- Are they prepared to learn from other people?
- How do they feel about members being involved with other traditions?
- Do they value previous experience?
- Do they value creativity and extemporization, or do they prefer more formal rituals?
- Can you meet the existing members?
- Is there a training or acculturation process before the commitment phase?
- Can you attend an open ritual before deciding whether to embark on the training?
- Do they distinguish between "sacred time" and "ordinary time"?
- Do they seem to control members' lives?

You could also ask yourself a similar set of questions.

- Do you want a group that has ground rules?
- How far are you prepared to travel for meetings?
- How many meetings per year are you willing to commit to?
- How do you feel about people with opinions that are different from yours? Are you prepared to be challenged in your thinking?
- Do you have the time and energy to be involved with more than one tradition?
- What skills and experiences can you bring to the group?
- What style of ritual do you prefer?
- Are you prepared to put in the effort of engaging with the training process and learning new things?
- Are you comfortable with the idea of commitment?

The answers to these questions will vary from one individual to another, and from one group to another. Hopefully, you can find a group whose answers to the questions are a fairly close match with yours.

Unethical groups

Beware of groups that try to coerce you into committing to more than you are ready or willing to do.[120] I would strongly advise against joining any group that exhibits two or more of the following behaviors:

- Charges excessive amounts of money for attending events or learning the tradition
- Claims that sexual intercourse with senior members or leaders of the group is required (this is seriously unethical)
- Claims that it is completely unproblematic for a senior member of the group to enter into a sexual relationship with a junior member of the group
- Dismisses large numbers of legitimate members of the tradition as insincere adherents
- Tries to limit social contact between members outside of meetings
- Tries to limit your social contact with other people outside the group
- Tells you not to read certain books
- Peremptorily dismisses any concerns you have about something that makes you uncomfortable
- Tries to prevent you from reading widely and critically about the tradition;
- Dismisses and belittles anyone who disagrees with them
- Fails to set a clear boundary between "sacred time" and "ordinary time"
- Has members who strike you as unduly dominated or controlled by the leaders
- Works entirely from one particular person's teachings and does not allow deviation from those principles or allow people to question them
- Makes it difficult to leave the group and claims you will not find another group if you do leave
- Refuses to provide verification that they are what they say they are, and cannot seem to keep their story straight

---

120   Yvonne Aburrow (2015), "Fraudulent and unethical groups." *Gardnerian Wicca*. https://british-wicca.com/warnings/

Some of these may be more relevant to one type of tradition than another, but they are good rules of thumb for evaluating a tradition or group.

Exercises, journal prompts, and reflections

- What do you experience as sacred? What do you regard as important, special, emotionally significant?
- What do you regard as taboo and/or profane?
- Where do you get your inspiration?
- What amuses you? What makes you happy?
- What makes you feel safe? Conversely, what makes you feel threatened?
- Whom do you trust?
- What are you thankful for?

Meditation: The sacred

Close your eyes and choose something—a place, a concept, an
object, a person—that you regard as sacred. What is the quality
in it that evokes the sacred for you? What values or virtues does it
represent? Are they values or virtues that find an echo within you?
Is the sacredness an inherent quality of it, or does it shine through it,
as if its source is elsewhere? Focus for a while on your sacred place,
concept, thing, or person. Allow its virtue to shine for you. Hear its
inner music, smell its perfume. Now let the place, concept, thing
or person fade from your mind and just focus on the virtue itself.
Recognize its reflection in your own heart.[121]

121   Yvonne Aburrow (2012), *Many Names*. Lulu.

Chapter 7.
Syncretism: blending paths

It turns out that, when you are faithful to the
path rather than to the map, you sometimes find
yourself in unfamiliar territory. What I have found
sometimes seems a little strange to people, myself
included, but I can't deny the beauty of what I
have seen.

—Cat Chapin-Bishop[122]

I was meditating in the upper room of the house at the Chalice
Well in Glastonbury. The room is designed to evoke the upper room
where the Last Supper was held. It is filled with wood: The sloping
ceiling is lined with wood, the floor is polished planks, the table and
chairs that represent the table at which the Last Supper was held are
made of wood, and the plates and goblets on the table are also made
of wood. Also in the room is a powerful artifact that represents the
Holy Grail. Both Glastonbury in general, and particular sites in and
around it—including the Chalice Well—are sacred to both Pagans
and Christians. As I meditated, I became aware of the presence of
Jesus, and so did my then-husband, who was also present. He said
that he did not get the impression that Jesus wanted to talk to him,
but that Jesus wanted to talk to me. I believed at the time that Jesus
wanted me to form a relationship with him. I had a number of other
visions of Jesus around that time. One was when I was in my back
garden, and Jesus appeared with Aslan. Another time, I was doing
some spiritual healing, and both Jesus and Kwan Yin showed up to
help.

---

122   Cat Chapin-Bishop (2017), "Quaker and Pagan Means What, Exactly?" *Quaker Pagan Reflections*. http://quakerpagan.blogspot.com/2017/10/quaker-and-pagan-means-what-exactly.html

I did not know what to do with these experiences. I was and am a witch, not a Christian. At times I thought that Jesus wanted me to become a Christian; at other times, I thought I was suffering from delusion. It is hard (but not impossible) to syncretize Wicca and Christianity, and I had some as-yet-unresolved anger with Christianity that was hiding a well of fear in my psyche. These visions, along with my studies of liberation theology, queer theology, and process theology, removed the anger and forced me to confront the fear.

Some people are excellent at syncretism, at blending two or more spiritual paths together. They are able to move smoothly between two or more different religious paradigms, and make contact with Spirit in both settings. It is very hard for me to do this (perhaps because my thinking tends to be theological and analytical).

I also found that the effort of defending one's syncretism to people who do not believe that it is possible to be a member of two different communities at the same time was too hard. But there are many people who have successfully created a syncretic practice—and deepened their relationship with Spirit as a result.

❀⤜•°•⤛❀⤜•°•⤛❀

Some people's response to discovering a new religion is to add it to their current practice. There are a variety of ways of doing this, and an increasing number of people are beginning to identify as belonging to more than one spiritual tradition—not merely in the sense of selecting attractive ideas from each tradition, but in trying to be faithful to the ethos of both traditions.[123]

Questions that might arise about syncretism are whether and how it is possible to combine traditions, especially if there is potential conflict between their worldviews, or their worldviews are mutually exclusive; how a particular person came to follow more than one tradition; what constitutes membership of a tradition; whether

---

123   Yvonne Aburrow (2011), *Dual-Faith Practice*. https://hcommons.org/deposits/item/hc:20907/

identification with a tradition is sufficient; and whether practicing more than one faith is merely part of the "subjective turn" of contemporary culture.

In many religions, the idea of practicing more than one tradition is uncontroversial—for example, many people practice Wicca and Druidry alongside each other, or Paganism and Unitarian Universalism, Judaism and Unitarianism, Quakerism and Unitarianism, or Buddhism and Shinto—but for those faiths that claim the exclusive loyalty of their followers, practicing more than one tradition may be seen as deeply problematic. Even in very liberal traditions, not everyone is comfortable with people practicing two traditions alongside each other.

Examples of religious syncretism range from explaining one religion using the symbolism and terminology of another, to a full-blown mingling of the two traditions.

It seems that, whenever one religion encounters another religion, a need is felt to make some form of accommodation with its truth claims—sometimes by denying them, sometimes by recasting them in the language of one's own tradition, and sometimes by assigning the other religion's holy figure a position in one's own tradition. For example, Hindus regarding Jesus as a "supremely religious soul."[124] The outcome of this process depends on the willingness of the faith communities to co-exist. At the level of the individual, religious belief is always more "messy" than a cursory examination of the creeds and teachings of the religion would indicate.

More than one form of syncretism can be identified, depending on the relative political and cultural status of the two systems being syncretised. High syncretism is when the core values of the original religion are retained, with only a veneer of the incoming religion; low syncretism is when only the surface trappings of the original religion are retained, and its core values are replaced by those of the

---

124   Woodburne, A.W., (1927) "The Indian Appreciation of Jesus." *The Journal of Religion*, 7 (1)., pp. 43-55. https://www.journals.uchicago.edu/doi/abs/10.1086/480633

incoming religion.

Another form of syncretism is "coinherence," where two religions that both make sense to the practitioner are followed side by side and held in dialogue or creative tension with each other.

There have also been examples of deliberate syncretism, such as Ryōbu Shinto, a formal mixture of Buddhism and Shinto; the reorganization of ancient Roman paganism in response to Greek and Etruscan paganism; the Romanization of the indigenous deities of other parts of Europe, for example the cult of Mercury and Rosmerta; and the creation of the syncretistic Din-I-Ilahi religion by the Mughal emperor Akbar.

In today's global culture, encounters between faiths no longer occur only at the boundaries of their traditional heartlands. The interfaith movement is growing, both to make peace between conflicting traditions and to explore the idea that all religions are honoring the same Divine, or numinous.

At the same time, there seems to be a growing polarization between liberal, tolerant, inclusivist views of religion and ecstatic or evangelical practices, which are frequently associated with fundamentalist and exclusivist views. The people who are attracted to this type of religion tend to long for a stable and ordered society but also want to feel their faith inwardly. Church-going in general has sharply declined in Britain and in North America, whereas spirituality in the holistic milieu has been increasing.

So it seems there are a range of possible responses to diversity: to embrace it and celebrate it; to tolerate it; or to reject it and seek to impose norms. However, no matter how a particular tradition responds to diversity, it is impossible to ignore it.

Much of the criticism of dual-faith practice seems to revolve around the issue of authority and whether it is derived from the individual, the group, the tradition, or the Divine.

Other criticisms include: the idea that each tradition is complete in itself and does not require outside input; and "pick'n'mix" spirituality, in which the dual-faith practitioner chooses only the parts of each tradition that appeal to them, avoiding aspects that seem difficult.

There are also issues like loyalty to a tradition and to the martyrs who died for its principles or values. It is hard for a contemporary Pagan to also embrace Christian beliefs when so many ancient pagans were killed, pagan temples destroyed, and witches persecuted. Conversely, many Christians look askance at the Pagan revival, and at Christo-Pagan syncretism, because of the early Christians who were martyred by ancient pagans.

Particularity versus universalism

The degree of difficulty in combining two or more traditions depends on how exclusive the truth claims of each tradition are. A useful distinction can be made between exclusivism (claims of completeness) and sectarianism (claims to sole possession of the truth).

This distinction is sometimes framed as particularity versus universalism. Particularity may refer to the features of a religion that arise out of a specific culture or history; when used in the phrase "the scandal of particularity," it refers to the weirdness of the idea that God would choose to reveal himself only to a small group of people in first-century Palestine. Universalism may refer to the idea that all religions are different paths up the same mountain, or it may refer to universal salvation (also known as apocatastasis), the idea that everyone is "saved."

A totalizing system[125] is one that is either sectarian or exclusivist and that seeks to subsume all other paradigms, rather than accepting that other paradigms exist alongside it. It regards itself as a complete

---

125   Yvonne Aburrow (2018), "Totalizing systems." *Dowsing for Divinity.* https://dowsingfordivinity.com/2018/02/25/totalising-systems/

and universal system that can explain all experience and needs no supplemental systems.

A non-totalizing or pluralist system recognizes its particularity to its local culture and sees that philosophies emerge from specific cultural contexts and local histories. A totalizing system ignores local contexts or seeks to explain them through its paradigm.

A totalizing system assumes that its style of religion, philosophy, theology, and/or culture is best for all humanity, and it may seek to convert others or impose it on them—the most obvious example being Christianity. Islam recognizes other "religions of the book" as valid, although it does seek converts. Ironically, atheism is also a totalizing system when it assumes that all religion is wrong, or that all religion is the same, or that it is all literalist in its beliefs. Buddhism is also mostly a totalizing system, in that it views itself as a potential overlay to other systems, but it replaces their core beliefs with its own metaphysical and philosophical assumptions.

Pagan religions are not totalizing systems. They can operate as a framework within which local folklore and stories and festivals may be inserted; but they do not seek to impose themselves on the whole world or assume that everyone should be a Pagan. They view themselves as emerging from a specific cultural context (they are usually open to people from other cultures but they do not seek converts), and they recognize that other perspectives are possible.

Judaism is not a totalizing system because it views itself as a religion of a specific people; other peoples have their own religions.

Totalizing religions are usually not compatible with each other; but they are also not compatible with non-totalizing religions because they seek either to convert others to their paradigm or to subsume others within their paradigm.

Pagan and occult traditions are usually compatible with each other because they are pluralistic, viewing themselves as one possible perspective on the world—not as the only valid perspective.

Whether a totalizing system sees itself as an overlay on local and indigenous traditions or a replacement for them, it is still largely incompatible with a worldview that says "this is my perspective, but other perspectives are possible."

Hence, Pagan and occult traditions (such as Freemasonry and Thelema) can be practiced alongside each other, and so can indigenous traditions (including Judaism, Taoism, Shinto, Hinduism, African traditional religions, First Nations religions). None of them seeks converts or regards itself as an universal system or explanation of how the world works.

Individuals (or even whole subtraditions or denominations) who are part of a totalizing religion may have adopted the perspective of particularity, localism, and an acknowledgement of other possible worldviews, but at a system level, these religions do not recognize other paradigms as valid. They may permit some, most, or all of the cultural and spiritual practices of the autochthonous[126] traditions that they have replaced or overlaid, but they regard the autochthonous religions' theology as either subservient to that of the totalizing system or invalidated by it.

Individuals within pluralist religions might have adopted a totalizing view, but at a system level, these religions are pluralist.

If a member of a totalizing system joins another tradition, they often feel a need to make it fit within the worldview of the totalizing system. The syncretic approach that they adopt will be one where the core of their belief (drawn from the totalizing system) is likely to remain unchanged, and only the practices of the other tradition are followed.

A member of a non-totalizing or pluralist system is more likely to be able to practice dual-mindedness, where they regard their two

---

126   Autochthonous: local and indigenous, literally 'sprung from the earth'.

practices as equally valid paradigms but different perspectives on reality.

People who have had direct mystical experiences of the numinous often find it difficult to fit them into the norms of the traditions they are following. Various mystics, especially female mystics, attracted the attention of the Inquisition to determine whether or not their mystical revelations fit with Catholic doctrine and whether their miracles or stigmata were genuine. Some revelations cannot be accommodated in the existing paradigm: new religions were founded on the teachings of Buddha, Jesus, and Mohammed because they were not accepted by the traditions from which they emerged. Sometimes people will break away to form or join a new tradition because of dissatisfaction with some feature of their existing tradition; this may involve a total rejection of the existing tradition and/or a return to an earlier tradition. An example of this can be seen in Goddess feminists' rejection of Christianity on the grounds of its patriarchal associations and their resulting creation of new traditions. Alternatively, the new tradition may be a syncretic amalgam of the old with the new, as early Christianity was an amalgam of the new insights of its founders with its Jewish heritage and the Greco-Roman religions that were contemporary with it.

Another possible criticism of dual-faith and syncretistic practice is the charge of cultural appropriation. This issue has been raised by Indigenous Peoples of Turtle Island (North America) in objection to the "borrowing" of their ideas, rituals, and practices. They view that as another form of imperialism. Using ideas from other cultures should be done respectfully and with sensitivity to their original context.

Whatever models are used to describe or explain dual-faith practice, it is clear that dual-faith practitioners are not merely "spiritual shoppers," but rather people who are attempting to follow what they have experienced as a call, coming from a source perceived to be external, but heard inwardly.

It seems that it is possible to follow two or more traditions simultaneously, but it is never easy. It is sometimes painful, because of contradictions that may be felt internally and because of hostility from people whose religion is almost entirely a matter of external authority.

Many people successfully combine more than one spiritual tradition, and some of them have thereby created a third thing. Examples within the Pagan sphere include Druidcraft (a combination of Druidry and Wicca), Chaos Craft (a combination of Chaos Magic and Wicca), and Heathen witchcraft (a combination of Heathenry and witchcraft). Examples where people have successfully syncretized Pagan practice with religions outside the Pagan sphere (or have straddled the boundaries) are Pagan Quakers, Jewitches, Unitarian Universalist Pagans, Taoist Pagans, and Buddhist Pagans. These examples tend to be successful because the traditions they are syncretizing do not have sectarian or exclusivist views.

There are also Christo-Pagans. There are numerous ways to be a Christo-Pagan: You can be a Christian who enjoys Pagan ritual and liturgy. You can be a Pagan who maintains a connection to Jesus and/or Christian saints alongside Pagan gods. You can honor Yahweh and the Shekhinah as your God and Goddess. You can create your own syncretization of the two faiths.

One fascinating example of a blend of Christianity and Paganism is the story of Mark Townsend. Mark was an Anglican vicar who had a crisis of faith. He started exploring Pagan ideas and became a Druid. He is now an independent minister and ordained member of the Progressive Christian Alliance (PCA), as well as a member of The Order of Bards, Ovates and Druids.[127] He is also a stage magician. He wrote three excellent books about his experience of changing paths, *Diary of a Heretic, The Path of the Blue Raven,* and *Jesus Through Pagan Eyes. Diary of a Heretic* chronicles his year of exploration, and the joy and creativity he found in Druidry. It shows how some

---

127   Mark Townsend, "Independent Minister." https://www.marktownsendministry.co.uk/independent-minister.html

Anglicans were still welcoming towards him, while others were deeply suspicious of his newfound Pagan leanings. In The Path of the Blue Raven, Townsend shares the story of his exploration of Druidry, and the stories of other people exploring nature-based paths.

On writing the book about Pagan views of Jesus, some Pagans became suspicious that Townsend was trying to sneakily convert us to Christianity, which was definitely not the case. Many other Pagans enjoyed the book. The first part of the book is a summary of contemporary liberal theological perspectives on Jesus; the second half has contributions from Pagan authors on their views of Jesus (some of which are quite surprising). This story shows that there are open-minded and closed-minded people in every tradition, and it is not always obvious who the open-minded ones will turn out to be. Some of the more positive encounters described in Diary of a Heretic were with evangelical Christians.

Combining two or more spiritual traditions is not impossible, but it is difficult and time-consuming. There is nothing inherently wrong in trying to be a dual-faith or syncretizing practitioner; but it can be very painful trying to juggle the values, loyalties and demands of two traditions. It helps if both traditions have very closely aligned worldviews and values and focus on similar areas of spiritual practice.

Exercises, journal prompts, and reflections

- If you have a daily spiritual practice, which of your traditions does it most resemble? Who or what are you worshiping / honoring? Have you read about the history and traditions of both religions? Could you comfortably lead a ritual or service in both traditions? Do you feel the presence of the Divine or deities in both traditions? If you try to import a practice from one tradition to the other, does it fit, or do you have to adapt it in significant ways?

- Compare the beliefs and values of your two traditions. Where do they intersect or overlap, and where do they diverge?

- Do you regard one of your traditions as the main one, or are they both equally important?

- What is the function of each of your traditions in your spiritual life? Do you gain different things from them?

- How did you become attracted to your traditions?

Meditation: The Divine

What is the Divine? Is it the still small voice that whispers to your conscience in the watches of the night? Is it love that leaps like a spark from heart to heart? Is it inspiration, stirring the mind to insight and poetry? Is it power and glory and might? Or is it humility and integrity and wonder? Is it compassion that pities the poor and friendless and alone? Is it the power of creativity that continuously creates all existence? Is it the power that sustains the universe? Is it the source of all that is? Is it the beauty and grandeur of Nature? Is it eternally one and the same, unchanging, ceaseless and beyond all thought? Is it constantly changing and evolving, growing like a tree into the vastness of time? Is it the void, the nothingness and silence beyond existence, where we can let our minds rest?

It may be all or none of these things, but we feel its touch when we let our minds rest in the ultimate ground of our being, the silence and awe and wonder. Now go within, to your own silent contemplation of the Divine.[128]

---

128   Yvonne Aburrow (2012), *Many Names*. Lulu.

Yvonne Aburrow

Part Two:
Joining Paganism

It will be a long way (Koen Jacobs/Flickr)

Chapter 8.
Joining a Pagan tradition

We ask, then, for peace for the gods of our fathers
and of our country. It is just that all worship should
be considered as one. We look at the same stars,
the sky is common, the same world surrounds us.
What difference does it make by what pains each
seeks the truth? We cannot attain to so great a
secret by one road.

—Quintus Aurelius Symmachus (340–402)

I will never forget my first Pagan ritual. It was at Jack Scout Cove
in Lancashire, England, and it was Samhain. We trekked up to the
ritual site at dusk. Two of us went to gather wood for our small fire,
and saw a procession of tiny faeries walking across the woodland
floor. The ritual itself lingers mostly as an impression of firelight
playing on faces, and illuminating the trunks of trees around us, and
a feeling of being in the right place with the right people. A Wiccan
priestess had given us a ritual script to work with. This included a
chant to the goddess Hekate. It was thrilling to be out in Nature, in
the dark, with a few friends, among the trees. Jack Scout Cove is a
liminal place, a headland that is surrounded by the sea and covered
in trees. There is something deep and true and real about being in a
wood with a campfire in the dark. It is primal and wild.

❀⤝•°•⤜❀⤝•°•⤜❀

There are a variety of Pagan traditions, plus eclectic Pagans
who do not belong to any particular tradition. What they all have
in common is a view that Nature is sacred, and a celebration of
pleasure. Pagans who believe in deities or the Divine view divinity as
immanent in Nature. The concept of immanence expresses the idea
that deities (or the Divine) are the soul of Nature. Atheist Pagans,

127

although they do not believe in deities or spirits, still regard Nature as the focus of their practice.

Pagans believe that the realization that you are a Pagan wells up from within,[129] as a response to the beauty of Nature, the call of the Pagan deities, or a growing convergence with Pagan values and a Pagan worldview. We do not believe that it is "cosmically necessary" to be a Pagan—our gods want willing adherents, not forced ones, and they do not punish people who do not believe in them.

Coming home to Paganism

Most Pagans feel that you cannot be converted to Paganism, and we do not attempt to convert others—because being a Pagan is not about the acceptance of a set of propositions or a creed, but a sense of connection with Nature, the old gods, the Earth, or the land. Instead, we call the realization that we are Pagan a feeling of coming home.

If you expressed an interest in Paganism, you would not be turned away, but the person you ask is more likely to recommend you a book to read, or perhaps invite you to a moot (a Pagan social event) or a seasonal celebration. The word moot is an Old English word for a meeting or a debate.

Most Pagans will seek to help you find your spiritual path, so if you mention to a Pagan that you are interested in Buddhism, then they would be likely to try to help you with that.

Very few Pagans are born into a Pagan tradition. Most people join as adults, often after a gradual process of changing their ideas. Pagans often develop a set of ideas and only later discover that the name for that collection of ideas is Paganism. That is how it worked for me, and also for Judy Harrow.[130]

Most Pagans do not identify with the term "conversion," seeing it

---

129   Yvonne Aburrow (2015), "Why Pagans don't proselytize or evangelize." *Dowsing for Divinity.* https://dowsingfordivinity.com/2015/06/19/why-pagans-dont-evangelise/

130   Judy Harrow (2002), *Spiritual Mentoring: A Pagan Guide,* Toronto: ECW Press, pages 113-125.

as something that happens to adherents of "revealed religion," and preferring to talk about how they have always been Pagan really, and when they found Paganism, it was like coming home.

However, there is a process of becoming part of the Pagan community. People read books, they talk to other Pagans, they develop a Pagan worldview; they learn where the boundaries of the discourse are. Tania Luhrmann described this process as "interpretive drift." People start out not believing in magic, or the occult, and gradually come to believe in it after experiencing magical rituals. She writes:

> [T]he slow shift in someone's manner of interpreting events, making sense of experiences, and responding to the world. People do not enter magic with a set of clear cut beliefs which they take to their rituals and test with detachment. Nor is their practice mere poetry, a new language to express their feelings. Rather, there seems to be a slow, mutual evolution of interpretation and experience, rationalized in a manner which allows the practitioner to practise.[131]

However, she also identifies different positions that people can take in relation to religion and magic, ranging from a view of magic as metaphorical or psychological to a view that the magical world is a separate reality from the physical world. So I do not think that everyone's interpretation is drifting towards the same conclusion.[132] I think it is reassuring that the shift is slow and informed by experience, rather than a sudden change. It is also evident that people's beliefs in magic fluctuate over time; they do not make a steady progression from nonbelief to belief. Instead, their belief waxes and wanes in response to their experiences.

131   Tanya M. Luhrmann (1989, 1991), *Persuasions of the Witch's Craft: Ritual Magic in Contemporary England*. Harvard University Press.
132   Yvonne Aburrow (2008), "Do Pagans see their beliefs as compatible with science?" MA thesis, Bath Spa University. https://hcommons.org/deposits/item/hc::20905

Most contemporary Pagan traditions tend to focus on practice rather than belief, preferring to talk about how we do ritual rather than why we do ritual. So Pagans (who often arrive at their understanding of the world in relative isolation and are then delighted to find others who think similarly) often do not notice the subtle shifts in their outlook and ideas when they join a Pagan group or tradition.

However, I believe that it is important to have a theoretical explanation for your practices, beliefs, and values (otherwise known as theology). Theology is not dogma, it is a discursive approach to understanding your relationship with the numinous and with the world around us. If we do not have a theoretical or theological framework for our practices, we are likely to unthinkingly reproduce the oppressive structures of mainstream society.

Types of Pagan groups

The most open and accessible type of Pagan group is a moot. This is usually an open discussion circle and will generally meet in a pub or a café. Moots are free to attend and fairly easy to find: Type "Pagan moot near me" into your favorite search engine. They generally have their own social media groups and events pages. Some moots have guest speakers or round-table discussions on Pagan topics; others are purely for socializing, and some are a mixture of formats.

Some moots also host open rituals for the eight festivals of the Wheel of the Year. These are generally eclectic and often held outdoors (weather and climate permitting).

A group of Druids is called a grove, or sometimes a seed group. Not all Druids identify as Pagan. There are many different Druid orders. One of the largest is OBOD (the Order of Bards, Ovates, and Druids), which has groups in many countries. An OBOD grove is usually run by someone who has attained the Druid grade. An

OBOD seed group may be run by someone who is just starting out on the Druid path. Another very large Druid organization is Ár nDraíocht Féin: A Druid Fellowship (ADF). They are mainly based in the USA but also have groves in Canada, Brazil, Australia, and Germany.

A group of Heathens is often called a hearth. There are many different Heathen organizations. I would recommend searching for inclusive Heathenry and checking to see that the Heathen group is anti-racist and inclusive of LGBTQ2SIA people. A range of levels of commitment is possible within Heathenry.

A group of witches or Wiccans is known as a coven. Joining a coven involves a lot of commitment and training. An initiated Wiccan is both a witch and a priest/priestess/priestix, so most covens are looking for people who are capable of performing in that capacity. Most covens have a training course or group before initiation. This is sometimes known as an "outer court." I do not like this term, personally, but it has crept into the terminology.

AtheoPagans (also known as Atheist Pagans and Naturalistic Pagans) have started to organize affinity groups and have a thriving online community.

There are various types of polytheism. Many (perhaps most) polytheists do not identify as Pagan, but they are worshiping ancient pagan deities and share many of the same values as people who do identify as Pagan. Whatever ancient culture you feel drawn to, there is probably someone practicing the polytheism of that culture. There are Kemeticists (ancient Egypt), Hellenists (ancient Greece), people who worship the gods of ancient Rome, ancient Gaul, ancient Slavic peoples, and so on. Some of these groups also have right-wing and nationalistic elements, so researching their views online is advisable before approaching them.

Some people practice Paganism and/or witchcraft on their own, without joining a group; they are generally known as solitaries.

There are books available for the solitary practitioner, and this is a good option for people who want to try a few things to see if this path is for them before committing to a group.

There are also numerous online communities with regular meetings and rituals that happen through video chat. These range from discussion groups to ritual groups to sharing circles.

Pagan values and virtues

A value is a shared norm or expectation of a group—something that is considered desirable. A virtue is a quality that is considered desirable. Pagan values emerge from an appreciation of life and the enjoyment of being physically embodied.[133] Many traditional Pagan ethical codes were lists of virtues that were considered desirable, and not a set of rules to be kept. The cultivation of virtue was said to lead to eudaimonia, a happy and balanced state of being. The concept of cultivating virtue is an ancient pagan concept that was later co-opted by Christianity, and the Pagan virtues are somewhat different from Christian ones (for instance, obedience does not feature on Pagan lists of virtues).

Hospitality was, and remains, a very important virtue in just about every traditional culture. It is reciprocal, and it governs the behavior of guest and host. If you were riding in the wilderness at midwinter, like Gawain in the story of Gawain and the Green Knight, the offer of shelter and food may literally have saved your life. If you were shipwrecked on a strange coast, in an age when there were no coastguards and few lighthouses, like Odysseus in the story of The Odyssey, Nausica and her maidens coming to rescue you would have been a gift from the gods. The ancient Greeks regarded hospitality as a sacred obligation.

The guest must also behave honorably toward the host, and know how to behave while staying in the house, and when to leave. Many

---

133   Yvonne Aburrow (2015), "Paganism for Beginners: Values." *Dowsing for Divinity.* https://dowsingfordivinity.com/2015/06/08/paganism-for-beginners-values/

cultures still have the beautiful custom of the guest-gift—something that the guest brings the first time they visit your house.

Another important concept in Paganism is that of reciprocity and balance. This is linked with the idea of hospitality, which is a relationship between host and guest (indeed, the two words stem from the same Indo-European root word). "A gift for a gift" says The Hávamál.[134] Connections between people are maintained by the exchange of gifts (not necessarily physical objects, but the gifts of time and attention).

Everything in Nature is balanced, and the same is true of society and culture—as in the saying "what goes around, comes around." This is related to the Pagan concept of cyclicity, which maintains that everything goes in cycles: night and day; the seasons; birth, life, death, and rebirth.

The land is sacred in Pagan traditions and, looking back at non-hierarchical cultures, we can see that it was either held in common by the people or not owned at all. The persistence of the idea of communal land, despite the Enclosures, the Highland Clearances, and the theft of land from Indigenous Peoples around the world, shows what an important idea this is. Many ancient cultures recognized the Earth as a sacred being, and realized that we share the Earth with other beings. They understood that if you take too much, Nature cannot renew itself, and the common treasury will be depleted.

Honor, or the upholding of personal integrity, appears in lists of virtues compiled by a number of cultures and traditions, including the eight Wiccan Virtues (listed in The Charge of the Goddess by Doreen Valiente), and the Nine Noble Virtues of Heathenry.[135] What honor means to me is being honest in my personal dealings, and

134   *Hávamál: The Words of Odin the High One* from the Elder or Poetic Edda (Sæmund's Edda) translated by Olive Bray and edited by D. L. Ashliman, https://sites.pitt.edu/~dash/havamal.html
135   The Nine Noble Virtues are: Courage, Truth, Honor, Fidelity, Discipline, Hospitality, Industriousness, Self-Reliance, Perseverance. (Other sites give them different names.)

Patti Wigington (2018), "The Nine Noble Virtues of Asatru." *Learn Religions.* https://www.learnreligions.com/noble-virtues-of-asatru-2561539

doing the decent thing: fighting against injustice and speaking up for the vulnerable.

Most Pagans value embodiment and celebrate being alive. We value physical pleasure: eating, drinking, making love, seeing and experiencing beautiful things. We find that the enjoyment of these things increases our spiritual connection, because we love trees, rocks, mountains, flowers, beautiful art, the ocean, animals, birds, other people, the Moon, the night, the Sun, rolling hills, water, the pleasures of intimacy, eating, making merry. The Charge of the Goddess, written by Wiccan priestess Doreen Valiente, says that "All acts of love and pleasure are [Her] rituals."

The idea that the Divine/deities is/are immanent in the world (intimately entwined with physical matter) also contributes to the sense that being alive in this world is to be celebrated and enjoyed.

Sovereignty, or personal autonomy, is another Pagan value. "Women desiren sovereigntie," wrote Chaucer, at the end of The Wife of Bath's Tale. Sovereignty is the ability to determine your own destiny. Pagans love to be free, and do not like being coerced. We do not like to be told what to think, what to do, or how to live. This extends to bodily autonomy and not being coerced or cajoled into having unwanted sex or other physical contact.

Paganism is life-affirming, and most Pagans view the physical world as sacred. Pagan values flow from that and embrace it. Pagans do not usually regard spirit as more important or more valuable than matter. Most Pagans view matter as entwined with spirit, or perhaps as a denser form of spirit.

Deciding which tradition is right for you

There are many Pagan and polytheist traditions, and it can be confusing to be presented with all of them at once. I tried to create a Venn diagram with a broad overview of current Pagan traditions, and it got very complicated. The categories overlapped, and there were lots of shared ideas among them.[136]

However, we can divide the current Pagan, polytheist, and magical milieu into some broad-brush areas: eclectic Pagans (who do not belong to a specific tradition), Wicca and witchcraft, Druidry, polytheism (which includes Heathenry, Religio Romana, and other groups that are reconstructing ancient polytheistic religions), occultism (including Thelema), AtheoPaganism, and pantheism. Where it gets complicated is that you can be a polytheist witch, Wiccan, or Druid, and you can be a Druid who is reconstructing ancient Celtic polytheism, and you can be a member of more than one group. Wicca is a subset of witchcraft and also of Paganism. The Feri tradition and its better-known offshoot Reclaiming are both Pagan witchcraft traditions. There is a polytheist Druid fellowship (Ár nDraíocht Féin: A Druid Fellowship) that incorporates other polytheistic traditions into its practices. There are also polytheists who do not identify as Pagan. There are universalist and cultural Druids who are not Pagans. There are traditional witches who do not identify as Pagan. There are Wiccans whose practice is inspired by Heathenry. There are Heathen witches.

In practice, not all of these options are likely to be available in your area, so the first step is to find out what is nearby and attend their events and open rituals. Go to your local Pagan pub moot (you can find listings online) and see what is happening in your local area. Be aware, though, that not all Pagans attend a local pub moot.

There are several Pagan umbrella organizations, polytheist groups, Heathen groups, Wiccan groups, Druid groups, and witchcraft

---

136   Yvonne Aburrow (2020), *Basics of the Craft*. https://youtu.be/8xJtRX6B0YI

groups that can provide you with more information. These all have their own websites, and should have a clear explanation of what their traditions are about and how you can go about getting involved. There are groups at local, national, and international levels, but these groups are largely independent of each other. Some attempts have been made to create umbrella organizations, such as the Pagan and Heathen Symposium (UK), the Pagan Federation (UK), the Covenant of the Goddess (USA), and Pagan Federation International.

Many people make a choice of Pagan tradition based on the archetype that attracts them. People who are drawn to the archetype of the wizard tend to find Druidry or occultism attractive; people who are attracted by the image of the witch tend to join Wicca or another witchcraft tradition; and these archetypes tend to be skewed by gendered expectations. However, women and nonbinary people can be wizards, and men and nonbinary people can be witches. So my advice would be to choose based on the culture or pantheon (group of deities) you feel drawn to and the style of ritual that you prefer. Most Pagan and occult traditions are flexible about theology (you can be a pantheist, a panentheist, a polytheist, an atheist, or an agnostic), but they all have a specific ritual style and many are based on specific ancient cultures.

Different Pagan groups and traditions tend to have different focal points of their practice and interests. These fall into four broad categories: self-development, the community, deities, and Nature/Earth/land.

Nature tends to be conceived of as the totality of existence (the sky, stars, Moon, Sun, Earth, flora, and fauna). The Earth refers to planet Earth and all her inhabitants. The land refers to the local landscape where you live and all the other-than-human people that live there, including animals, birds, land-wights, trees, and plants.

Many eclectic witches are very focused on self-development. By virtue of being solitary, they tend to be less focused on in-person communities, but often form groups or loose networks online.

Wiccans tend to be focused on Nature and deities, though some are very interested in the land, and most tend to be environmentally aware and active. Most Wiccans regard self-development as a helpful byproduct, rather than the main aim, of spiritual practice.

Heathens and polytheists tend to be more focused on land and deities. Druids tend to be focused on the Earth and deities (or the Divine) and will often be very environmentally active.

The good news is that if you have time, you can belong to more than one Pagan tradition, and some people also attend a liberal church such as the Unitarian Universalists or the Quakers. There are also people who are both Pagan and Jewish. Eventually, you may find that your commitment to one of your choices deepens, and the other path recedes into the background or falls away. Some people can sustain a fusion of two traditions for a lifetime. Either way, you have plenty of time to make your choice, and most Pagans are perfectly comfortable with people having more than one path.

Exercises, journal prompts, and reflections

- What aspect of Paganism are you drawn to? Is it magic and witchcraft? Nature, the Earth, or the land? Ancestors? Trees, stars, and stones? A specific pantheon of deities or a specific ancient culture?

- Once you have listed what aspects you are drawn to, see if you can match them to a specific Pagan tradition.

- Which of the Pagan values explored in this chapter appealed to you the most? Is it associated with a specific Pagan tradition?

- Reflect on your preferences for ritual styles. Do you prefer formal or informal, indoor or outdoor, structured or spontaneous?

- Make a list of the pros and cons (or strengths, weaknesses, opportunities, and threats) of the tradition you are considering joining.

- Read up on the history of your chosen tradition.

- Watch YouTube videos, read blogs, and/or listen to podcasts by members of the tradition. How do you feel about the tone, style, and content of these offerings?

Meditation: The four elements

Face the North, direction of Earth. Be aware of the bones in your body that hold you up, of the solidity and physicality of your body. Your body is made of the food you eat and the lands where that food grew.

Face the East, direction of Air. Breathe in and out, focusing on your breath. The air is the source of life and the conveyor of sound. Imagine the air you are breathing filling every space in your body.

Face the South, direction of Fire. Feel the warmth of your body, the energy within you. This is how fire manifests in your body.

Face the West, direction of Water. Feel the fluid in your body. Feel your blood pulsing through your veins. Be aware that your body is mostly made of water.

Chapter 9.
Arriving in a group

"Any ritual is an opportunity for transformation.
To do a ritual, you must be willing to be
transformed in some way. The inner willingness is
what makes the ritual come alive and have power.
If you aren't willing to be changed by the ritual,
don't do it."

"Ritual affirms the common patterns, the values,
the shared joys, risks, sorrows, and changes that
bind a community together. Ritual links together
our ancestors and descendants, those who went
before with those will come after us."

—Starhawk [137]

The first time I ever stepped into a Wiccan circle and heard the
beautiful words of the first degree initiation rolling over me, I knew
I was home. There was a power in those words and in that circle:
the power to evoke the Divine, to awaken an inner connection with
the powers of Nature. It was an utterly magical experience and the
visions that it caused for me are still fresh and vivid in my mind more
than thirty years later.

My journey with Wicca has not always been easy, but it is
absorbing, exhilarating, and powerful, and I feel that Wicca is my
true spiritual home.

❀⚶•°•⚛⚶•°•⚛❀⚶•°•⚛

Arriving in a new spiritual community can be exhilarating, but
also intimidating. There are new terms to learn, new concepts to

---

absorb, new people to meet, a new style of ritual or liturgy to get to grips with. At first, the new member tends to forget that the new group is likely to have its own cliques, controversies, feuds, and dysfunctional aspects—just like every other group of humans— because they are excited to encounter and explore the community and the tradition.

In chapter four, we looked at finding a group and all the questions you may need to ask when you are looking at joining a group. This chapter is about the process of joining a new community.

Membership and identity

Joining a new group brings up questions of membership and identity.[138] Many people identify as being of a particular religion; but what constitutes membership? In Christianity, the boundary between membership and identity is fairly blurred—it could be measured by attendance, baptism, belief, or adherence to the Nicene Creed.

In Paganism, identity and membership of the community are largely informally negotiated at festivals and gatherings, which people attend both to discover the self and to develop the self. Festivals bring people together and create a temporary community.[139]

Peter Chapin-Bishop (a Quaker Pagan)[140] believes that membership in a tradition consists of having received Divine communication in that setting. Liz Opp (a Christian Quaker)[141] writes that identity is a sense of one's personal values being close to the group identified with, whereas membership is participation in that group and its norms, values, and social life. She adds that identity is the foundation of a person's being, and may come into conflict with membership of a group. In her formulation, identity seems more important than membership; but she also talks about

138 Yvonne Aburrow (2011), *Dual-Faith Practice*. https://hcommons.org/deposits/item/hc:20907/
139 Wendy Griffin (2002), "Reviewed Work(s): Earthly Bodies, Magical Selves: Contemporary Pagans and the Search for Community by Sarah M. Pike." *The Journal of Religion*, 82 (3), pp. 499-501
140 Peter Chapin-Bishop (2007), "Membership and Identity." *Quaker Pagan Reflections*. http://quakerpagan.blogspot.com/2007/05/on-membership-peter.html
141 Liz Opp (2007), "Membership and Identity." *The Good Raised Up*. http://thegoodraisedup.blogspot.com/2007/04/membership-and-identity.html

experiencing an inner call. There is clearly a subtle balance between membership and identity whenever people participate in a group. Perhaps people join groups because they admire their values and want to become more like the people in them. Perhaps people join because they admire the practices of the group but then find that the values are not what they expected. Or they find that they are expected to transform their own identity, values, and insights to conform with that of the group to a degree that violates their identity. Either way, the formation of a person's identity happens in a social context,[142] and groups that someone becomes involved in will reflect that identity. Many groups have rituals or ceremonies or oaths that confer membership. There is no membership ceremony for being an eclectic Pagan—you identify as a Pagan and seek to learn more about Paganism. Traditions within the Pagan movement, however, such as Wicca and Druidry, do have membership ceremonies in the form of initiations.

Cat Chapin-Bishop (a Quaker Pagan) comments about eclectic Paganism:

> Pagans, I think, look to bestow membership
> where identity as a part of a group already exists.
> Quakers . . . look to develop identification with a
> group through the formal relations of membership.
> It's probably a chicken and the egg type of issue,
> really—membership shapes identity shapes
> membership.[143]

Clearly membership involves dialogue among the members of a group—to ascertain what the core values of the group are and how those are played out in the lives of its members—and often this does involve some kind of formal commitment to the group. A person may identify as belonging to a religious tradition, but for them to be

142   Edwards, D. N. (2005) "The archaeology of religion." *In:* Diaz-Andreu, M., Lucy, S., Babić, S., and Edwards, D. N., *eds. The Archaeology of Identity.* London and New York: Routledge. Page 116.
143   Chapin-Bishop, C. (2007) "Quaker, Pagan, Quakerpagan or Paganquaker: Moving Beyond the Cool Kids' Table." *Quaker Pagan Reflections.* http://quakerpagan.blogspot.com/2007/05/quaker-pagan-quakerpagan-or-paganquaker.html

a member of a group, they have to be recognized as a member by other members of the group.

It could be argued that if a person identifies with a group, the criteria of membership need to expand to include that person. On the other hand, it might be held that the person has to adjust to the mores of the group to belong. However, if the practices of the group contradict its stated ideals and values, perhaps the newcomer, bringing a fresh perspective, is the very person best placed to call attention to that contradiction. Most groups are not very receptive to the insights of newcomers, however.

Furthermore, the exclusion of certain categories of people from membership of a group may be of disservice to the group, as Cat Chapin-Bishop points out:

> To the extent that my spiritual community does
> not accept my membership, or discounts it as
> merely individualistic "self-identification," I will
> be cut off from exactly what Marshall sees self-
> identifiers as withholding from their communities:
> that interdependence, the right not so much to
> make demands on the group or to shape it to
> my liking, as to serve the group, offer it my gifts,
> and be transformed by the experience of that
> mutuality.[144]

In Pagan communities and traditions, the more commitment and effort is required to be a member of a group, the more you can expect to encounter a need to learn about what it means to be a Pagan and a member of that tradition, and the less likely it is that membership will be automatic just because you identify with that group.

That is why it is a good idea to attend low-commitment groups

144   Chapin-Bishop, C. (2007) 'Quaker, Pagan, Quakerpagan or Paganquaker: Moving Beyond the Cool Kids' Table.' *Quaker Pagan Reflections*. http://quakerpagan.blogspot.com/2007/05/quaker-pagan-quakerpagan-or-paganquaker.html

and events such as pub moots and open rituals, so that you can test the waters before committing to anything more involved.

Commitment

Many groups have a phase of exploration or seeking before you make a commitment. This is important for both the seeker and the group, in order to ensure that everyone feels comfortable with each other. The more commitment and trust that are involved in being part of a group, the longer the period of getting to know each other will last. The first step is a series of meetings, usually in a café or other public place, or by video chat. You will probably not get invited to the leaders' home for the first meeting, and this is as it should be. The process of seeking a Pagan group is a bit like internet dating, and all the same safety rules apply.

In Wicca, there is a tradition of getting to know the seeker for a year and a day before initiating them. This period is often occupied by some sort of training course, which may or may not include rituals. Some covens' training period lasts for two years.

In OBOD Druidry,[145] anyone may attend public rituals and Bardic rituals, but once you start attending a Bardic grove, you are usually expected to work toward Bardic initiation. When you are getting involved with a Druid group, find out what their expectations and requirements are.

Heathen and polytheist groups vary in their requirements for making a commitment to the group.

It is a good idea to find out what level of commitment is expected before joining any group. Some groups expect that members make a reasonable effort to attend every ritual. This is mainly because numbers are small, and it is frustrating if the leader has gone to the effort of preparing a ritual for six people, and only four people show up. Also, if the leader is trying to coordinate a program of training,

---

145   The Order of Bards, Ovates, and Druids. https://druidry.org/

it gets really difficult if people's attendance is erratic, because then they have to play catch-up. However, most Pagan groups meet every three to six weeks on average, so it is not too difficult to commit to attending all the rituals. Though obviously the rest of the group will want you to stay away if you have a cold, flu, covid, or some other contagious illness.

Politics in groups

There are group dynamics in every group of people,[146] and spiritual communities are no exception. You will likely find that you are drawn to some people more than others, and there may be people you do not like—or who do not like you.

I would strongly advise you not to jettison your existing friends (unless they are trying to drag you back to your previous religious tradition) in the excitement of joining a new group.

Before you join a group, it helps to ensure that you have dealt with most of your issues and can relate to other people in a balanced way. If you are still suffering from unresolved trauma, it may be best to deal with that in a less intense setting before attempting to join a coven or any other small and committed group.

It takes time to make friends in a community that you have joined, whether it is a reading group, a knitting circle, or a spiritual group. Try not to be discouraged. A common pattern for people suffering from post-traumatic stress is to tell new acquaintances their entire life story on first meeting. However, it is best not to share so much straight away; let information about you emerge gradually, in a reciprocal way. People may ask you about your previous spiritual journey, which is fine. But how much you share, and when you share it, is up to you. If you are seeking to join a coven or other high-commitment group, however, do expect to be asked to work through your issues and to be asked about your prior spiritual experience and

---

146   Yvonne Aburrow (2015), "Paganism for Beginners: Group Dynamics." *Dowsing for Divinity.* https://dowsingfordivinity. com/2015/09/14/group-dynamics/

knowledge.

Group dynamics are complicated, but key questions to ask are: "Where does the power go in the group?" and "Who is wielding the power?"

Many groups elect or appoint their leaders. In Wiccan covens, the leader is usually the high priestess, who is probably the founder of the coven. In a Druid grove or a Heathen hearth, there may be a single leader or a small group of leaders.

In a small group, it can be an excellent idea to rotate the leadership role. Different members of the group take it in turns to write and facilitate a ritual. Most progressive and/or inclusive covens encourage their members to create and facilitate rituals.

Many people prefer working in a group with a flat hierarchy to one with a very top-down hierarchy. Flat hierarchies are characterized by shared decision-making and informal communication among group members. Some people like groups where decisions are made by the leaders; this requires a high degree of trust.

Groups often go through a process of forming, storming, norming, and performing. First the group forms. Then there is a struggle to resolve the group's differences—storming. Once that has been resolved, the group's values, goals, and beliefs converge (and it helps if their values were already fairly close together). This is the process of norming. Once that process is complete, the group starts to perform.

During the formation of the group and the convergence of its ideas, it will begin to become apparent who is in the group, and who is outside the group. This is known as the in-group/out-group dynamic. The formation of the in-group can be a positive thing, in that it makes the group feel closer together, but it can be dangerous, because if the in-group projects its shadow onto the out-group, this can result in persecution of the out-group.

The projection of group members' shadows onto other people in the group can be a dangerous dynamic. The shadow is the aspect of our psyches that we have repressed because we do not like it, and we often project it onto other people—especially if they resemble a repressed aspect of our personality. It is also possible that this happens to the person who just does not fit within the group.

Another interesting dynamic in groups is "somebody has to do it" syndrome. This is where one person takes on more responsibility than the others, and an expectation comes about that they will always do the tasks that they have taken on.

It is a good idea if the locus of power in a group is visible. If it is not obvious who holds the power, then it will default to the person with the loudest voice or the most stubborn resistance to new ideas. Either that, or it is necessary to firmly establish that the group norm is consensus process.

The role of the leader of a coven is to empower others and enable them to develop as priestixes, priestesses, or priests. This model is sometimes known as servant leadership, because the leader is mindful that the group is not there to serve them. Instead, their role is to create safe space for the group, to hold the space, and to empower others to be creative.

Why join a group?

After all of this, you are probably wondering why on earth you would want to join a group! The answer to that question may vary from one person to another, but in my experience, the joy of sharing ritual and companionship on the spiritual journey with other people outweighs the pitfalls of being in a group.[147] When you have a group of people to do rituals with who really understand you and accept you without judgment, and you feel safe with them, it is a wonderful feeling. The necessity of feeling safe and held is why

147   Yvonne Aburrow (2015), "Paganism for Beginners: Finding a group." *Dowsing for Divinity.* https://dowsingfordivinity. com/2015/07/30/finding-a-group/

covens are selective about who can join. It may seem rather like a clique, but when you are going to do something strange and unusual like practicing witchcraft with a group of people, you need a shared understanding and feeling of closeness. This is not something that happens overnight, but something that takes time to develop.

A group provides companionship along the way, and new friends. However, I would advise against joining a group just to make friends; that should be a happy byproduct of being in the group, rather than the main aim of joining it. Also bear in mind that the main aim of the group is not to provide therapy, though that may be a beneficial byproduct.

Having a group of people to create and share rituals with gives you a different perspective on spirituality, mythology, and life, and it challenges you in unexpected ways. Being in a group rubs the sharp corners off people and makes us more human.

Exercises, journal prompts, and reflections

- Keep a note of all the new terms and concepts you encounter as part of your exploration of Pagan traditions and events.

- Have you ever identified as part of something, but then been told you are not a member of it? How did you feel?

- Have you ever noticed the exertion of power in a group setting that surprised you or disturbed you?

- Read stories about groups in mythology and history, such as Jason and the Argonauts, Robin Hood and his Merrie Men, King Arthur and the Knights of the Round Table, Scottish clans, witches' covens, and so on. What, if anything, is attractive to you about these groups? Did their members have to sacrifice their individuality or their identity to join?

Meditation: Groups

What are you looking for in a group? Reflect on groups that you have been part of. Allow yourself to gently disconnect the tendrils that connect you to groups that may have harmed you in the past, and unclench the bits of you that are clenched as a result of those experiences. Allow an image of an ideal group to form in your mind. How would you feel in your body in that ideal group?

Chapter 10.
Unexamined baggage

"Everyone you meet comes with baggage, find someone who cares enough to help you unpack."

— Ziad K. Abdelnour

"In our unpacking process, we must own it before we can disown it!"

— Evinda Lepins

"In order to understand your pain, you have to understand your healing."

— Karl Stewart

I have always had a rather earthy attitude to my Pagan spirituality, and am not embarrassed about farting or belching. I am completely baffled by men who think it is acceptable for them to fart, but not acceptable for women. So (as is normal for me), one beautiful sunny day, I let rip with a particularly loud fart. The man I was with said something along the lines of "the Goddess doesn't fart" (because in Pagan thought, all genders are regarded as manifestations of the Divine). I replied, "Yes She does! What do you think volcanoes are?"

The inability to cope with ordinary bodily functions, especially when women exhibit them, seems to me to be an example of some unexamined baggage from patriarchal Christianity.

A more dangerous example of patriarchal baggage is when rape culture rears its ugly head in Pagan communities, with ugly consequences like slut-shaming and double standards, sexual assault, and assumptions about sexuality and consent.[148]

---

148   Christine Hoff-Kraemer and Yvonne Aburrow, editors (2016), *Pagan Consent Culture. Building Communities of Empathy and Autonomy.* Asphodel Press.

People often bring spiritual baggage from their previous religion or philosophy with them into their new group.[149]

Everyone is likely to have intellectual and emotional baggage from the tradition they grew up in, even if that tradition was atheism. Before you assume that something is just a given in your personal worldview or the worldview of your tradition, you might want to find out where it came from and whether it gets you to where you want to go.

When I first started writing about Pagan theology, I got a lot of pushback. People said, "We don't need theology, that's a Christian concept." This is incorrect; the classical text De Natura Deorum, "On the Nature of the Gods" was written by Cicero, a Pagan.

They said, "If we have theology, we will get orthodoxy." I think they were thinking of dogma, not theology, which is generally discursive. Some people wondered how discussing the nature of the gods was relevant to our lives—but theology is about ethics and praxis, not just the gods.

We need discursive theology because otherwise we just repeat the ideas we have been taught by mainstream culture, or we repeat nineteenth century ideas of what Paganism is, or evangelical tropes about Paganism, or we parrot 1950s ideas of what is radical. We need to examine our baggage, unpack it, repack it, and do our laundry.

Look at your ideas about gender, tradition, nature, ancestors, and the land. What are your concepts of polarity, gender, and fertility? What are your ethics based on? Are your ideas about these things based on something you got from your upbringing? Maybe on an outdated view of science? Or are they based on a Pagan book that you read? Where did the author of that book get their ideas? Did

149   Yvonne Aburrow (2021), "Unexamined Baggage." *Dowsing for Divinity*. https://dowsingfordivinity.com/2021/12/29/unexamined-baggage/

you read the book in a critical manner, checking its assumptions and examining its baggage? What are the political views of its author?

If we do not have well-thought-out theology, then bad theology will fill the void caused by its absence. You only need to look at the unexamined baggage about polarity, gender, and fertility that some people carry around to figure that out.

Having more theological discussion does not lead to orthodoxy; it leads to different schools of thought. There were many schools of thought in ancient Pagan religions, just as there are in contemporary Hinduism. In Ancient Greek and Latin, a school of thought was a haeresis, from which we get the modern word heresy. Heresy ultimately means choosing your own path, which seems like a good thing to me.

If you want your Pagan or Wiccan or Heathen or Druid or polytheist practice to serve your spiritual goals and not hinder them, then you need to examine your emotional, intellectual, and spiritual baggage.

The most obvious forms of Christian baggage that people are likely to bring on their Pagan path are puritanical attitudes to sex, gender, and the body, such as homophobia, transphobia, biphobia, misogyny, fatphobia, and so on. An example of this is holding to notions of modesty derived from purity culture, or believing that women should not fart, be loud, be overweight, or have too much sex.

Sometimes people react to leaving Christianity by jettisoning sexual ethics. While fundamentalist and evangelical Christians have a warped attitude about sex and gender, that does not mean that anything goes outside of their restrictive rules. It is still necessary to be honorable, truthful, and not to lie, cheat, or steal. If you are monogamous with your partner, it is better to negotiate a polyamorous relationship than to cheat on them. Numerous guides to ethical polyamory are available, if that is your preference.

However, there are subtler items of Christian baggage to look out for. One of them is seeing religion through the Protestant lens. What this means is that, owing to the cultural dominance of Protestant Christianity in many countries in the West, people tend to assume that it is the norm, and that all other religions must have similar features (such as concepts of sin, salvation, an afterlife, a single holy book that is the sole source of truth, a view that only one religion can possibly be right, and a monotheistic view of the Divine). This is not true. Religions have many ways of viewing the world and the human relationship with divinity.

The concepts of sin and salvation have no meaning in Pagan religions. The concept of sin can vary even within Christianity, but it is generally regarded as something (an attitude, a state, or an action) that separates us from the Divine. The concept of salvation can mean saving us from the consequences of sin, or it can mean healing the rift between the human and Divine.

In Pagan religions, we are not separate from the Divine or deities. The Divine is immanent in the world, and therefore we are never separate from it. We can choose to ignore its presence and get out of balance with Nature, but consensual pleasure will never separate us from the Divine.

Pagans do not have a holy book with commandments from a deity. We tend to derive our ethics from reasoning about the world around us. We cultivate virtues rather than following commandments.

Some traditions may derive their ethics from the traditional body of lore of a particular culture. This wisdom from the past, embedded as it was in experience and an ethic of responsibility toward other beings, is an excellent source of ethical guidance, but it is important to note that we have wider knowledge and experience in some areas, and that science, technology, engineering, and medicine have made some things possible that could not have been imagined by our ancestors.

I think the foundation of Pagan ethics is the idea that everything is sacred because the Divine is immanent in everything.[150] If you believe that the physical universe is an embodiment of the Divine, and life is something to be celebrated, then your mythology, and your ethics, will flow from that.

Pagan stories and mythologies illustrate the idea of deities and spirits being involved in the world, and of people taking care of each other and of animals and plants. Each Pagan story, myth, and legend reinforces the view that everything is sacred, but the stories are not necessarily the source of that insight. The insight emerges from our emotional response to the world around us, a sense of being in "right relationship" with it when we treat it as a Thou and not an It.

Another issue that can arise comes from the experience of interfaith dialogue, which can have the result that participants see all religions as different perspectives on the same mountain and become attracted to a more universalist or perennialist view of religious traditions. However, religions do have distinct perspectives and are particular to the culture from which they emerged.

Rather than all religions being different perspectives on the same mountain, I wonder if we actually each have our very own mountain[151]—not just a different mountain for each tradition and religion and denomination, but personal mountains. Maybe our mountains are on the same mountain range, or on the same continent; maybe they are on different continents. And because continents move around as the tectonic plates shift, new mountain ranges are created and new continents are formed. The Pagan continent (like the mythical Atlantis) was submerged for a while, but now it has re-emerged. Now we can explore it again, with its polytheist mountain range, its monist mountain range, its pantheist mountain range, and other geological formations. Being

---

150   Yvonne Aburrow (2013), "The foundation of Pagan ethics." *Dowsing for Divinity.* https://dowsingfordivinity.com/2013/04/16/foundation-of-pagan-ethics/
151   Yvonne Aburrow (2014), "Your mountain is not my mountain and that's just fine." *Dowsing for Divinity.* https://dowsingfordivinity.com/2014/03/11/mountains/

a Pagan sacred landscape, it either has no centers, or its centers are everywhere, and it has no periphery (unless you want a bit of liminality).

Indeed, who is to say we are all climbing up mountains? Maybe some of us are exploring lush valleys, hanging out in the forest, taking a dip in the ocean, building a beautiful eco-village, or whatever takes your fancy. You can define your own journey, you can walk (or run or hop) on a predefined path, or discover your own bit of the lush Pagan continent. There is room for all.

Atheists also have emotional and intellectual baggage—such as the notion that all religions believe in the supernatural. This is not true. Pagans believe in immanent deities and spirits, which Michael York has labeled "preternatural"—a quality that "comprehends the magical, miraculous, numinous, mysterious yet non-empirical quality of the sublime" and "does not demand belief or faith but instead encounter and experience."[152] Atheists are often skeptical of any notions of energy or spirit, but that is often because they operate within a post-Cartesian dualist worldview, where matter and spirit are viewed as separate. Western thought has been fairly consistently dualist since the time of Descartes.

Enlightenment values have also had a tremendous impact on religion and philosophy. The Enlightenment elevated reason above all other forms of thought and experience, and there was a huge conflict between a priori reasoning and empiricism (the idea that everyone starts life as a blank slate and has to experience things to make sense of the world). The conflict between rationalism and empiricism was not resolved until the early twentieth century. The first stirrings of the Pagan revival happened during the Enlightenment, as people rediscovered the world of the ancient Greeks and Romans and developed a new interest in Graeco-Roman gods, philosophy, and values. They also began to become

---

152   Michael York (2008), "A Pagan Defence of Theism." *Theologies of Immanence Wiki*. http://pagantheologies.pbworks.com/w/page/13621955/A%20Pagan%20defence%20of%20theism

disillusioned with the Christian worldview and to rely more on science for their understanding of the world.

However, during the nineteenth century, as the Industrial Revolution was in full swing, people started to become disillusioned with science and technology. The intelligentsia began to turn more toward Romanticism, looking for meaning in their own culture, languages, folklore, and folktales. People began to explore mystical states such as the sublime (an experience of awe and wonder at natural phenomena), and to want to experience new places and sights. The dark side of Romanticism, however, was a turn toward nationalism. There was also a renewed interest in the internal processes of spirituality, which could be seen in the rise of Evangelicalism and Methodism. New German scholarship (known as the Higher Criticism) exploring the historical and literary processes that produced the Bible became available. To many Christians, this was more threatening than Darwin's theory of evolution. The backlash against both the theory of evolution and the Higher Criticism gave rise to the Fundamentalist movement, which had become so popular by the mid-twentieth century that people started to view Christianity (from both the inside and the outside) as entirely fundamentalist. Many liberal Christians were driven to leave Christianity altogether.

The tendency to view all Christians as fundamentalists has expanded into a tendency to view adherents of all other religions as fundamentalist, or to assume that fundamentalism is the "real" version of a religion, and more liberal expressions of it are somehow less real.

This view has sometimes been brought into Pagan discourse, where people who stick rigidly to a "traditional" version of a religion or worldview are referred to as "hard" (not to be confused with hard polytheism, which is a different concept). However, we need to guard against importing stereotypes like this into Pagan discourse.

Recently there has been a horrific new version of the use of the term "traditional" as a screen for bigotry. A very small group of transphobes in Gardnerian Wicca have claimed that their transphobic bigotry is somehow "traditional." They claim it is necessary to have a biologically male person and a biologically female person to make polarity, and are using this claim to try to exclude trans and nonbinary people from Wicca. There is so much wrong with this view that it is hard to know where to start. For one thing, the categories of "biological" male and female are a gross oversimplification of the complexities of sexual characteristics, which can vary dramatically and are determined by numerous subtle genetic and hormonal differences—any one of which could be missing in an individual and result in variation. For another thing, polarity has never been such a significant part of the Wiccan tradition as they claim, and polarity can be made by any complementary pair (extrovert and introvert, morning person and evening person, and so on). . And as Jack Chanek pointed out in a YouTube video on the subject,[153] it is particularly invidious for them to claim that their bigotry is "traditional," as they are thereby seeking to invalidate anyone who does not agree with them.

I would definitely suggest that transphobia and homophobia are a distinct case of unexamined baggage being brought into Pagan traditions, because several ancient Pagan religions were largely relaxed about gender and sexual diversity (most notably the ancient Greeks), and had practices that accommodated them.

As you learn things about your new tradition and community, try not to view them through the lens of your existing assumptions or weigh them down with baggage from your previous tradition. Try to view things in a fresh way, as if they were completely new to you.

---

153   Jack Chanek (June 2022), "'Traditional' versus 'Reform' Gardnerians." https://youtu.be/6Y0_s31Dmhk

Exercises, journal prompts, and reflections

- Write a description of your current theological views. You could also do an online questionnaire such as the Belief-o-matic from BeliefNet, but be aware that BeliefNet has financial links with right-wing organizations.

- Check your baggage. What ideas or values or assumptions are you carrying around from your original religious or philosophical tradition? Which ones do you want to jettison, and which ones do you want to keep?

- Make a list of every piece of received wisdom, 'common sense', things your parents told you, and that your community told you, and review them to see if they are still helpful to you. If not, jettison them.

Meditation: Unpacking

Visualize a bag or suitcase full of clothes. Pull out the items one by one and hold them up to light. Are they new or ragged? Would you still wear them? Do they suit you any more? If you still want them, visualize folding them neatly and putting them back in the bag. Otherwise, set them aside. When you are done, visualize zipping up the bag and leaving the room with it in your hand, leaving the unwanted items behind.

Chapter 11.
Pagan values and ethics

> In Wicca, darkness does not symbolize evil.
> The darkness is necessary for rest, growth, and
> regeneration. Death is not evil, but a necessary
> adjunct to life. If there was no death and
> dissolution, there could be no change or growth.
> The cycle of birth, life, death, and rebirth is part
> of the interaction of the polarities. Suffering is
> also part of the process of growth; just as a tree
> is shaped by the wind, we are shaped by our
> experiences. It is only by experiencing suffering
> that we acquire sufficient depth to know the
> fullness of joy. It is then that the full light of
> consciousness dawns in us, and we achieve mystical
> communion with the divine.

— Yvonne Aburrow[154]

I was standing in a circle at a Druid open ritual. It was Beltane, and participants had been invited to share their experiences of romantic love. Several people shared the joy of their relationship with a significant (heterosexual) other. I noticed that the gay members of the group were not there that day; I was the only LGBTQ+ person present, as far as I was aware. I could have shared about the beauty of same-sex love, but I was put off by the overwhelming number of heterosexual anecdotes. Nobody intended to be excluding of LGBTQ+ people with their enthusiasm for heterosexual romance, but nevertheless I felt excluded. I think I physically took a step back. I mentally shifted from participant to observer—not intentionally, it just happened.

---

154   Yvonne Aburrow (2015), "What color is your witchcraft?" *Dowsing for Divinity*. https://dowsingfordivinity.com/2015/07/18/what-colour-is-your-witchcraft/

This story illustrates why explicit inclusion of marginalized groups, and an explicit statement and clear demonstration of your values, is important. If you do not make it obvious that the celebration of same-sex love is welcome in your group, LGBTQ+ people will stay away. If you do not make it clear that you are actively trying to dismantle white supremacy, BIPOC people will stay away. If your ritual setup does not make provision for disabled people, they will not attend.

❀�•°•ᔓ❀�•°•ᔓ❀

Pagan values are life-affirming, celebrate sexual and gender diversity, and respect and celebrate the natural world. This is related to the celebration of the divine feminine principle and of darkness. For centuries in Europe, goddesses were a literary and folkloric phenomenon not admitted to the realm of religion. Although the Virgin Mary and female saints function like goddesses in many ways, they do not represent a celebration of female sexuality, which was relegated to the realms of the demonic and darkness. One of the themes of the Pagan Revival has been reclaiming the sacredness of sexuality and the beauty of the night.

Pagan values are grounded in an appreciation of life, the enjoyment of being physically embodied,[155] and the desire for others to enjoy the same experience. A value is a shared norm or expectation of a group—something that is considered desirable. A virtue is a quality of a person or a group that is considered desirable and contributing to human flourishing. Traditionally, most Pagan ethical codes were lists of virtues that were regarded as desirable, instead of a set of rules to be kept. The cultivation of virtues by the individual was said to lead to eudaimonia, a happy state of being.

Pagan morality is centered around the principle of human and environmental flourishing, the community of all beings in an interconnected web of existence. Deities and spirits are often

---

155   Yvonne Aburrow (2015), "Paganism for Beginners: Values." *Dowsing for Divinity*. https://dowsingfordivinity.com/2015/06/08/paganism-for-beginners-values/

seen as part of that community of beings, but their needs exist in relation to everything else; they do not supersede the needs of other beings. Being in relationship with our fellow embodied beings, and in relationship with our ecosystem, will do more to bring us into relationship with our deities than any amount of worship.[156] We do need to make an inner connection with the spirits of place, the spirits of the land, and the deities as part of our awareness of all the interconnected relationships of the nested interconnections of being in which we live, but deities, land-wights, animals, and humans are all part of that web of relationships. The deities are not more important than other aspects of that interconnectedness, any more than humans are.

When weighing up the ethics of a situation, we have to consider the needs of everyone involved—humans, animals, plants, and the environment. This is why, when an Indigenous hunter took the life of an animal, they traditionally thanked the animal for giving its life, and they did not take too much or slaughter all the animals in the area.

Sometimes the needs of humans will conflict with the needs of animals, or with the needs of other humans. If that is the case, we have to weigh the conflicting needs carefully.

It is also worth considering the principle of eudaimonia, the practice of living rightly to promote human flourishing. This ought to include the flourishing of the biosphere and other animals and plants.

Nature is a key concept in many Pagan paths. It is more diverse than our wildest imaginings. It is not a rigid structure or a "great chain of being" or a hierarchy. It is creative and wild and constantly moving and changing. It is not bunnies, rainbows, and dolphins, but it is not all fierce competition and struggle either. A better model for evolution is one of cooperation and community, as promoted by Peter Kropotkin.

---

156   Yvonne Aburrow (2015), "Relational Polytheism: Standing Beside the Gods." *Dowsing for Divinity*. https://dowsingfordivinity.com/2015/08/24/relational-polytheism-standing-beside-the-gods/

Being in touch with nature necessitates acknowledging the diversity of nature and living sustainably. Eco-spirituality is about acknowledging that we are part of nature, not in dominion over it. It is about being embodied and aware of nature all around us.

My ideas about Nature are informed by science, art, folklore, and mythology. I try to keep up to date with scientific insights (especially on LGBTQ+ topics). I think we need the creative and playful approach to Nature represented by art, folklore, and mythology, but we also need to be open to the wonder inspired by scientific discoveries about the universe and the natural world.

My criterion for deciding whether anything is right or not is, "does it harm anyone?" Of course it is impossible to completely avoid harm, but we can and should reduce the harm caused by our actions. I also draw on the Eight Wiccan Virtues (mirth and reverence, honor and humility, strength and beauty, power and compassion) as a guide to how to act. Other Pagans and polytheists draw on the lists of virtues or the body of lore from their own traditions. Druids have the Welsh Triads. Heathens have the Nine Noble Virtues.

An important source of ethical decision-making in Wicca is the Wiccan Rede, which is the saying "An it harm none, do what ye will" (or "If it harms no-one, do your will"). Many people respond to the Rede by saying that it's impossible to harm no-one, so it doesn't make sense; every action you take can cause harm. This is exactly the point of the saying. It is impossible to completely avoid harm: so you can't just do what you want. It basically means, think about the consequences before you act, and seek to minimize the amount of harm that you do. It is based on a saying from Rabelais.[157]

There is a lot of talk on the internet about the so-called Threefold Law, but this is not actually part of initiatory Wicca as it is commonly understood.[158] The actual law enjoins that when we receive good, we should return good threefold; there's nothing about

157 Yvonne Aburrow (2021), "The Wiccan Rede." *Dowsing for Divinity.* https://dowsingfordivinity.com/2021/02/15/the-wiccan-rede/
158 Yvonne Aburrow (2021), "The Threefold Law." *Dowsing for Divinity.* https://dowsingfordivinity.com/2021/02/14/the-threefold-law/

some cosmic law of karma that you will get back threefold what you give out. However, a sensible interpretation of this idea, offered by Patti Wigington, suggests that consequences of actions occur in the physical, mental, and spiritual realms, which means that we need to think about how our actions will affect our body, mind, and spirit.[159]

Some Pagan communities derive their ethics from the traditional body of lore of a particular culture.[160] This wisdom from the past, embedded as it was in experience and an ethic of responsibility toward other beings, is an excellent source of ethical guidance. But if there is a conflict of ideas, then that should be solved by weighing the needs of the parties involved. Many Pagan groups are keen on the notion of tradition. As far as I am concerned, tradition is not fixed and immutable. It is fluid and evolving, and it should change to meet the needs of practitioners. We should be in dialogue with tradition, but we should also be very clear that tradition should serve humans and not the other way around.

Authority in matters of tradition should rest with the community, not with an elite. Some more conservative Pagans use their definition of deity as a justification for exclusive ritual practices and rigid notions of tradition; but many in the community have now adapted to a more fluid model of gender and more flexible ritual practices. We need to look at how we make our spaces welcoming and inclusive of other marginalized groups, and we need to resist the development of authoritarian tendencies and far-right ideology within Pagan traditions, such as rigid notions of tradition, and ideas of heterosexuality and the gender binary being the only valid expressions of gender and sexuality.[161]

The Pagan Revival is now a global phenomenon that has moved beyond English-speaking countries. It has been adapted to its new locales, so it should not exclude people of any ethnic group.

159   Patti Wigington (2018), "The Rule of Three: The Law of Threefold Return." *Learn Religions.* https://www.learnreligions.com/rule-of-three-2562822
160   Yvonne Aburrow (2021), "Nature, Tradition, and Ancestors." *Dowsing for Divinity.* https://dowsingfordivinity.com/2021/11/26/nature-tradition-and-ancestors/
161   Amy Hale (2019), "The Pagan and Occult Fascist Connection and How to Fix It." https://medium.com/@amyhale93/the-pagan-and-occult-fascist-connection-and-how-to-fix-it-d338c32ee4e6

However, we still have work to do as a community in ensuring that we do not perpetuate Eurocentric stereotypes, structures of whiteness, colonialism, or ideas about what practices are appropriate for certain types of people.

Many Pagans talk a lot about ancestors. I think it is important to broaden this concept to include more than just our genetic ancestors. We also need to acknowledge that some of our ancestors did toxic things. If we live on stolen or colonized land, we should acknowledge that fact.

In Wicca, we talk about the Mighty Dead (Wiccans who have died). We talk about the Beloved Dead (a phrase borrowed from the Reclaiming tradition, meaning people we love who have died). Some of us borrow the terms "ancestor of spirit" (people from the past who inspire us), "ancestor of blood" (genetic ancestors), and "ancestor of place" (people who lived where we live now) from Druidry. I also speak of queer ancestors: the LGBTQ2SIA people of the past who can inspire and guide us.

How we relate to other spiritual and religious communities is important, and one of the ways we ensure that we do so ethically is by avoiding cultural appropriation. I have written extensively on this topic, and my suggested definition of cultural appropriation is outlined as follows:[162]

- Taking someone else's practice without permission or proper handing-on of the tradition and making money out of it—especially if the originators of the practice have a tradition of freely teaching it to people
- Taking someone else's practice into a completely different context where it does not fit
- Taking someone else's rituals, practices, or stories and pretending they are your own

162   Yvonne Aburrow (2013), "What is cultural appropriation?" *Dowsing for Divinity.* https://dowsingfordivinity.com/2013/03/25/cultural-appropriation/

- Taking someone else's ritual and then excluding them from it
- Doing someone else's practice and pretending that you have been authorized to do it
- Claiming a fake identity as an Indigenous practitioner
- Doing others' spiritual practices and changing the meaning, and/or failing to build in the appropriate safeguards, and failing to acknowledge that you've changed the meaning
- Failing to acknowledge the history of oppression suffered by the people whose practice is being copied
- Doing something that has nothing to do with a culture but dressing it up and claiming it as part of that culture—when you are not a member of that culture
- Wearing an item of clothing that expresses someone else's identity and sacred traditions as a fashion statement or a joke
- Anything that adds to a culture that misrepresents and mythologizes Indigenous Peoples and makes their real struggles invisible. For example, "noble savage" discourse.

I also repudiate any suggestion that a predilection for a particular culture is based on genetic makeup. Culture is not transmitted genetically.

Pagan values and virtues should be an expression of living in harmony with Nature and ensuring that all beings can flourish. This implies that diversity is to be celebrated, because what flourishing means for each person is different, depending on their context and inclinations. The only limitation on this is when one person's concept of flourishing means another person's erasure or annihilation. I would argue that in this case, it is not true flourishing. The flourishing of all beings is interdependent because we inhabit an ecosystem.

Exercises, journal prompts, and reflections

- Make a list of your personal values and virtues that you hold sacred.
- Are any of them in conflict with each other?
- Are any of them unexamined baggage from your previous tradition?
- Are there any ethical statements in your current or previous tradition that you disagree with?
- What does flourishing mean to you?
- How do you see yourself as part of a wider ecosystem?
- How do you relate to, or connect with, Nature?
- What do you think is the basis of Pagan ethics?

Meditation: The sit spot

A really great way of experiencing yourself as part of nature is to incorporate the sit spot into your practice. The sit spot is a place in nature where you can sit comfortably for about fifteen minutes. While there, you slow your breathing, quiet your mind, and listen to the sounds around you: the rustling of the wind in the leaves, water flowing or falling, bird song. Return to the same spot on a regular basis to become attuned to that particular place and its sounds, energies, spirits, seasons, and moods.[163]

163 Yvonne Aburrow (2016), "The Sit Spot." *Dowsing for Divinity*. https://dowsingfordivinity.com/2016/01/10/the-sit-spot/

Chapter 12.
Changing paths within
the Pagan sphere

I am Pagan. I am a part of the whole of Nature.
The Rocks, the Animals, the Plants, the Elements,
and Stars are my relatives. Other humans are my
sisters and brothers, whatever their races, colors,
genders, sexual orientations, ages, nationalities,
religions, lifestyles. Planet Earth is my home. I am
a part of this large family of Nature, not the master
of it. I have my own special part to play and I seek
to discover and play that part to the best of my
ability. I seek to live in harmony with others in the
family of Nature, treating others with respect.

— Selena Fox[164]

The first Pagan tradition that I tried was Wicca, and it has always
felt like the right choice for me. So when I went to check out Druidry,
I always felt that I was only visiting. It was interesting, but it was not
my spiritual path. I enjoyed the rituals, and they were sufficiently
similar to Wicca that it felt comfortable, but it never felt like home
in the way that Wicca does. I am sure there are many people who
have tried other traditions in the Pagan community, and found them
interesting to visit, friendly and comfortable—but not home. For
others, the first tradition they check out is not the right one for them,
and they keep looking for the one that feels like home.

❀⚶•°•⚶❀⚶•°•⚶❀

Sometimes people change from one Pagan tradition to
another. This may not be as dramatic as changing paths between

---

164   Selena Fox, "I am Pagan." *Circle Sanctuary.* https://www.circlesanctuary.org/index.php/about-paganism/i-am-pagan

two completely different traditions, but it shares some of the same features: a change of worldview, and perhaps a sense of disenchantment with the tradition that you are leaving. In some cases, the tradition you are leaving may actually be oppressive. Not everything in the Pagan garden is rosy.

Sometimes people select their tradition based on an archetype (for example, they choose Druidry because they are drawn to trees and wizards, or they choose Wicca because they like stories of witches). This is a valid reason for choosing a tradition, but sometimes the archetype that we identify with can change, or another tradition turns out to express your version of the archetype better.

Sometimes people get involved with a particular community because it is the only option in their area, and then they move to a place where more traditions are available. This is also completely understandable.

The good news about changing paths within Paganism is that it can be done gradually, and you can be part of more than one community at the same time (if you have time). Pagans are generally keen to help people find their right path.

One thing to guard against is the tendency to look for ever more intense spiritual experiences. A lot of people jump from one tradition to another looking for a better spiritual high. This is fair enough if a tradition is just not working for you, but give it time and try a few different versions before giving up. Different groups within a tradition have different ways of working and emphasize different aspects of the tradition.

I like my religion to give steady spiritual nourishment without massive highs or lows. The occasional peak experience is good, as long as it is not followed by a massive trough or withdrawal symptoms.

As mentioned in the chapter on leaving religions, though, there are some groups within Pagan traditions that are abusive, and it is definitely advisable to leave those as soon as this becomes apparent.

Often, When people first encounter Paganism, they get involved with some form of eclectic non-initiatory Wicca—either in a small-group setting or based on popular books. While this is a valid spiritual practice, it is not the be-all and end-all of Wicca. People often do not notice the lineaged initiatory traditions of Gardnerian and Alexandrian Wicca, or other more organized forms of Wicca, and assume that the eclectic practice is all there is. Or they think that the lineaged traditions are the same as the eclectic practice.[165] To add to the confusion, some of the eclectic groups offer a version of the three degrees of initiation, which may confer some sort of spiritual experience, but that may be wildly different from Gardnerian and Alexandrian initiations.

There are many articles online where people say that they started out practicing eclectic Wicca and then moved on to Heathenry or other forms of polytheism. This might be because there is a general assumption that Wicca is duotheist or monist, and that you cannot be a polytheist and a Wiccan. Or it might be that most "beginner" books on Wicca fail to be LGBTQ-inclusive. There are many polytheist Wiccans, and many Wiccans have adapted their rituals to be more inclusive of LGBTQ2SIA people (see my earlier books, *All acts of love and pleasure: inclusive Wicca; Dark Mirror: The Inner Work of Witchcraft;* and *The Night Journey: Witchcraft as Transformation*).

The assumption that all Pagan paths are "Wicca-lite" is sometimes called "Wiccanate privilege" because it is assumed that the spread of Wiccan-flavored rituals is somehow helpful to Wiccans, or that Wicca-lite is privileged over other paths because it is so widely recognizable.[166] The problem with this approach for non-Wiccans is that for at least a decade, the Pagan book market was flooded with

165   River Enodian (2018), "Bashing Wicca As A Polytheist Or Occultist Doesn't Make You Cool And You Know Nothing About It Besides." *Tea-Addicted Witch.* www.patheos.com/blogs/teaaddictedwitch/2018/06/bashing-wicca-doesnt-make-you-cool/
166   Yvonne Aburrow (2014), "Wiccanate Privilege and Polytheist Wiccans." *Dowsing for Divinity.* https://dowsingfordivinity.com/2014/03/10/polytheist-wiccans/

175

"Wicca 101" books. This means that a lot of Pagan terminology is based on the language of Wicca 101 books, and there is a set of assumptions out there in the public domain about what Pagans do that is based on these books—that all Pagans celebrate the festivals of the Wheel of the Year, that all Pagans think the deities are archetypes and expressions of a single underlying divine energy, that all Pagans are duotheists, that all Pagans do magic, or that all Wiccans perform rituals based on the Key of Solomon and/or Kabbalah, and so on. Workshops and rituals at events are often based on these assumptions.

Some of these assumptions are problematic for Wiccans, especially Wiccans who do not conform to general expectations and assumptions of what Wicca is about. These 101 books often contain an assumption that you are a Wiccan if you have read one of these books and you do the rituals in them; but more problematic for me is the fact that books on Wicca often contain an assumption that Wicca is duotheistic. Most Wiccans I know are polytheists, pantheists, animists, or non-theists. But because it says in these books that we are duotheist, other polytheists often refuse to believe that a Wiccan can be a polytheist. But many Wiccans regard "the Lord and Lady" as patron deities of the Craft, two among many; and many covens in the UK and Europe honor a different pair of deities as their coven patrons and honor a number of deities alongside them.

Another problem is that books on Wicca are often heterocentric and seem to have forgotten that the ultimate goal of the mysteries (especially in the Hermetic Order of the Golden Dawn) used to be seen by many practitioners as spiritual androgyny.

Add to that the fact that these 101 books are often prescriptive about what Wicca involves, and you get the imposition of a set of norms that it is difficult to challenge in our particular culture (because people tend to respond with "but I saw it in a book so it must be true"). And you face assumptions from non-Wiccans that that is what Wicca is like.

However, it is also entirely possible that Wicca was not the right path for many of the people who moved on to some other Pagan or occult tradition. So in their situations, moving on was the right decision for them.

Because different Pagan and polytheist religions tend to believe in the same deities, and some of them celebrate broadly the same festivals, it is pretty easy to move from one Pagan or polytheist tradition to another. However, each of them tends to be focused on a different aspect of the religious experience: self-development, relationship with Nature, devotion to the gods, or building community. Some practice magic, and some do not. Some are Goddess-oriented, some have a non-theist focus on Nature, and some are polytheist. As Christine Hoff-Kraemer wrote:

> Because this makes for a diverse set of attitudes, beliefs, and concerns, though, the outliers in this Venn diagram tend to struggle with the idea of "Pagan" identity. Pagan identity is most stable where the three categories overlap. Polytheists who aren't particularly earth-based or interested in gender politics may feel marginalized, as may indoor worshippers of "the Goddess." Those practicing "deep ecology"—a nature-based spirituality that has little to do with deities at all— may also feel out of place in the Pagan midst.[167]

If you have begun to feel uncomfortable or marginalized within the eclectic Pagan community, it may be time to find a community that is more closely aligned to your interests. Given the diversity within the "big tent" of Paganism, polytheism, and occultism, it is quite likely that such a community exists.

If you are uncomfortable with theism (belief in divinity or deities) and belief in magic, you might find AtheoPaganism or

167   Christine Hoff-Kraemer (2013), "Three Legs on the Pagan Cauldron, or Must Pagans Be Polytheists?" *Dowsing for Divinity.* https://dowsingfordivinity.com/2013/01/11/must-pagans-be-polytheists/

eco-spirituality more attractive. If you are uncomfortable with polytheism, there are monist, pantheist, and Goddess-oriented groups. If you are equally drawn to magical and spiritual practice, community, and ancient mythology, then Wicca or Druidry might be the right fit for you. If you are uncomfortable with monism or duotheism or pantheism, there are many polytheist traditions available. If none of these are the right fit, animist groups are starting to emerge.

There are approaches to polytheist practice and beliefs that may also cause practitioners to look for a different group. One of these is devotional polytheism, which can be broadly characterized as the desire to put the gods at the front and center of one's practice. Devotional polytheists usually regard deities as being discrete or distinct entities with agency. The concept of deities having agency (and not merely being an instrument of human wills) is very important to many polytheists.

Another approach is relational polytheism, which is focused on being in relationship with the world, including the gods, but also includes Nature, animals, birds, trees, other humans, ecosystems, and so on. Relational polytheists tend to regard the gods as potential partners with humans.

A difficult aspect of polytheism is the belief that everyone has a personal deity.[168] Some polytheists argue that you do not choose the deity, the deity chooses you. I disagree. You have the right to choose your deity or deities, and you have the right to refuse them. Not everyone has or even wants a personal deity, and it is not a "required" element of Pagan or polytheist practice. You can have zero, one, or many personal deities. The Hebrew Bible mentions "household gods" which I think refers to the group of gods that one has a relationship with (not necessarily all from the same pantheon).

---

168   Patchwork Crow (2018), *Thinking About Personal Deities*. https://patchworkcrow.wordpress.com/2018/11/11/thinking-about-personal-deities/

Gus di Zerega (2012), *Encountering Pagan Deities*. https://www.patheos.com/pagan/encountering-pagan-deities-gus-dizerega-08-24-2012

Some people become god-spouses. There can be an issue of consent with that concept, but it can and does work for many people. If you feel that you are drawn to being a god-spouse, read widely on the subject to make sure that you can engage in the practice safely.[169]

For some people, it can take a long time to find their personal deity. It is a good idea to read about deities from cultures that you feel drawn to. Maybe you have a personal connection with a particular place and feel drawn to connect with the spirit of the place. You will know you have found the right one when you get visions or dreams of them. You can also do divination to check if they are the deity for you. Once you have established a connection, you can maintain it by having a small shrine or statue of your personal deity and making offerings or prayers to them on a regular basis.

The great news about changing from one Pagan tradition to another is that most people in the Pagan community will encourage you to follow your heart and find a tradition that works for you, rather than trying to coerce you to stay in any tradition.

The key to changing paths is to follow your heart and not to slam any doors behind you, as you may find yourself returning to the community you are leaving if your needs or priorities change. The goal of spiritual practice is to create meaning in your life, to find beauty and balance and community. If your current practice is not providing that, and the conditions for creating it are not present, then it may be time to move on.

---

169   Bat Bruja (2018), *Godspouse 101: FAQs and my experiences*. https://batbruja.wordpress.com/2018/08/17/godspouse-101-faqs-and-my-experiences/

Exercises, journal prompts, and reflections

- Make a list of the ideal features of your path. What should it focus on mainly? Do you practice magic, or want to practice magic? Are you more of a mystic? Is your path focused on Nature?

- How well does your ideal path match the tradition you are currently practicing? Can your current practice be adjusted to match your ideal one?

- How well does your ideal path match with other current traditions? Can any of those be adjusted to match your ideal scenario?

- Is your path primarily Nature-oriented, Goddess-oriented, or polytheist, or is it a mixture of all three? How does that fit within the tradition you currently practice?

- If you are a polytheist: Are you a devotional polytheist, who wants to put the gods at the forefront of your spirituality? Or are you a relational polytheist, who wants to enter into partnership with the gods?

- Does your practice focus on self-development, creating community connections, or devotion to gods and spirits? Does that sit comfortably with the tradition you currently practice?

- Can you create a new group or practice within your current tradition that meets your needs?

Meditation: Personal deity

Find an image of a deity you feel drawn to, or go to a place that feels sacred to you. Try to connect with the deity or the spirit of that place. Allow the image of the deity to form in your mind, and see if they are a deity you could connect with on a long-term basis. Ask if they are drawn to you and what their sphere of influence is.

Chapter 13.
Finding beloved community

We'll weave a love with roots growing deep
And sap pushing branches to wake from their sleep
Bearing leaves burnt amber with morning's full
sweep
Together my friends we'll weave on,
we'll weave on.

— Carolyn McDade, Song of Community[170]

Roots hold me close; wings set me free.

— Carolyn McDade, *Spirit of Life*[171]

I was at a Wiccan gathering and there was a symbel hosted by two
people who are very dear to me who practice Heathenry as well as
Wicca. A symbel is a Heathen ritual where a consecrated horn or
cup of mead is passed around.[172] First the mead is hallowed with a
hammer, the symbol of Thor, by the host and the cupbearer. Then
it is passed from hand to hand. The first round is the brag round,
where you can speak of something you have achieved. The second
round is the boast round, where you may make an oath over the
vessel of mead. This oath is sacred and you are bound to fulfill it; you
have made the oath in a sacred setting, in front of your community
and the gods, and over a consecrated vessel. The third round is a
round of toasts. These are usually toasts to a deity, but they may also
be to an ancestor (this does not have to be a genetic ancestor), or to
someone physically present at the symbel.

---

170   Carolyn McDade (1981), "Song of Community." From the album *Rain Upon Dry Land* (1984).
http://hamiltonsings.ca/wp-content/uploads/2020/09/song-of-community_Carolyn_McDade.pdf
171   Kimberly French (2007), "Carolyn McDade's Spirit of Life: Unitarian Universalism's most beloved song, the woman who wrote it,
and the communities that sustain her spirit." *UU World*. www.uuworld.org/articles/carolyn-mcdade-spirit-life
172   John Wills (2012), "Symbel: The Heathen Drinking Ritual?" *Odroerir*, Vol. 2.
https://www.academia.edu/2060520/Symbel_The_Heathen_Drinking_Ritual

It was the second time I had attended a Wiccan gathering since my massive spiritual wobble. Up until that point, I had been practicing Unitarianism and Wicca, but this was becoming increasingly difficult, and things had come to a crisis point with my practice of Unitarianism. I realized that practicing both paths was not working for me. I was so happy to feel fully back in the Wiccan community, which accepts all aspects of me and where the ritual works for me and makes me happy.

At the symbel, when it came to the round for oaths, I knew what my oath would be. I made an oath to devote my spiritual path to Wicca full time, because Wiccans are my beloved community. (Even when they are annoying, they are still family.) I believe that the energy to write my books about Wicca ultimately came from that oath.

❀ई•°•ॐ❀ई•°•ॐ❀

A beloved community is a place where you feel safe and accepted for who you are, where you can connect with other people in an atmosphere of mutual trust and friendliness, and where you can connect with the numinous without reservation. In such a community, you experience a sense of fellowship and pleasure in the company of the other members. There may be individuals in the community that you find harder to get along with, but nonetheless, you have the shared focus of the community as a bridge between you.

A community can be gathered around a number of different things: the people who live in your neighborhood (a geographical focus), people of your cultural group, people in your bridge club or hockey team or football team. It can gather around a volunteer effort, or in a church, synagogue, gurdwara, sangha, or mandir. It can be a Heathen hearth, a Druid grove, a Wiccan coven, or a group of polytheists practicing their tradition together.

There are open communities and closed communities. An open community is one where it is easy to join and easy to leave. A closed community is harder to join, and harder to leave. This sounds cultlike, but it does not have to be. It can simply be intended to create a safe space for the ritual or activity that happens in that space. To determine if a group is cultlike, it is best to examine other behaviors of the group—like their attitude to having other friends outside the group, how controlling they are of members' other activities, and so on. Check their behaviors and attitudes against the Advanced Bonewits' Cult Danger Evaluation Frame.[173] (See also the earlier chapter of this book about finding a group.)

Some communities are more tolerant of their members' belonging to other groups. If the belief system spiritual community subscribes to is a totalizing system (one that believes itself to describe reality completely and to provide all that is needful), it will be harder to be a member of another spiritual community. If the group is a "high-control" group (one that expects to have control over every aspect of members' lives), then it is unlikely to tolerate membership in other groups, whether they are secular or spiritual. Being a "high-control" group is definitely a warning sign that the group is a cult, and therefore best avoided.

A community that cares about you as a person is likely to make space for your personal and family stories.[174] This includes celebrating rites of passage for all aspects of your life, whether that is birth, coming of age, coming out, transitioning to another gender, getting married, getting divorced, losing a parent, your kids leaving home, menopause, old age, or death and bereavement. It includes celebrating those rites of passage in ways that respect the history of individuals and families, and that include the stories and symbols that are important in your culture, heritage, and family.

Your spiritual community should also accept and celebrate you for

---

173   The original Advanced Bonewits' Cult Danger Evaluation Frame is at www.neopagan.net/ABCDEF.html and there is a list of cultlike groups at https://rationalwiki.org/wiki/Cult

174   Herbert Anderson, Edward Foley (2001), *Mighty Stories, Dangerous Rituals: Weaving Together the Human and the Divine*. Jossey-Bass.

who you are, and that includes your gender and sexual orientation. The rituals and festivals of the tradition should reflect the diversity of the participants and not value or center heterosexuality, monogamy, cisgender identity, whiteness, neurotypicality, youth, or any other category above other ways of being human. It should instead value consent culture, inclusion, diversity, and equality. It should stand against rape culture, racism, homophobia, transphobia, and ableism. It should be a safe, welcoming, and inclusive space for BIPOC people, LGBTQ2SIA people, and disabled people.

If you feel that some aspect of your true self is not valued or celebrated by your community, and that aspect does not harm others, it can be very disheartening and destructive of self-esteem.

To be truly safe and welcoming spaces, many communities have a probationary membership period in which the group and the prospective member can assess whether they are a good fit. From the perspective of the group, this means assessing whether the prospective member really subscribes to and embodies the core values of the group. From the perspective of the prospective member, it means assessing whether the group practices what it preaches.

Once you have become a full member of the community, you are typically then entitled to a say in the running of its affairs and in the group guidelines, and a veto over prospective members.

When you have found your beloved community, there is a sense of comfort, of being at rest in a safe space, of feeling at home. There is little or no conflict between your values and those of the majority of the community. The rituals and celebrations of the group become a necessary part of your life; you feel as if there is something missing if you do not celebrate the high days and holy days. Stepping into the community and taking part in the rituals feels nourishing, safe, normal, and energizing. You are comfortable with other members of the community and with the ancestors and other beings that it venerates.

I feel that one of the signs of being in a community is that you form real friendships with other members of the community— friendships that would endure if you left that community. For example, I have some very dear Unitarian friends whose continuing friendship I value very highly.

I think it is important to maintain or develop friendships outside of your spiritual community—to get a bit of perspective, and to interact with people who do not necessarily share your worldview.

It is interesting to look at your community and see who belongs to it. Do all or most of the people share the same characteristics (such as gender, sexual orientation, socioeconomic group, ethnic group)? Is that a historical, geographical, or cultural accident, or is a group being excluded on purpose or because of some belief or assumption held by the majority of the community?

How does the community respond when one of its members is in trouble, hardship, or pain? Do they rally to offer help and support, or do they abandon the person or family? Are there rituals to support the person or family in the difficult situation?

How does the community deal with a situation where one of its members abuses another? A safe and supportive community should have a code of conduct for large gatherings and events that makes it clear how they will deal with conflict, unwanted sexual advances, sexual assault, and the like. It should also have workshops to promote consent culture and ensure that all members of the community are aware of the guidelines.

There are circles of trust within communities. Your innermost circle of trust is the people you are most comfortable with, whom you trust not to violate your personal space and not ask you to do something you are massively uncomfortable with, and with whom you feel safe to let down your guard and be vulnerable and intimate. Beyond that, there are people who are vouched for as safe, or whom you assume to be vouched for as safe.

Consent culture

There are many environments (especially spiritual communities) where people assume that everyone in the community is safe and trustworthy. These are often called high-trust environments. This is why it is so devastating when someone violates that trust by committing a sexual assault, for example. It is doubly devastating when the community supports the perpetrator rather than the victim.

We should not let the desire for peace and harmony in the community override the need to hold accountable people who violate and harm others. If we allow such incidents to pass without some form of consequence, whether it is being barred from community events (temporarily or permanently, depending on the nature and seriousness of the violation), we are eroding that trust, peace, and harmony.

In the anthology co-edited by Christine Hoff-Kraemer and me, *Pagan Consent Culture*, members of various communities examine what it means to create safe and welcoming communities that promote consent culture and how to ensure that people are not violated in our communities.

One of the issues that occurs when a community is confronted by the possibility that one or more of its members is an abuser is that people strenuously deny that anyone they know could possibly be a rapist or an abuser, because they are "good people." And once someone is revealed to have perpetrated abuse or rape, they are immediately cast out into the outer darkness, with no hope of rehabilitation. People assume that they are completely bad and want to obliterate their memory.[175]

This makes it extremely hard to bring abusers to justice or to hold

---

175   Yvonne Aburrow (2016), "Binary Thinking and Dealing with Abuse." *Dowsing for Divinity*. https://dowsingfordivinity. com/2016/09/16/binary-thinking-and-dealing-with-abuse/

them to account because the stakes are so high. That is why those who defend abusers feel the need to assert that they did nothing wrong.

But life is more complex than that. People are a mixture of good and bad impulses and behaviors.

The biggest problem with this binary view of "good people" and "bad people" is that people tend to take the view that preventing abuse and rape is simply a matter of getting rid of the "few bad apples in the barrel." They think that if only we had a perfect means of identifying abusers and preventing them from getting into the community, we would be able to fix this problem. If only we could eject abusers from the community once and for all when they were discovered to be abusers, they think. And surely the intuition of community leaders is good enough to prevent abusers from getting in, they claim. Ah, but what if the abuser is one of the leaders? Or they claim that the members of the community are strong enough to protect themselves from abusers. And why should the onus be on anyone to protect themselves? They also think that once we have gotten rid of these abusers (who obviously have an evil look about them so are very easy to spot), the community will be safe for everyone.

That is why abuse gets swept under the rug, because people do not want to face up to the fact that the "good person" they hang out with is abusing others, and they know that there will be no hope of them ever being rehabilitated within the community once it has been widely accepted that they are abusers.

Sadly, we will not get rid of abusive behavior by culling a few bad apples from the barrel. We live in a rape culture, which creates social conditions that make rape easy to get away with. We live in a society where violation of consent is routinely validated, approved of, and promoted and where the existence of valid consent is constantly erased and undermined. The view of mainstream culture is that women should not have sexual desire, and a woman who does have sexual desire is viewed as deviant and a "slut." Because she is viewed as an object and not a subject, once she has become sexually available, she is therefore available to all men and can be raped with impunity. A "pure" woman, on the other hand, has to be cajoled and persuaded into sex. Because she is seen as not wanting sex, she can only consent if she is offered an inducement—the security of marriage, a nice dinner, a few drinks, a compliment. (Obviously this is a caricature of mainstream society's views, but you can see echoes of this as being the underlying attitude in many conversations and interactions.)

Paganism is a subculture that seeks to regard women as subjects and to validate women's sexual desires. However, the attitudes of the mainstream can and do find their way into Pagan discourse. Not everyone is perfectly acculturated to the Pagan worldview, and we are still subject to the influences of mainstream society. Thus it is not bad apples that taint the barrel—it's the conditions in the barrel that causes some apples to rot.

If it is not a matter of finding and ejecting abusers, what is the solution? There is no simple and easy quick fix. It is something we all have to work toward.

In their chapter in *Pagan Consent Culture*, Kim and Tracey Dent-Brown present a four-part model, which is summarized below. I would strongly recommend reading the chapter, as it explains in considerable depth how they arrived at this conclusion.

1. Reducing motivation to abuse—this needs to be done on a societal/communal level (what are the wider societal factors that promote abuse, i.e. rape culture?)

2. Reinforcing internal inhibitions (shame, knowing right from wrong, empathy for others, understanding what valid consent is). "How can we all develop a state of mind that makes us more likely to take others' consent very seriously."

3. Strengthening situational barriers (procedures or systems that protect potential victims). "This is the area most ripe for action, because it is where communities, groups, covens, organizing committees and so on can have influence."

4. Reinforcing the individual victim's own defenses (to coercion, physical means etc). "This is the last level of defense and if the rest of the pagan community does nothing at levels 1-3, this puts the potential victim in the position of being entirely responsible for defending themselves. Hopefully the more active the community has been at earlier levels, the less likely action at this level is to be needed."

This is how I think we need to go about creating consent culture, which is an essential part of creating a beloved community that is safe and welcoming for everyone.

- Promote consent culture within Paganism and wider society. Methods can include running workshops about consent, promoting conversation about what consent and consent culture are, etc. Embed consent culture within the Pagan worldview by relating it to Pagan theologies and mythologies. (These were some of our aims in continuing and spreading the conversation about consent culture by editing the book, *Pagan Consent Culture*.)

- Promote the Pagan and Heathen Symposium Code of Conduct,[176] because this creates a situation where both potential victims and potential perpetrators know that the event staff and organizers take consent and violations of consent seriously, and will act on reports. The Code of Conduct is not going to fix the issues on its own—it is only one part of a multifaceted approach that includes holding workshops, writing articles, and so on. We didn't invent this approach; it has worked really well in the science fiction and

---

[176] Pagan and Heathen Symposium (2015), *Pagan and Heathen Symposium Code of Conduct.* http://pagansymposium.org/code.html

information technology communities.

- Educate everyone about consent and what it means, as this will strengthen individuals' resistance to violations and discourage potential perpetrators from committing violations.
- Reduce our tendency to binary thinking, in order to prevent abuse being swept under the rug.

The role of leaders

The roles of leaders, elders, and teachers in the community are also very important. In a safe and welcoming community, it should be possible to have doubts, ask questions, and explore new ideas. Community leaders should be accountable, and there should be a mechanism for voting them out.

Leaders should see their role as keeping the community safe, promoting consent culture and other community values, welcoming new members and helping them to become full members of the group, and providing support to members. I have written extensively about the role of leader in my book T*he Night Journey: Witchcraft as Transformation*. I would also recommend reading *The Pagan Leadership Anthology*.[177]

The best Pagan leaders are those who listen—to the promptings of spirit and to their group members.[178] Pagan leaders should be people who empower, nurture and teach others. They should not regard their community as serving them, but instead feel that they are serving the community (which includes other-than-human beings). Elders get that title by being acclaimed by others —not just by virtue of being old, but by having wisdom and experience. In return, the community should value those who serve.

In my experience, even if some leaders of Pagan groups let it go

---

177   Taylor Ellwood and Shauna Aura Knight, editors (2016), *The Pagan Leadership Anthology*. Megalithica Books.
178   Yvonne Aburrow (2014), "Pagan leadership." *Dowsing for Divinity*.
https://dowsingfordivinity.com/2014/07/11/pagan-leadership/

to their head for a while, they soon learn that they are leaders by consent of the group, and if they do not care for the needs of all the members of the group, and nurture and empower their members, people will leave.

Ideally, the values of the leaders and the community should be in harmony with each other, and subject to an agreed set of community guidelines and norms that can be reviewed and adjusted by the group when new circumstances require it.

Putting down roots

When you join a new spiritual community, there is a honeymoon period where you only see the good parts of the tradition. After a while, you start to see the flaws and the drawbacks as well as the good parts. Once in a while, there may be things that bore you, or people that annoy you, or practices that are frustrating. When the honeymoon period has worn off, what makes people stay in their new religious tradition? It is most likely that the good that they found outweighs the frustrations.

Every tradition has a shadow side; quite often, its shadow side is a consequence of its positive aspects. Traditions emphasize one thing and this means that there is something else that gets repressed. A discourse makes certain utterances and thoughts a natural consequence of other thoughts, and thus excludes certain other ideas from the discourse. They are also reflections of the cultural period in which they were born.

For example, Wicca was born sometime between the 1930s and 1950s. When it arose, the idea of a Goddess was new and radical, and so was the idea of the Goddess being married to the God. It absorbed lots of ideas from the zeitgeist, as documented by Ronald Hutton in *Triumph of the Moon: A History of Modern Pagan Witchcraft.*[179] However, the consequence of having the Goddess married to the

---

179   Ronald Hutton (1999, 2019), *Triumph of the Moon: A History of Modern Pagan Witchcraft.* Oxford University Press.

God is that people tend to elevate heterosexual love above all other kinds, despite the line in The Charge of the Goddess that states that all acts of love and pleasure are rituals of the Goddess.[180]

If you look at the history of Christianity, it was born during a period when people were syncretizing different religions together, and there were many mystery cults springing up everywhere. In its early years, Christianity closely resembled a mystery cult; for example, only those who were already baptized could witness a baptism. It also had a strong ascetic streak, possibly absorbed from the Essenes, or from the general philosophical turn against the body that was prevalent at the time. This ascetic tendency led to a rejection of the body and of women. It also led to Christianity's first major schism, between the Gnostics and the mainstream church, as the Gnostics rejected physical reality. Early Christians also believed that the end of the world was going to happen very soon, and many of Saint Paul's letters are written with this belief in mind. We can still see these themes in many versions of Christianity today. Their consequences are authoritarian attitudes toward women and a rejection of all sexuality except that which results in procreation. Some branches of Christianity have had a rethink and have reframed their ideas in a more liberal direction.

Once you have decided that you can live with the shadow side of your chosen community, the next step is to put down roots. It is a great idea to meet in person with your chosen community as often as you can, while also building connections with other types of community. Online communities are helpful, but it is easy to build a false picture of people online. They are showing you only their best side most of the time. When an argument breaks out, because of the lack of context, nuance, and body language, it is very easy to misconstrue what someone else has said—or pick on one tiny aspect of it—and blow it out of all proportion. So meeting in person is

---

180   Doreen Valiente (1957), *The Charge of the Goddess*. https://www.doreenvaliente.com/doreen-valiente-Doreen_Valiente_Poetry-11.php

Patti Wigington (2019), "Charge of the Goddess: History and Variations." *Learn Religions*. www.learnreligions.com/charge-of-the-goddess-history-and-variations-4151704

better.

How often you meet with your beloved community is up to you—but take time to share stories of your lives and get to know each other as people. In our circles, we regularly schedule time for sharing personal feelings, within ritual and outside of it.

It is also good to have social time with your community that is focused on having fun together, not necessarily on ritual or your religion. Examples include going for walks or hikes together, planting trees together, having picnics, and just hanging out together. I always say the best way to get to know other people at Pagan camps is to help dig the firepit, or to help with meal preparation or washing the dishes afterward.

On a personal level, take the time to learn the history, culture, and rituals of your new community. Who were the founders? What motivated them? What brought them to found this community? Who are the main movers and shakers now? This is a good idea even if your new community is atheism (look at early atheists like Eerasmus Darwin, Bertrand Russell, Frances Wright,[181] and so on). What are the rituals of your community? How did they develop, and why are they important? Get to know the mythology, gods, spirits, and ancestors of your new community. Perform or attend rituals in your tradition, and connect with its deity or deities, on a regular basis. How does your community feel about Nature, and how do they maintain or develop a connection to it?

When you love a community or a tradition, it is natural to want to immerse yourself in it, but it is also a good idea to read about other related topics, in order to see it in context and deepen your engagement with it. You can only read so many Paganism and Wicca 101 books before you want to move on to the next level.

Check out the governance structures of your new tradition: Who

---

181   Sharon Presley (2018), "Neither Gods Nor Masters: 19th Century American Women of Freethought, Part 1." *Libertarianism.* https://www.libertarianism.org/columns/neither-gods-nor-masters-19th-century-american-women-freethought-part-1

makes decisions? Where does the power reside (in local groups, and at a more global level)? How are difficult dilemmas and conflicts resolved?

Community is a precious thing when it is working well. Like friendship, we need to work at it, nurture it, and tend it to ensure that it develops in a healthy way. We need to have open and honest conversations about what our community values are (preferably in advance of potential conflict instead of in reaction to actual conflict). And we need to ensure that we have customs and procedures that allow us to reinforce and teach values of respect, kindness, and celebrating and affirming diversity, equity, and inclusion. Above all, your membership in a community should bring you joy, resilience, friendships, meaning, hope, and connection.

Exercises, journal prompts, and reflections

- What does it mean to belong to a community?
- How do you feel about belonging to multiple communities?
- Does your spiritual community make space for, or include, your personal and family stories?
- Do you feel that everything about you is accepted and welcomed by your spiritual community?
- In a community setting, what makes you feel safe and accepted? What makes you feel excluded, unsafe, or rejected?
- What do you think are the characteristics of a beloved community? How should it treat its members? Who belongs, and who does not? How should it respond to abusive or controlling behaviors by one of its members?
- Who do you see as being included in your community? Does it include ancestors, spirits, deities, the Divine, animals and birds, trees and rocks, rivers and lakes, the land itself?

Meditation: Beloved community

Visualize yourself sitting in the shared silence of a beloved community. Be aware of the connections of love and friendship that connect you with all those around you. Imagine that each of our hearts is a beacon lit in the night, a fire of hope and courage and love at which others can warm themselves. Sometimes we have failed to share our warmth. But many times we have made a difference to the lives of others by reaching out to them in love. See all the shining threads of love and care that connect you to others, and see the threads of love wound around the whole world, as we are all interconnected—a network of shining beacons of love embracing the world.[182]

182   Yvonne Aburrow (2012), *Many Names*. Lulu.

Chapter 14.
The road goes ever on

顿悟之前砍柴挑水，顿悟之后砍柴挑水

Dùnwù zhī qián kǎnchái tiāo shu,
Dùnwù zhī hòu kǎnchái tiāo shu.

Before enlightenment, chop wood and carry water;
After enlightenment, chop wood and carry water.

—Wu Li (吴力)[183]

I remember vividly the times when I felt in my bones that Wicca is home. It happens to some extent every time I step into a Wiccan circle, but there have been specific occasions when I have felt this: when someone just gets what I am talking about; or they said something that deeply resonated with me. One of these times was when I was giving a talk about the experience of initiation. I mentioned a specific experience in ritual, and people just knew what I was talking about without my having to explain it in great depth. Another occasion was the very first time I stepped into a Wiccan circle, at my initiation. Another was at the symbel where I vowed to devote my energies to Wicca. I have felt comfortable in other traditions, but it is Wicca that feels like home. If you have found a tradition that feels like home for you, I hope it will be a nourishing, challenging, supportive, joyful experience.

❀⤐•°•⤜❀⤐•°•⤜❀

After all the upheaval of a spiritual wobble or a change of paths, life settles down into something resembling normality. Maybe you

---

183   Kelly (2011), "Quotes and Idioms." *Red Leopard*. http://www.redleopard.com/2011/05/quotes-and-idioms/

have left one tradition and joined another; maybe you have returned
to your original tradition.

I grew up in Christianity, became an atheist at the age of fifteen,
and then joined Wicca at the age of twenty-three. Years later, around
the age of forty, I found that I had some unresolved issues around
Christianity and needed to revisit that tradition. This re-evaluation
was partly as a result of getting involved with interfaith dialogue.
By revisiting Christianity, and then discovering Unitarianism, I got
things in perspective. But in the end, I found that you can take the
girl out of Wicca, but you can't take Wicca out of the girl.

When we take the perspective that all religions are paths up the
same mountain, we enter a sort of spiritual no-man's land. This
perspective is all well and good, but it is too rarefied an air for
ordinary mortals to breathe. It is exhausting trying to maintain such
an abstract view of religion. That's why, as Andrew J. Brown says, we
need to focus on the "radical particularity" of our traditions—not as
a way to denigrate other traditions, but because ours is what will get
us up that mountain. Someone else's tradition won't, and maybe we
are all climbing different mountains, anyway.

Assuming that there are universal, perennial principles behind all
religions is overly essentialist and has sometimes been used to support
racist and colonialist perspectives. Even when it is used for liberal
purposes, it can still turn your religion into weak tea. As Brown says:

> Liberal religionists have had a long love affair with
> the idea that it was possible to express religious
> faith through certain "essential and universal
> principles" hoping that, in so doing they could
> articulate a kind of pure, "neutral" religion that
> would suit all and offend none. It is a project
> which, though admirable in many ways, has
> failed and the continued decline of liberal religion
> as a vital force in our contemporary culture is

extremely worrying, especially at a time when
religion as a major political and social influence
is back with a vengeance and when right-wing
political forces across Europe are once again
gaining ground.[184]

I cannot find the comment or article now, but when I decided
to settle down and focus on one tradition, Brown quoted to me the
saying from Wu Li that is the epigraph for this chapter: "Before
enlightenment, chop wood and carry water; after enlightenment,
chop wood and carry water." In other words, get to grips with the
particularities of your tradition, because that is what will sustain
you. Brown is not interested in imposing his perspective on others;
he is interested in building liberal religious community around a
particular set of ideas. And that is as it should be. We cannot be "all
things to all men"; we can only speak as we find things. I find his
ideas profoundly interesting and helpful.

Changing from one religious tradition to another can be a deeply
unsettling experience. Even when we join another tradition, we
still have to deal with the baggage from our original tradition—
whether we were born into it, or joined it as an adult. We absorb the
metaphors, mythology, stories, and rituals of any tradition that we
engage with seriously, and we inevitably carry them forward with us.

My sojourn in Unitarianism[185] came about because I am very
interested in social justice. I still value many of the ideas and
practices, and most importantly the people, from that tradition.
It was a wonderful place to get over the wounds inflicted by
Christianity, and it is a deeply welcoming and inclusive community
with a commitment to creating space for people to work out their
own personal theology. In the end, it was not my spiritual home, but
it was a great place to visit. I have certainly absorbed many ideas

---

184   Andrew J. Brown (2009), "The Flower Communion—Hard particularities with profound love and trust." *Caute: Making Footprints, not Blueprints.* http://andrewjbrown.blogspot.com/2009/06/flower-communion-hard-particularities.html
185   In the USA, the tradition is known as Unitarian Universalism, because Unitarianism and Universalism merged in 1961 to form the Unitarian Universalist Association. In the UK, where I was involved in it, the tradition is known as Unitarianism.

from it and met many wonderful people.

For me, a true spiritual home is a place where I can connect with the numinous, and with other practitioners, without difficulty (whether philosophical, spiritual, theological, or intellectual).

The Pagan community, being made up of human beings, is flawed like any other community. But it is a place where I feel free to seek, to find, and to be my authentic self and to connect with the numinous. One of the aspects of the Pagan quest is to find the authentic self. We are also seeking to become more deeply connected with the land, the Earth, and Nature and to recover our connections with our ancestors and their gods. Different Pagan and polytheist paths tend to focus more deeply on one or two of these aspects.

But each person's path through life, love, community, spirituality, and religion is unique. If there is not an existing path that suits you, make your own. It is good to travel with fellow travelers, but it is to be hoped that they will recognize that you have your own story and your own way through the woods. You do not have to know where you are going, you just need to live authentically. Your commitment to your path will ebb and flow, your spiritual practices will come and go, you will experience faith and doubt, times of abundance, times of drought. Andrew J. Brown says:

> . . . it is only when you genuinely let things flow
> and we allow ourselves to move with them, without
> being fixed in one position, that we begin to
> develop a truly flexible, living philosophy that is
> not "set up like the solution of a puzzle, worked
> out with all the pieces lying there before the eye"
> but something that is "more like the clarification of
> what we know in our bones."

> But this clarification is always coming into the
> light out of the relative obscurity of existence itself
> and this means. . . that the basic meanings of our

unfolding lives can never be anticipated—they can
only dawn upon us.[186]

This is excellent advice and reminds me of my favorite quote from
Laurens van der Post, "Only one heart had to find its true position
and travel on from there and all the rest would follow. . ." quoted at
the start of chapter five.[187]

It is possible that the true position of your heart can move and
change; but it may very well be that it has something to do with
relationships, whether they are with other people, Nature, the
Divine, deities, the transcendent, the immanent, or the numinous.
But once you have found the waters from which you draw joy,
nourishment, inspiration, and sustenance, and other people who also
draw from those waters, then you have very likely found your beloved
community.

Perhaps the conclusion to this book is that there is no conclusion:
as Wittgenstein once said, "Alles fließt" ("Everything flows"). It is
the journey that matters and not the destination. We can only find
our way through the thickets of uncertainty—and hope for some
signposts and helping hands. No religious tradition has all the
answers; most liberal traditions will tell you that their job is to help
you deal with uncertainty. Alan Watts said:

> Faith is a state of openness or trust. To have faith
> is to trust yourself to the water. When you swim
> you don't grab hold of the water, because if you do
> you will sink and drown. Instead you relax, and
> float. And the attitude of faith is the very opposite
> of clinging to belief, of holding on. In other words,
> a person who is fanatic in matters of religion, and
> clings to certain ideas about the nature of God and
> the universe, becomes a person who has no faith at

---

186   Andrew J. Brown (2014), "The reflection worth indulging doesn't know where it is going—Leaving behind only footprints and never
blueprints." *Caute: Making Footprints, not Blueprints*. http://andrewjbrown.blogspot.com/2014/07/the-reflection-worth-indulging-doesnt.html
187   Laurens van der Post (1978), *A Far-Off Place*, p.304. Mariner Books.

all. Instead they are holding tight. But the attitude
of faith is to let go, and become open to truth,
whatever it might turn out to be.[188]

All that we can do is follow our hearts, remaining "open to new light, from whatever source it may come" as the Quakers say,[189] and approaching new ideas with discernment, to see whether they are conducive to creating joy, connectedness, and peace.

Your journey may involve being in more than one spiritual community, either consecutively or in parallel, and that's okay. It takes courage to change paths, and also to sustain a connection with two or more traditions at the same time. It helps if neither of the traditions is a "totalizing system" that tries to claim an exclusive hold over its participants, but if you can sustain both connections, it can be very fulfilling to hold them in creative tension, or creative union, with each other.

Your spiritual path might be a solitary one, and that's okay too. You might find your beloved community in other ways.

A spiritual tradition worth its salt should provide a variety of ways to nourish your mind, body, and spirit, and share significant times in your life—of joy and of suffering—with others. It may not answer your questions about life, death, and the meaning of suffering, but it should provide you with a spiritual toolkit to travel through life in all its complexity, and some convivial companions along the way.

---

188   Alan Watts, *On Faith*. Quoted in: Jackson (2009), Being open to truth, whatever it might turn out to be. https://truthaparadox.
wordpress.com/2009/12/11/
being-open-to-truth-whatever-it-might-turn-out-to-be/
189   The Religious Society of Friends (1995-2022), *Quaker faith & practice* (Fifth edition). Chapter 1: "Advices and queries," item 7.
https://qfp.quaker.org.uk/passage/1-02/

Exercises, journal prompts, and reflections

- How has your spiritual practice ebbed and flowed? Can you identify internal and external triggers for these changes?
- Do you believe that all religions are paths up the same mountain, or up entirely different mountains?
- What drew you to your chosen religious tradition? Is that what sustains you, or are you compensating for a psychological wound of some kind?
- Pay attention to what your body is telling you. Where do you feel most comfortable, most nourished?
- What inspires you and nourishes your creativity, your spirituality, your sense of relatedness? How can you make more space for it in your life?

Meditation: Multiple perspectives

Visualize a vast many-faceted crystal, suspended in space, absorbing and refracting light within its many angles. You can look into the heart of the crystal through any of the facets. Try looking through the different facets until you find one that fits with your vision of the universe.

> The Road goes ever on and on,
> Down from the door where it began.
> Now far ahead the Road has gone,
> And I must follow, if I can,
> Pursuing it with eager feet,
> Until it joins some larger way
> Where many paths and errands meet.
> And whither then? I cannot say.

— J.R.R. Tolkien[190]

---

190 There are various versions of this song in *The Hobbit* and *The Lord of the Rings*. "The Road Goes Ever On (song)." *Tolkien Gateway*. https://tolkiengateway.net/wiki/The_Road_Goes_Ever_On_(song)

Part Three:
Experiences of Changing Paths

This part of the book contains personal stories from various contributors, about their journeys through and experiences with various traditions. Some I know personally; others are people I met online through the Missing Witches podcast community. My call for contributions asked for people to share their experience of changing from one religious or spiritual tradition to another. I felt that it was important to include other people's stories to show how varied the terrain is.

Forest Path. (Riza Nugraha/Flickr)

A bad Buddhist but a good witch—Jasmin

"You're not being a very good Buddhist." I hear echoes of my mother's voice as I reflect on the past fifteen years of trying endlessly to find myself. Of thinking that I had to conform to what was perceived as spiritually acceptable to be myself. Of accepting, at one point, that I was never going to be able to be "out" with my spirituality if I thought of myself as a witch.

Masking is something I am all too accustomed to as a neurodivergent, fat, and chronically ill person. It is the act of assimilating into a space, of contorting your mind, body, and spirit to fit inside the systemic box that was made by a small group of powerful people. I was all too used to overcompensating for my size, covering my pain, and pretending to be "normal" like everyone else. In the current power structures we live within, masking is something I believe that everyone does; it's a form of survival.

A strong Hungarian man who sacrificed a lot to raise his family in Montreal, my late Opa[191] was a beautiful violin player, a very emotional soul who (in my opinion) lived with a neurodivergent mind that lent itself to creativity and worry. In the end, his mind left him. The music was still there, though—songs like Au Claire de la Lune. And, I noticed, he smiled more. Perhaps his dementia was a result of the lifelong masking of a mind that was somewhat outside the norm, of being too tired to hold on to worry. We all need a rest. Sometimes. I hope that wherever he is (when he isn't visiting me in dreams), he is playing music and smiling.

In my first year of university, I took an elective course called "Witchcraft, Magic and Occult Traditions." I always enjoyed the strange and unusual and figured this would be a course that could raise my average and get me into the history department. As a child I enjoyed making potions in the backyard, talking to birds, and listening to loud music to relax myself after being social with people.

---

191   Grandfather

So I was known as an emotional kid. A strange one. I flitted like a hummingbird from friend group to friend group, never really settling until I moved to Ottawa to pursue my studies in classics and English. I worked at the Haunted Walk of Ottawa giving ghost tours, and it was there, and through completing the elective course on witchcraft, that I found her* (note that I use the terms her and them, acknowledging that the witch is anything and anyone, as a cisgender woman I tend to lean to the feminine, but I acknowledge the importance of the nonbinary as a central part of our witchy communities).

The witches welcomed me in. They helped me discover friends and allies—fellow weird ones who were totally O.K. with who I wanted to be. I was still, however, not open with my folks. But they were far away in Halifax, Nova Scotia.

In my mid-twenties, I was working as a teacher up north. Realizing that this witch stuff just wasn't (at the time) conducive to my profession, and worried I would shame my family, I abandoned the practice and looked for a "legitimate" spiritual group I could finally be open with.

So I went to Buddhism.

I was not a good Buddhist; I couldn't have been even if I had tried harder. From 2015 to 2018 I became vegetarian, spent way too much money on meditation supplies, and watched Dalai Lama lectures on YouTube for hours on end. I paid membership fees to a Halifax Buddhist community, and I paid tuition fees to complete several "levels" in order to eventually, I thought, truly become a central part of the community.

I thought I was home. Buddha seemed like a cool dude.

I abandoned the witch for Buddhism, the Goddetc.[192] for the Guru, and candle magic for prayer beads. I believed that Buddhism

---

192   Goddetc is Jasmin's gender-neutral term for Goddess, God, etc.

was the right fit because I could post about it on my social media and not be afraid of losing friends or being silenced by family members. I believed that I had to take a "respectable" path, and, for a moment, I thought I had finally figured out who I was.

Then, like one of those claw toys, I was plucked by the universe and placed in front of the witch again.

By mid-2018, the leader of the Buddhist community had released a statement admitting to several counts of sexual impropriety. That statement, like a crack in a dam, unleashed a flood of stories from other survivors accusing not just the leader themselves, but other teachers within the community. The red flags were flown. and so I flew out of the community. I no longer felt safe, and I also felt deceived.

I still have very little trust for the idea of a spiritual community. I'm working on it.

So I found them again. The witch. She was right there the whole time waiting for me to come back. As if I had never left the practice, I picked up a candle and organized an altar. I started connecting with something I had tried to convince myself I could no longer connect with. I tried to give up the witch because I was afraid, but the witch created a safe space for me to be myself, to explore, to learn, and to connect.

In truth, even if the walls hadn't come proverbially crumbling down on me, I don't think that I would ever have been a good Buddhist. I do not believe my neurodivergence (ADHD) or my innate desire to follow a non-patriarchal spiritual path (or my love of being alone) would have ever let me truly become a full-blown member of that community. I grew up in a family who chose not to baptize me because they believed that choosing faith, any faith, should be just that, a choice. My parents' European heritage (German/ Hungarian and Dutch) informed our somewhat traditional practices of Christmas, Easter, and trying to avoid meat on Fridays, but it felt more like culture than Christianity. Hanging chocolates on the tree or filling shoes with gifts on December 6 was more about my parents sharing the best parts of their culture with me, rather than indoctrinating me to believe a certain dogma (or dharma).

So now I have fully embraced the witch. I like to tell folks that for me, Witch is a verb—an act of resistance, of love, of unmasking and of connection. For years I have been a happily solitary and private witch, but no longer. With a partner who loves and celebrates all parts of me, parents who are pretty cool with it, a podcast (shout out to Amy and Risa of Missing Witches) that inspires me to act on my values about equity, justice, and love, a motivation for radical self love (as coined by Sonya Renee Taylor), and a connection with a deity that helps me get to my pre-Christian roots (hail Freyja), I feel like I can finally get to know myself. My whole, neurodivergent, strange self. It feels good to take the mask off.

After officially being diagnosed with ADHD, anxiety, and living with a chronic condition, I have learned that life is way too short to be afraid of being yourself.

So here I am, and I see you too.

As Frida Kahlo said, "I used to think I was the strangest person in the world but then I thought there are so many people in the world, there must be someone just like me who feels bizarre and flawed in the same ways I do. I would imagine her, and imagine that she must be out there thinking of me, too. Well, I hope that if you are out there and read this and know that, yes, it's true. I'm here, and I'm just as strange as you."

So, channeling the strange energy of Kahlo, I will conclude my story of coming, leaving, and coming back to the witch with a poem. It is dedicated to you, my fellow strange one, my fellow witch. I see you, and I love you:

Witch

Is a verb

An action

A practice

A spell

An intention

A way of life

Witch is a verb

Polarizing

Yet, non binary at its core

The witch is goddetc

In all its forms

A child of chaos

Perfectly happy

To swim against the current

Witch is a verb

And it is a fine way

To live a life

Blessed be, blessed be, blessed be.

—Jasmin

Jasmin (she/her) is a fat, chronically ill, and neurodivergent second-generation settler in Halifax, Nova Scotia. She has been a witch in the proverbial broom closet for over a decade, but no longer. Along with her Ph.D. work that focuses on anti-ableist pedagogy and pre-service teacher education came a deep desire for radical self-love (a term coined by Sonya Renee Taylor), and her late diagnosis of ADHD has cemented her passion to unmask, embrace the craft, and share her thoughts and ideas about how she understands that the word Witch . . . like love . . . is a verb. She looks forward to continuing to be a part of building a community

The God's Honest Truth—Ambrose Heath

How did I go from being a Christian fundamentalist to becoming a witch? I would love to be able to tell you that it was the result of a thorough theological inquiry and academic study. I wish I could provide you a well reasoned argument for conversion to a Pagan spirituality. I wish I could say that I became disillusioned with my faith because of my church's leanings toward homophobia or misogyny. But that is simply not how it happened. Besides, I never actually gave up faith in "Christ."

I grew up in a fundamentalist Christian home. At age 19, I preached my first sermon. I led youth groups and adult Bible studies. I was a lay preacher and missionary all through university. Point being—I was a true believer.

It began with an incredibly vivid dream. Or what I thought was a dream...

I was sleeping on the couch and an older man suddenly appeared out of nowhere. He sat by my feet on the couch. I sat up. I asked him who he was. He told me He was "God." He had appeared because he understood I had some questions for him.

As a matter of fact, I did. I explained that I was troubled by some of his rules. Particularly around human sexuality. I simply didn't understand the necessity for regulating harmless, pleasurable activities, among consenting adults. I just didn't get it. It didn't seem right to condemn people for being gay, or trans, or any other aspect of the LGBTQ+ community.

He sighed heavily and said, "Rather than answer your questions I'm sending you to speak to ... well ... for now, let's just call her ... my other half." He snapped his fingers and disappeared.

His other half?? What was that supposed to mean??

I had just fallen back to sleep, when I found myself standing at a distance from a great huge Greco-Roman-like palace or temple. It had seven great huge white pillars across the front of it. I could hear voices in my head. They were all female voices, and I knew they were coming from inside the palace. It sounded like a party of some sort. There was a general mix of voices from multiple conversations. Then suddenly the voices stopped. I could feel their minds focusing their attention on me. Then one loud commanding voice, a mature woman's voice, demanded, "Who are you??"

"I am . . . 'I am' sent me to you."

With that I was instantly transported to a room inside the palace-temple.

I was lying on a bed inside a large room. I was unclothed. As I lay on my back, I felt the warmth of a woman's body as she lay down beside me. I could feel her as she gently snuggled against me. I could not see anyone.

I looked toward where I thought her head would be. I whispered to her, "Who . . . who are you?"

Her invisible, warm body rolled on top of me. The sensation of skin on skin was astonishingly real. I felt her breasts press against my chest.

She whispered softly in my ear, "My dear, I am the woman of your dreams."

With those words I woke to find myself on my friend's couch. Alone. And very much clothed.

I am sure you're thinking: It's a dream, right? No "mystical" explanations required. I have to admit, that's pretty much what I thought too.

The next morning, I got up and got ready for class. I was in my final year at university. I had about one and a half semesters' worth of credits to complete my B.A. in English.

I wasn't absolutely certain what I was going to do with that degree. I loved writing, but I had no desire for the life of a would-be/starving-artist. Teaching held little appeal. I started looking into journalism as a possible career path. I had done some writing for the local newspaper. In any event, even if I didn't know how, I figured a degree of any kind would assist me.

I got a bus to Warden Station. From there I caught the subway train.

I was contemplating the weird dreams I had the night before, when I noticed a dark-haired, professionally dressed woman with dark brown eyes. She was probably in her mid-thirties. She dropped the book she was reading on the empty seat beside her. Her expression turned from one of indifference, seeming to ignore my presence, to sudden and intense interest. She stood up and took the few steps she needed to stand directly over me. She leaned over suggestively, until the cleavage in her blouse was level with my eyes.

"I am the woman of your dreams," she said with a sly, suggestive smile.

Then she returned to her book swiftly and began reading again as though nothing had happened. I looked around. The bounty of smirks and grins confirmed that I hadn't been hallucinating. I was tempted to approach her, in need of some clarification. But intuitively, I decided against it and she exited the car two stops later, seemingly oblivious to what had transpired. I began to realize that I was dealing with something—or someone—I clearly did not understand. I needed help. But from where? Who could I talk to? Did God have a . . . wife? If so, who was She?

But if She was God's wife, why was she so interested in me??

"Have you tried bibliomancy?" asked my friend Mark as he sipped his beer. I had called him and asked him to meet me. Of all my friends, he was the most open-minded and thus the one friend

I figured I could share my story with. We met at a typical Toronto British-style pub near campus, with a Tudor façade, subdued lighting and sturdy hardwood furnishings. We sat in a booth near the back, and I told him I didn't even know what "bibliomancy" was. He began to describe it.

"Oh, of course!" I almost shouted. I had used the technique a few times over the years, starting when I was a kid.

It was simple enough. Approach God in prayer with a question. Open a Bible quickly and at random. Pick a passage to read from at random. See if the words contain an appropriate response to the question. But I found that it didn't always work.

Mark suggested that She, whoever She was, was obviously trying to communicate with me, and thus might be able to answer some of my questions through bibliomancy.

It might not work, but there seemed no harm in trying. He suggested also that spiritual communication often took the form of symbols and metaphor and may or may not be intended literally. I should keep an open mind and keep questioning.

I wasn't in any hurry. Truth was, I was spooked by the whole damn thing and kept putting off the whole bibliomancy exercise. A week later, I remembered that I was supposed to prepare a study on the topic of the Holy Spirit as part of an adult Bible class. I was staying with another friend, Jason, that weekend, out in the east end, Scarborough. It was a warm sunny afternoon, which was unusual this late in September. So, I took my Bible and a notepad and pen out onto the balcony of his apartment.

As I began flipping the pages of the Bible, I began to feel . . . funny. It felt like I was dizzy, but not entirely. My vision seemed to be blurring a bit, and I felt an unusual sense of calmness. Having never experienced this before, I did not know that I was slipping into a trance.

I began reading the passage in front of me. Soon I was praying my questions and flipping randomly through the Bible for responses.

My eyes widened in amazement. The responses were coming with alarming constancy and clarity. Our "conversation" went on for quite some time. Some of it I was told not to share. But what I can say is that She, for me, became "the Voice of the Holy Spirit in female form." I was to see, relate, and speak to the Holy Spirit in her female form.

To be clear, She did not say that She didn't or couldn't assume other forms. She had simply chosen to reveal herself to me in this form. I did not choose Her. She chose me.

"Why?" you ask? I have no freaking idea.

I was writing a sermon for the following Sunday when I began slipping into a trance again. I couldn't think of any questions, so I just started reading random passages from the scriptures. But nothing seemed to jump up at me. I sighed heavily and closed the Bible. Then it hit me: The one constant in every passage had been a reference to going to Jerusalem. But since Jerusalem was easily the most commonly referred to location in the Bible, it might be hard NOT to come across a reference to it at random. So, I put the Bible back on my desk and went to the kitchen to make some coffee.

And I heard her whisper inside my head. It was a still, small whisper. But it was clear and sudden: "I do want you to go to Jerusalem."

I dropped the coffee pot in the sink. The water splashed me.

"Alright then!" I shouted to my empty apartment, "I'm fucking going to Jerusalem! Now, can I please make myself a cup of coffee??"

As I sat musing over that coffee, I had an urge to call Mark. There was no way his talk of Israel, only days earlier, could have been a coincidence. That bastard knew more than he was letting on, and I was ready for some answers.

I called three times. No answer.

I called again an hour later. Still no answer.

I went to my classes the next day and tried again in the evening. This time an electronic-sounding voice said that the number was no longer in service.

I was officially on my own in dealing with this problem. Well, unless you include Her. But, to my mind, She was the problem!

This whole business was extremely troubling, and I wasn't sure how to deal with it. I had no desire to expose myself to ridicule by claiming that God was whispering to me. After all, I might be insane—and if that should prove to be the case, I would rather people not know about it. In addition, the church I was attending believed that since the Bible had been written, God did not need to communicate with people directly any more. So, any assertion to the contrary bordered on heresy.

As an active lay preacher, I was often called upon to present classes on biblical topics and give sermons. I told my "Beloved" that if anyone asked directly why I was going to Jerusalem, I would tell them the truth. But I would not be making any references to it in any sermon or Bible class.

She seemed okay with this arrangement.

There was one last church function to attend before I started my journey, and, to this day, I am not sure why I chose to go—other than perhaps habit. I typically attended the weekly Adult Bible Class, which usually had no more than a dozen people. Among them would be close friends with whom I had already shared my story about the whispers of God. And they'd probably told the rest.

So that Wednesday, I went to the church hall and took a seat. I was relieved as each person greeted me as they had always done, and the class went on as though my "heretical craziness" had been forgiven— if not forgotten.

After class, though, one of the church elders offered me a ride home. I should have realized it was a trap. Fortunately, he was one of the more open-minded people in the church, and he seemed more curious about my story than anything else. But, make no mistake, he was acting as my inquisitor.

As we neared my apartment, he asked me three last questions.

One: "Have you considered going into therapy?"

I told him that I was already in therapy and that my therapist supported my decision to go.

Two: "Are you certain this is God and not your own imagination?"

I told him that no, I was not at all certain of that.

Three: "Then why are you intent on going?"

I told him that my spirituality, my faith, and my commitment to God were more important to me than anything else—including my own life. That being the case, what was the worst thing that could happen?

Was it feeling like a fool thousands of miles from home, realizing I had deluded myself?

No.

For me, the worst-case scenario would be to stay home, only to one day discover that God had, indeed, asked me to go to Jerusalem— and I had refused. In either case, the only way to find out was to go.

With that explanation, he shook my hand and wished me well.

Hebrew Union College was a Reform Jewish Institution. In the heart of downtown West Jerusalem and walking distance from the Old City, it was a "schul" or school in every sense of the word. It was a university campus with a good library of Jewish texts, many of which were available in English translation. They held religious services every shabbat and on Holy Days. In those days, it didn't seem to matter that I was not Jewish, Israeli, or even a student. As far as I could tell, the religious services and the library were open to the public.

It is here that I found the Talmud in English translation. But it was a difficult read. I didn't have the cultural background to make sense of many of the references or idiomatic expressions in their literal English translations.

I had made contact with a couple from my denomination who lived in Jerusalem, Ed and Leslie Livingston. The Livingstons knew a Rabbi who was willing to include non-Jewish learners in his weekly lessons, so I started going. It was a fascinating time for me. Jewish perspectives were so similar in many ways, and most definitely not in others.

I started reading what I could from the Hebrew Union College Library. I attended "schul" there as well. I went every Saturday morning and went to regular Torah instruction one evening a week. I desperately wanted to know more about Kabbalah, but I kept getting steered toward regular Jewish learning. After initial frustration, I realized that approach probably made sense. I would simply have to be patient.

I also started studying more about Islam, archeology, and ancient Near Eastern mythology.

It was all very exciting, but also dangerously disorienting. I was starting to connect dots that I had never realized needed connecting. The Fellowship I belonged to had made a great habit of pointing out the Pagan origins of many things that most people assume are Christian. But the more I studied, the more uneasy I felt about even that version of Christianity—my Christianity!

The Fellowship I belonged to was convinced that they had sanitized their faith from all things Pagan in origin. But what if they were wrong? What if the very foundation of that faith actually came

from ancient pagan spirituality? What then? What if everything
that distinguished Christianity from Judaism was actually Pagan in
origin?

I thought I had stumbled upon a truth that no one else was aware
of. And I had no idea what to do with it. (I was wrong, of course.
If you are intrigued by the connection between Christianity and
Paganism, check out Tom Harper's book *The Pagan Christ*.)

Ed and Leslie Livingston had established contacts within various
parts of Jerusalem's religious communities—and apparently a
few others besides. They held a religious service at their home on
Saturday nights for the same Christian Fellowship I belonged to. I
would attend, and I often remained a guest at their house for the rest
of the weekend. One Sunday afternoon, Ed invited me to go with
them to see the fabled "Quarry of Solomon" the next morning. I
was intrigued, as I had neither heard of it nor come across it in the
books I had read. But I was more than a little skeptical. Archeologists
had yet to discover any trace of Jerusalem's first Temple. Maps,
ancient and new, seemed to make no reference to Solomon's Quarry.
I wondered if it might turn out to be another touristy "supposedly"
and "probably not" sham historical site. But it would be interesting
to investigate, nevertheless.

So, we made a plan to meet the keeper of the site first thing
Monday morning.

Most of our religious exploration trips produced little more
than idle curiosity, which was how I was feeling about the quarry
adventure. If anything, I was prepared for disappointment. But not
the Livingstons. We got up very early, and their excitement was
evident and infectious. They bustled around like it was Christmas
morning.

After gentle prodding of "Come on! We don't want to be late,"
I did my best to match their pace of preparation. But if anything,
based on what I'd been told about the general area, I was fairly

certain we would be arriving ahead of time.

And we did—about thirty minutes before the appointed hour. There was a gate, as we'd been expecting, secured by a great iron chain and an ancient-looking padlock. But there were no posted hours. In fact there was no sign at all—not even a simple plaque to indicate what lay beyond this ancient gate. The only thing that I could see was a dark tunnel descending into the earth behind that gate.

We decided to find something nearby to drink and munch on, but the Livingstons didn't want to lose sight of the gate. Ed managed to find and buy some juice bottles, and we waited for their friend and guide. The gatekeeper arrived precisely on schedule. He smiled warmly at the three of us as we shook hands in welcome, and he gave Ed a big brotherly hug. He took out his keys and unlocked the gate. Holding it open, he welcomed us in—and then closed it and locked it with all of us inside. This took me by surprise, and I was beginning to wonder if the site was usually open to the public at all. Our guide seemed to sense my thoughts and explained that the site was occasionally open, but that the current political upheaval meant that it had to be closed for much of the time. We were honored guests, he said, and he was happy to give us a private tour.

We walked down a narrow passage that had the look of a mining tunnel. It soon opened up into a huge subterranean cavern with many smaller tunnels branching off from it like some enormous, hollow spider. There were several plaques on the walls and stone pillars throughout the cavern; most explained the history and process of excavation. I stayed behind to read the plaques as the Livingstons followed our guide down a side tunnel. Lights strung along the walls of the cavern gave the whole place a soft golden glow and differing shades of shadow.

I suddenly felt a hush descend upon the cavern as my friends disappeared. There was a kind of electricity in that silence, and the entire cavern radiated . . . energy. I could feel it.

I kept looking around and spied a large plaque: "Every year, the Freemasons gather in this place . . ." What?

The Freemasons? Suddenly the excitement and anticipation all made sense. This wasn't just another suspected holy site. This was "The Holy Site"! The Quarry of King Solomon! The heart and center of the entire world of Freemasonry, and my friends and I had been given an exclusive tour!

The central cavern started to spin, and I put my hands to my temples to try to mitigate the dizziness. I could hear my companions and tried calling out to them, but the words caught in my throat. I was still standing, but my vision blurred. I realized that what I was experiencing was no health or physiological issue—thoughts, symbols, words swirled around me like puzzle pieces caught in a tornado, and I was in the center. The pieces that were swirling around me were being pulled together, coming together of their own accord, and the puzzle picture was forming as it spun around me. Chaos and confusion were swirling into a new way of understanding. And it was all happening right there. Right then.

I began for the very first time to understand the new world I was entering, to grasp the reason behind my previous anxiety and confusion. It wasn't about learning. It was about unlearning, about releasing and ridding myself of all that I thought I knew about life, God, and the Universe. I just needed to stop and listen. I kept trying to interpret everything using my own frame of reference, and it was woefully inadequate for interpreting this new information.

If I was to avoid going mad, I absolutely had to let it go.

To adequately articulate the insights I gained would require a whole book in itself. There is a connection, a thread, a current running through the mysteries of Isis and Osiris, the Torah, the Descent of Ishtar, the account of Christ's death and resurrection, and the origins of Freemasonry.

More personally, and perhaps more shockingly, I was informed that I was becoming Her human lover and consort, Her human spouse . . .

Six months later, I was back in Toronto. I was engaged. My betrothed had obtained an engagement ring for me. I should clarify that I mean a human woman, my partner. Her name was Sarah. I worked with her sister; her sister had introduced us. Sarah gave me a thick gold band with a large diamond. My "Beloved" and Spirit-Wife told me to take the ring to a jeweler and replace the diamond with another stone—lapis lazuli. My long-suffering human fiancée was used to my eccentricities and didn't protest.

This new ring would be the symbol of my marriage, not to a physical human woman, but to the Divine in female form herself. The physical union with my new human bride was also the union between myself and my Holy Beloved.

Modern Wiccans and those who practice traditional Witchcraft will recognize the similarities here. This is similar to the celebration of the marriage between the Lord and Lady—which is why I would eventually make my way into the "Old Religion." But there was a significant difference. I was not representing the God.

I am certainly a human, and a flawed one at that. Much of my life has been spent vacillating among doubt, suspicions that I really am crazy, and feelings of inadequacy and complete unworthiness.

I once reflected in my journal, "How can the deep, vast, enormous ocean fall in love with a tiny speck of beach sand?" But my Beloved, Soul of the Universe, had done just that—with me.

I am surprised sometimes, that my claim of marriage to God (or Goddess) hasn't earned me a stay in a mental health institution. But maybe that's because I am not the crazy one. And the story isn't really about me. The story is about Her. She's the one who's crazy.

She claims that her love "is poured out upon all the earth" and that her law "is love unto all beings." Her love isn't limited to me. My story is just an extreme crazy illustration of how deep, extensive, and vast her love truly is.

Someone once asked me, "She is the Mother of All. So, does that make you my stepdad?"

"God, I hope not!" I replied, "Way too much pressure."

Besides, spiritual symbols and spiritual communication need not always be taken literally.

But just in case anyone's tempted to push that idea, I want you to do one thing for me, and how you do it is up to you.

Take time every day. Take time every day to remind yourself of this one, simple, God's honest truth (and I mean that literally):

Mother Loves You.

Reconnecting with the mystery—Èlia Viader

To me, the terms God and Goddess are interchangeable. The term Magic is synonymous with mystical experience, connection, openness, expansion. The term Pagan is inclusive. This is a first-person narrative of a real experience. I cherish and hold dear everything that is discussed here.

I look at the moon and feel my body respond. Its light shines on me. Its curvature is reflected in my figure. Finding its presence among the trees or peeking through a window makes me smile. At a very early age, without anyone explaining anything to me, without reading anything, I learned to let myself be touched by the subtlety of life. I had a near-death experience. My new baby brother had a strange disease that the doctors didn't know how to cure. The family business wasn't generating enough money for us to live. At school I was bullied by my classmates. I felt that I didn't belong anywhere, and at the same time I felt a huge need to belong. I learned that the world emanated in me, and I saw that simple things in life brought the world to me.

The moon, the wind, the rain, the animals. The wind blows, the thunder appears louder or longer, the animal looks at me, comes closer and is gentle with me. I feel in the depths of my being that each one, in its own way, responds to me. It's a reciprocal relationship; it's alive, there's communication, and I'm connected with what surrounds me. In moments of connection (which I call Magic), my feeling and sense of being are extended. I become light and wide. My limit ceases to be the barriers of the body and becomes "other." I feel an electric goodness emanating from everything and a vibrant fluidity all around me. I'm aware that I'm an active part of the system, that we're one and not separate, that I and the parts exist at the same time. There's communication without words. And I observe it, I'm aware of it.

It seems that no one around me notices the Magic, which makes it more interesting because it's a secret. It makes moments full of "nothing"—for someone else who looks at it. For me they were, and still are, Everything. My vision ceases to give importance to the parts, apparently inert, and focuses on what unites us and what's similar. "Like a drop of rain flowing to the ocean," the song says, the feeling of isolation and loneliness that "mundane" life generates in me, turning my senses and my inner world to these mystical experiences heals me. It integrates parts of me that a moment ago I thought were broken or lost. All disappointment, fear, anger . . . disappears. I feel alive and full. Without words, without effort, without anything else. I am because All is, and we are together at the same time.

I never decided that an adjective that was going to describe me was going to be witch or Pagan. To this day, to be frank, they are concepts that I use with caution, even though I feel they are true. I'm a very curious person, I need to understand. The advent of the internet made it easier for me. It was through reading articles and blogs that I discovered that the Magic that was normal in me was known in the concepts of Paganism, witchcraft, Druidry, Wicca, Neopaganism, Celtic culture, and so many more. Once the concepts were identified, the deep search could begin. I wanted to learn more and be able to have mystical experiences constantly. The information I found in the sources was of the "magic formula for X" type. I quickly realized that everything had a method, and following that method was the reason for the appearance of the Magical. That is, a formula had to be applied to be able to experience the mystical.

The information that I found changed me and inverted my innocent relationship with the Magical. Before, my practice consisted of letting things happen and simply staying receptive (which in Christianity is known as Grace). It reversed the situation, so that I was the cathartic agent for It to express itself. Magic depended on me, and I could break it down by applying a method to make it listen to me. In a way, this way of thinking was what confused me, because I stopped thinking of Magic as divine, free, spontaneous, and existing everywhere, and I became a controlling center. Mistrust and fear entered my relationship with Magic. Mysticism was cut off in my life.

We often talk about the spiritual path we walk. Using these terms gives the feeling that we must always go further. It's a path, a transit, a movement. We acquire and consume values, skills, information, and even objects. Once inside this dynamic, it seemed to me that I should always go further, look for more, learn more . . . because something in me was incomplete. And, in theory, the more knowledge I acquired, the more I advanced. Some speak of it as "development." The restlessness of not being whole and well as I am became the constant. What guided me in the end was discomfort and the desire for more. And this is not bad, in itself, for out of discomfort comes the search for belonging and connection.

Looking back, perhaps the root problem is that when I received some comfort from the practice based on accumulation of knowledge and goals, the consequence was to fall lower. And when I fell, I sought again relief through the Pagan. But I would fall again sooner or later.

As time went by, I realized that this emptiness inside me wasn't going to be filled no matter how much I filled it with things or the "magic formula for X." The truth was that it was what I knew. The hole was getting deeper and deeper, and the Magical experience was becoming more and more inaccessible. What I put into the hole to remedy the hole itself made my emptiness deeper and heavier.

And it hurts. It hurts a lot. I caused myself a lot of suffering because I became insatiable. I didn't know how to solve it, and I tried to get better. But it got worse. I ended up applying bandages that lasted a few days or even minutes, and just as the feeling of well-being had increased, it fell away again and left me lower than the previous time. I lost my vision and my North Star.

Very agitated and tired from all this coming and going, accumulating, seeking, researching, not finding . . . I put everything aside, sat down, and asked myself: "If what I want is to be happy, to feel alive, and to be closer to the Magical—what gives me that?" And I listened to the answer: "The truth is, all I'm looking for is a place (without a place) to rest and feel like I belong. Just like I found as a child in nature." At that time, I was twenty years old and starting college, and my decision was to abandon everything related to Paganism and become an agnostic. I threw away literally hundreds of books. I needed to clean everything out and let go. I felt that so much accumulation and attempt at control hadn't served me well. I felt disconnected from life. I rejected everything related to the spiritual and even looked down on it. Taking stock, I thought I had lost peace instead of gaining it.

Intermittently, I felt pulled or called. The mystical experiences weren't my present, but the memory of them sustained me internally. Sometimes I would allow myself to visit the esoteric section in the bookstore, buy incense, or talk about some mystery with colleagues. But I was still determined not to go in. I was frustrated. I thought the source of my suffering was Pagan, and I didn't want anyone to think I was a weird person. I decided that the solution to my woes was to become worldly and pragmatic. After a few years, realizing my disconnection with the body and feeling, I started to practice a hard sport: trail running. Through sport in nature, I took possession of myself again. I got in touch with my body, I learned that thoughts can help you to follow your goal or move away from it, I let myself be surprised by a deer crossing the road. A year later, pain appeared in my knees, and I looked for another sport. That's how I started practicing Hatha Yoga.

Hatha Yoga is a physical practice that generates in me a strong feeling of well-being. Tension in parts of the body that I can't detect is loosened and released. I stay relaxed during this physical exercise, perhaps stressful in another context, guided by the feeling of well-being to generate more well-being. Improving my posture. I seemed to have found a master key to another way of feeling and living. Suddenly I felt at peace with myself, body, and mind—and with the world. As the curious person that I am, I needed to understand and comprehend why this was happening, how it was happening. I wanted to build more of what was happening in the sessions. I studied for four years to become a Yoga teacher and did a two-year university master's degree in meditation.

This initial search for wellness on the physical plane over the years diverted me to the Advaita Vedanta philosophy. The truth is that Hatha Yoga is a physical practice that is closely linked to a religion (paradigm) and culture, so that as one practices, one also acquires Hindu habits and ideas without almost realizing it. Unlike Paganism, I found Yoga to be socially accepted and integrated. There are Yoga halls everywhere, and practicing Yoga is considered a healthy habit, even by government associations. I could show myself openly and proudly. This made me feel included and free, as if I had come out of the spiritual closet.

I found in Advaita Vedanta a very simple and logical description of existence. I seemed to understand reality—I could even make a conceptual map and have everything almost under control. In short, Advaita basically works with attention. The idea is as follows: We know we exist because we constantly observe. So "that" that observes and escapes when we try to know it directly, since it is the observer, is the final reality. It's a constant entity that silently observes. The only sure thing we know is that we are attention, and to know ourselves we must attend to our own attention. The ultimate reality is "Sat Chit Ananda" (being, knowing, loving), it's Brahman. If we put our attention on the very fact of attending (the atman, the part of the Whole contained in us) and stay there, without doing or touching anything, in the end we're just attention (or being); we are the Whole, Sat Chit Ananda, Brahman. These are enlightenment experiences. They explain that the reason we don't usually have them is because our "created self" (person) acts as a barrier, which they call the veil of maya. So, the practice is to stop being. Not to be a body, not to feel, not to be ideas, not to be a past or a future project. Not to be with the purpose of being everything.

It's a practice that in a way invites desensitization, disconnection of the senses, even ignoring oneself. This was my practice. My desire has always been to be in God, and meditation generated peace and moments of expansion. After a few years, while reading Touchstone magazine[193], I realized that my ability to feel had diminished. My senses were not grounded in the earth. This shocked me because, for me, animism is basic.

I was very involved in Advaita practice, but at the same time I felt some doubt. I felt that something was missing in me, that I needed to include Magic in my life, the connection, the feeling. What is enlightenment really? What is God like? I doubted how to answer and didn't know what reference to use to find answers. I looked for answers in books, and I read a lot! When I read, I find moments of understanding when everything fits together. But it's conceptual and therefore temporary; it ends. My dedication to Yoga was constant. Every available minute is an opportunity to finally get closer to God. I had high goals—from the more physical, like being very flexible, to the more subtle. I would wake up at 5 a.m. and adapt my daily schedule to Yoga. Yoga was my life. My life was adapted to Yoga.

One part that was hard for me to connect with in Yoga is that there's no place (without a place) where one belongs because place, as such, doesn't exist—it's an illusion. There is only emptiness, voidness, nothingness. In Yoga, one seeks the limits to realize that the limit is another illusion of maya. The practice advances according to how many limits you let go, how much you cease to exist as a person, and how much you integrate into emptiness. God is named as Brahman, but the truth is that Brahman isn't a God but is the whole of all that exists.

In Yoga, one seeks to become aware of everything that exists while one exists. This last phrase "to become aware of all that exists while one exists" is an experience very similar to how I experience Magic, cast a spell, or perform a Pagan ritual. In these, I'm attending to something that perhaps bothers me or that I want to change or seek

---

193   https://druidry.org/about-us/journals

to be guided by. I attend it with an open and nonjudgmental heart and remember the unconditional beauty and divinity that is, that nothing is separate or limited, as equal. And then I wait for this lived understanding that has taken place in me to move the petition or intention. The objects, whatever they are (incense, candle, flower, etc.), are aids in opening me to this understanding. Advaita seemed to provide a (Pagan) practice that was already in me, but simplified and less ritualized. But at the same time, as I was practicing it exclusively, I was missing elements of the Magic I had experienced before.

Even though I learned to disconnect my senses independently from external stimuli, I also had a strong desire to be alone and to not be disturbed. I began to avoid people, noises, and open spaces. The focus, the way to find God, remained in my inner world, and I had a very strict attitude. The rest was unnecessary; I even stopped laughing. I developed even more of an attitude of isolation. Despite my efforts and the mystical experiences that the practice brought me, my feeling of disconnection and of being far from a Magical life increased. Faced with this, I did what I knew how to do: study and put more effort into the practice. As much as the texts explain that one should not exert oneself or use one's mind, and I did, I was still missing something. I missed Magic.

I kept feeling called or pulled, and I experienced infinite longings to return to the place (without a place) where I had felt that I belonged without effort, places where I had encountered some of the faces of God, where I had felt that the world was a wonder. This longing was closely linked to Witchcraft. So, at some point I came back closer to Paganism. Suddenly, I began to find in various places the word "Glastonbury." Curiosity began to brew.

My life continued. Hard work, walks in the mountains with my dog, and the practice of Yoga. Sometimes I went through moments of desolation when I felt that everything was inert. Nothing was happening, nothing was moving, and I was further and further away from the Divine. I asked myself, what am I doing? In the end, what filled my existence were simple things like drinking tea, walking in the woods, taking care of animals, watching the moon and the sky in awe. Yes, I needed to feel It again. To feel alive, fulfilled, and connected. And with this need I went to Glastonbury. The first time I traveled alone. The first pilgrimage.

In Glastonbury, a town where the presence of the Goddess is felt in every pore, I felt very strongly that I had to stop following concepts, stop following predetermined ideas, realize the practices in an inclusive way, and connect with myself—with my own truth. To find my reference again. My origin, my feeling, my longing, was Pagan. At Glastonbury, I returned to the arms of the Goddess.

Each word has a meaning, one part socially created and the other of itself. Each one of us adapts a practice to our way of being, doing, and feeling, and I think it's important not to lose sight of it. My mistake was to look for what Yoga is out there and forget what Yoga is in me, what interests me, how it adapted to me. I forgot to let blossom what should blossom at its own pace—without an end goal to achieve.

Disciplines and practices are linked to the external: to ways of dressing, designing, lifestyle. You can consume and strive hard to fit into a concept, but the truth is that you always fall short because the concept is manufactured. Following a manufactured concept can turn into a long search that doesn't find anything. It is very frustrating and generates a lot of mental tension.

One of the things I found in Yoga is that it has a clear and simple central axis, something that can be very ambiguous in Paganism. Because let's not fool ourselves, we all have moments when we need a guide and reference, and in Paganism those can be hard to find. Another thing I missed in Paganism is that it doesn't have a fixed and public place; its simile in Christianity is the church, in Yoga it can be the Yoga room itself. While it's true that there are Pagan collectives and communities, I didn't belong to or have access to one. I knew they existed, but I didn't know how to find one similar to me.

Paganism is a minority practice, and it continues to move within secrecy. There's implicit social rejection, even though it's evident that people are very interested in it. But it's still embarrassing, and the witch wound (the collective and intergenerational trauma and pain passed down through our persecuted ancestors) is evident. The internet helps to make us feel closer to like-minded people, but that's why it's the internet. It's a distant, even idealistic relationship. What I missed was a physical collective, and I found it in Yoga. In Paganism, I'm a self-taught solitary practitioner.

As a final thought, I would like to end by saying that God, and therefore his experience, is uncontrollable. All this coming and going has taught me that all I can do to get closer to God is to undo. Open the door, empty myself, wait patiently, and quietly smile at Him. There are no magic methods or formulas for this. I will never be able to control His gaze, because there's nothing I can do that will force Him to come to me. It doesn't matter if I look for Him within myself or around me. It doesn't matter if I use words, feelings, my body, or objects. By themselves, they don't work. The sense of reverence, devotion, surrender, wonder, enchantment, mystery, tranquility, responsibility, celebration—that's what works. So it's a matter of developing a devotional attitude. I resonate with the Pagan (without closing myself to other disciplines). Others' methods of arriving at the same thing work for them. I believe that God isn't concerned about which discipline we follow. God uses a different language with everyone. We must do what we feel because that's the only way we will allow Him to show Himself.

Èlia Viader is a mystical Pagan and animist from Barcelona, Spain, currently living in Miami, Florida. She studied psychology, medicinal plants, and meditation at university. She is an animal caretaker and entrepreneur and enjoys being in nature and listening to the storms.

Wandering Away from Paganism—Nick Hanks

Introduction

Writing this feels like writing a "farewell" letter a decade after the event. I thought much about my decision at the time. Some of what I wrote back then included reflections on the issues I was having with Paganism in particular—and with spiritual practice in general. I have drawn on these and included extracts of what I wrote then, plus a few insights added with the benefit of hindsight. This is, of course, very much a personal response. What is written here may not accord with your experiences, but I hope my observations prove useful to some of you.

Background

About 10 years ago, I stopped doing all ritual. I have not done any since, nor have I felt any inclination to do so. I do, however, maintain an academic interest, as I write and lecture a little in academic circles on my area of research, which is ritual spaces. Back in those days I was doing a lot of rituals. I was co-running an initiatory Wiccan coven, dabbling in OBOD Druidry and Unitarianism, and occasionally doing a bit of mumming. In parallel to this, I had begun to take an academic interest in ritual space for my archaeology master's dissertation. This was playing to my spatial strengths as a dyslexic person. This research later became a conference paper and led to my co-writing a chapter in an academic book. (Out of this has come more general research on the concept of threshold, which is becoming a book.)

Then I hit a turbulent period of my life, which included the death of my mother, but my wobbles over following the Pagan path had started well before. Since then, I have had further significant life events, but I have not felt the pull to return to ritual, not even during the turbulent times of 2020 that led to the deaths from COVID-19 of my father and his new partner. I felt the practice was an obstacle, not a help. It got in the way. It was not a solace. The yearning I had was for the simplicity of walking and observing what nature I might encounter without any mediation of belief or ritual.

There is a book that has remained a companion on my journey. While at university for the first time in the 1980s, I acquired a number of books on spirituality. Two stood out. A book on Anglo-Saxon shamanism, *The Way of Wyrd* by Brian Bates, and Herrymon Maurer's translation of the *Tao Teh Ching*. The former nurtured an interest in Paganism, but the later had an immediate and enduring appeal. I would return to Maurer's translation from time to time, and I still do. (I have looked at other translations but have not found one that spoke so clearly to me.) Meanwhile, all my books on Paganism collect dust on the shelves.

Festivals

During that difficult time a decade ago, I found that my personal experiences were out of sync with the Pagan festivals. My mother died around Beltane, so I was not in the mood for that festival. I was feeling more inclined to the darkness of Samhain. And when the calendar got to Samhain, I had fallen in love and was feeling all Beltane. At the festivals, I would look out of the window and find more often than not that nature and the climate had not seen the calendar and were not doing the appropriate thing for the festival. So with my break from Paganism, I now just observe the nature I encounter, when I encounter it—without any need to place it within a ritualized calendar.

I still look for the winter solstice sunrise (a little practice I have done since I was small). For me, the Winter Solstice is when I see the sunrise from my home. The weather may make my solstice several days later than it is for others. For me it is "that moment" that matters, not the precise astronomical time of the sun entering Capricorn, which I do not directly experience.

I have returned to my roots before my foray into Paganism. I recently realized that I am "culturally Christian," just as someone

can be culturally Jewish. I do not do the Christian rituals or believe
in their theology, but I was brought up with Easter, Halloween,
and Christmas. These contain Pagan elements, but I enjoy the
service of nine lessons and carols, the choral music, and the church
architecture, and I don't feel the need to remove the Christian or
Pagan components from the secular Christmas. Both were marked
by me in my childhood and by my family. And I feel more of a
connection to my immediate and more recent ancestors than I do
to those from the evocative but ultimately unknowable deep past.
I can sing the actual songs my recent ancestors sang. Imaginative
reconstructions of the culture of the deeper past are fun, but for
me they lack something. I have, in fact, found books on Christian
spirituality more useful than those on Pagan spirituality. I can filter
out the tradition specifics from the universals more easily, as I have
not followed those practices and beliefs. Also, these books feel less
cluttered, somehow, with more on the core of the matter at hand and
less on the interesting, colorful surface of things.

Rituals

I have spent some time reading up on ritual theory across several
academic disciplines. But of all the definitions, the most helpful
and comprehensible that I came across was by Ronald L. Grimes
in his book *Beginnings In Ritual Studies*, which includes a diagram of
the spectrum of what could be called "ritual." The words "ritual,"
"magic," "celebration," "ceremony," and "liturgy" are used in
different and inconsistent ways by people. This leads to problems in
Paganism where people expect one "mode" of ritual but get another.
They are expecting a quiet "ceremony," but it turns out to be a lively
"celebration." Grimes' definitions of these modes, I think, are by
far the most useful, as they are expressed in the form of words in
a table. They cover the full spectrum of the fuzzy nature of ritual
without trying to nail it down with long tangled sentences. Reflecting
on this table, I found that the mode that most suits me is the one
least frequently encountered within Modern Paganism. Some of

the modes really switched me right off, and I would feel this in any tradition. There is no right or wrong mode. They are just different. But I think people seem to be naturally more suited to one mode over another, or at least have a strong preference.

Some of my issues with Paganism are driven by my neurodiversity. The heavy emphasis on wordiness is a joy to many, but my dyslexia made it hard. Also being naturally shy and probably on the autism spectrum the loud, colorful, very social nature of Paganism was also hard going. But in the coven I was in, we once did a standard Wiccan ritual in total silence. I found it greatly satisfying. For me the practice of simple silent meditation naturally appeals.

Though the coven I was in was in an initiatory tradition, we were never very conformist. We were always experimenting, trying out different things, and developing new practices. This sometimes did not sit well with people who were more traditionalist, but those traditions were new once. (Is tradition improvisation gone stale, or is improvisation rootless rambling? Discuss at your leisure.) Present action is a product of all pasts, whether intended or not. The question should be "does it work," rather than "is it traditional or correct." So, we tried out things to see if they worked. Maybe we did too much of that. I wrote so many rituals that I exhausted my ritual writing creative spark. As my ritual writing evolved, it became simpler. Some even had no words at all. And wordiness does seem to be a vital component in the Western Mystery traditions. I finally ran out of ideas and lost interest in them all. I have not written a ritual since.

I had begun to feel that the magical rituals, structures, and words were getting in the way. The idea of it all had gone from ideal to idol and blocked the view of the road ahead. I needed to find my way. I was struck by what Herrymon Maurer wrote in his introduction accompanying his translation of the *Tao Teh Ching*, that the Way (the Tao) is anti-ritual.

> The way of convention is to give names to all
> things in the universe out of a petty will to control
> life. The names may attach to matter or monsters,
> duties or deities, objects or operations, but they
> represent an effort to dominate reality through
> the agency of abstract cogitation . . . Lao Tzu
> disagrees. "When law and order arose," he writes,
> "names appeared. Aren't there enough already? Is
> it not time to stop?' His practice and his counsel is
> not to name things but to be intimate with them.
> Truth itself is beyond name, and the name of Tao
> cannot be its name . . .

For me, personally, perhaps it means to really look at the real—not
to build rituals over it.

Barbara Brown Taylor had a similar falling out of the practices
of the Christian tradition. She developed a more everyday and
integrated practice described in her book *An Altar in the World*. She
asked herself the questions: "What is saving my life right now? What
does my life depend on?"

> The answers I gave all those years ago are not
> the same answers I would give today—that is the
> beauty of the question—but the principle is the
> same. What is saving your life now is the conviction
> that there is no spiritual treasure to be found apart
> from the bodily experience of human life on earth.
> My life depends on engaging the most ordinary
> physical activities with the most exquisite attention
> I can give them. My life depends on ignoring all
> touted distinctions between the secular and the
> sacred, the physical and the spiritual, the body and
> the soul. What is saving my life now is becoming
> more fully human, trusting that there is no way to
> God apart from real life in the real world.

I was finding that trying to accumulate all of the Occult Knowledge within the tradition was a strain. All those names and correspondences were not at all good for my dyslexic brain. It felt like more and more that pertained to less and less, and I could not see how it would help me cope with life and behave better in the world. It was like hoarding gold ornaments: impressive, but not of any practical help. I had the same issues with the otherworldly non-practical nature of theology, be it in Paganism, Christianity, Taoism, or Buddhism. In Mark W. Muesse's DVD course on mindfulness, in the final lecture, he warns not to fall into the trap of collecting lots of mindfulness books, meditation mats, more courses, and so on. Keep focused on the core practice. Brown Taylor quotes Meister Eckhart, "God is not found in the soul by adding anything but by subtracting." The Tao The Ching says a similar thing: "To get learning, add to it daily. To get Tao, subtract daily."

At the time I wrote, "Is occult knowledge secret or obscuring? Occult means 'secret,' therefore something not to be shared or worn as a fashion accessory. But does it actually help in self-development, or is it just a load of smoke and mirrors? Obscuring rather than enlightening? Cluttering the path, rather than clearing the way? Why is the 'occult' secret? That knowledge which is hidden. Why? Too dangerous? Not for the unworthy? Or does it only really help you develop in the absence of the temptation to let ego in by showing off that knowledge?"

To look at it another way, I once wrote, "Each person has a method of spiritual practice. For some it is simple, for others it is elaborate. It is like a tower that aids us in reaching up toward the divine. Some put a lot of work into their towers, and we get very attached to what we put effort into. Others may come to admire our work, and so do we. And then we might get competitive with the towers of others. And then one is looking down at others below, looking down and at those admiring us and our work, but no longer looking at the sky. The tower of spiritual practice is a method, an aid, but we have to let go of it to actually reach the sky. Too heavy a tower will merely hold you down. But we can't all float up from the ground to connect, we all need a bit of tower to get us going. Thus, spiritual practice is both a help and a hindrance." Now I just pause when there is a glimpse of the sky and look, rather than try to reach. I feel no urge to fly.

People

During my time practicing Paganism, I moved among Wiccans, Druids, Unitarians, Buddhists, and non-Pagans. I kept seeing the same issues and arguments arising wherever I went. The practice does not seem to make them better people any more often than those outside the traditions. Sometimes some people were worse. The strong identification with the tradition led to an over-fueled sense of self-importance that was probably hiding inadequacy. I became disappointed in people. Not with anyone in particular, but with the general widespread occurrence of egoism and bitchiness. Individuals trying to control sites and control ideas. The self-appointed police of the boundaries of what is proper or real "Wicca/Druidry/Unitarianism/Buddhism/etc." That endless argument over authenticity.

At the time, I wrote the following: "RELIGION IS SOCIAL AND ANTI-SOCIAL. Science shows that we are social animals, and this sociability is the source of our morals. Religion provides comfort by building groups and extending altruism to others. But this same function which extends self-identity to the group leads to a sense of distance from others not of the group and, thus, conflict. (Paraphrased from Jonathan Sacks, Chief Orthodox Rabbi of Britain on "Something Understood," BBC Radio 4, 21st February 2010.) A problem of ritual is the tension between the social effect of the group and personal development. We use it to lose a sense of self in the group, but it increases the sense of otherness from those outside of the group. It increases the human universal of insider/outsider behavior, which is not helpful to spiritual development. Spiritual growth is aiming to connect with others in the widest sense—all people, life, and ethereal beings. It aims to transcend boundaries. The more you are bound to your group, the less you can link with those outside. If it is where you place your identity, then how can you connect with what you define as definitely not like you? There is also tension with those who should be like you, in a group, who are not 'behaving right' as seen by you. The group ritual work should be the first step: connect with them, then connect with others beyond. It is a means, not an objective. When a strong attachment is formed to a group/method, it holds you and others back. It needs to be held lightly as the Way in the Tao Teh Ching. So do not hug the spiritual path, or you will just end up eating dirt and blocking the way for others. Move along it, don't own it or set up toll booths, gates, or passport control. Effort and emotional investment hardens belief, whether the belief is right or not. It reduces flexibility to new ideas and situations."

I also wrote: "ACTS OVER BELIEFS. It is more important what you do rather than what you believe. Though beliefs influence actions, it is often implied that the relationship between the two is simple. It isn't. The way you do religion is important, not which one or if one at all. It is the way you enact, the way you behave, not the flag or the label used. The way one applies one's beliefs/ideas through our values. The Good Samaritan was good because of his acts, even though the others who passed the man by the roadside were the ones with the right beliefs (they were mainstream and not Samaritans). 'By their fruits so shall you know them' (Jesus); by the consequences of their actions, not their proclaimed beliefs."

Now I feel content by not trying to be anything, not a this or a that. Being nothing in particular feels right—freeing myself from the box of identity. Too much of Paganism seems to be about strongly identifying with a particular group, a strong personal identity, a special new name, and a particular deity.

Gods and Goddesses

I also became concerned not just with what people say to each other, but what they say the divine says. I even had misgivings about myself when speaking as a deity during invocation in Wiccan ritual. My break with this particular Pagan practice can be traced back to reading one article in New Scientist ('Dear God, please confirm what I already believe," 5 Dec 2009). Studies by a team led by Nicholas Epley of the University of Chicago in Proceedings of the *National Academy of Science*,[194] among others, have shown that Christians imbue God with their opinions on controversial subjects. Epley writes, "Intuiting God's beliefs on important issues may not produce an independent guide, but may instead serve as an echo chamber to validate and justify one's own beliefs." Christian volunteers were asked about controversial subjects, then asked what they think God's view was, then what they thought other Americans thought. The volunteers' own beliefs corresponded with those attributed to God. When the volunteers shifted their beliefs during another test, the views attributed to God also changed the same way, but not those they attributed to other Americans.

The knock-out blow for me was the end of the article, "Finally, the team used functional MRI scans of subjects' brains to show that contemplating God's beliefs activates the same brain areas as thinking about one's own views, while thoughts about other Americans' views activate a brain area used for inferring other people's mental states." So, it is all just in our own heads. We create the divine in our own image. Barbara Brown Taylor quotes Rabbi Sacks, "'The supreme religious challenge is to see God's image in one who is not in our image' for only then can we see past our own reflections in the mirror to the God we did not make up."

---

194   Nicholas Epley, Benjamin A. Converse, Alexa Delbosc, George A. Monteleone, and John T. Cacioppo (2009), "Believers' estimates of God's beliefs are more egocentric than estimates of other people's beliefs." *PNAS*. https://www.pnas.org/doi/10.1073/pnas.0908374106

Final Thoughts

Barbara Brown Taylor in her book *An Altar in the World* relates the experience of leaving the practice of her Christian tradition. In her chapter on "The Practice of Getting Lost,' she writes:

> By the time this unknown road dumps me back onto a highway I know, my detour has cost me ten minutes—a fortune, at the fevered pitch of my day—which I gladly pay for the liberating proof that I am still able to leave the thin paths I have worn with my frugal, fearful hooves. "If you do not start choosing to get lost in some fairly low-risk ways, then how will you ever manage when one of life's big winds knocks you clean off your course?" Then, "You are truly seriously lost, even though you know exactly where you are. . . . You may not be able to think about it until then, but something is happening to you in this wilderness that does not happen when you are safe at home. Some of it is purely physical. Because you are in danger, all the blood in your body has raced toward your heart, abandoning your hands and feet to an icy tingling. Your senses are on full alert. You can smell engine oil and spent rubber along with your own sweat. You can see the glow in the sky away up ahead, showing you where the next highway exit is. You can hear your heart pounding in the empty closet of your chest." "Even though you would rather not think about it, you are exquisitely vulnerable in this moment. You are vulnerable to this moment…."

Whence the spiritual quest now? Another person who got lost on the Way has some insightful thoughts. It seems that getting lost may actually be the point. John C. Parkin writes in Fuck It: The Ultimate Spiritual Way that we should say "fuck it" to searching:

We're all searchers. We're always looking for more
meaning. The search is relatively unconscious
for much of our life. We search for meaning in
relationships, in friendships, in jobs, in money, in
hobbies, in "missions" to help other people . . . For
whatever reason people get spiritual apparently
toward the end of their pursuit of meaning .
. . meaning creates tension and pain when it
comes into conflict with what life is. So the more
meaningful your belief/spiritual/religion is, the
more potential for tension and pain there is . . . So
here's another cosmic joke: the search in our lives
leads us to try to find meaning beyond what "is" in
our lives. Our loves, our money, our achievements
are not quite enough, so we look for more. And we
look for it in "spirituality," which usually involves
the "unseen." Whereas the answer to everything
possibly lies in this: not looking for more meaning,
but looking for less. When we strip away meaning
from the things that are already meaningful in our
lives, that's where we find peace and the divine.

God is not more than we know. He's less than we
know.

The less you search, the more you find.

The less you want, the more you receive.

The less you look, the more you see.

The less "You," the more "Is."

If God is less when we are looking for more, then
spirituality is not some preserve of believers.
Spirituality is everything as it is. Everyone is
spiritual, as is everything . . . This means that

there's nothing you have to do to be spiritual or "good." You don't have to go anywhere or achieve anything. You can truly say Fuck It to the whole thing and still be spiritual!

Brown Taylor writes:

> Whoever you are, you are human. Wherever you are, you live in the world, which is just waiting for you to notice the holiness in it. So welcome to your own priesthood, practiced at the altar of your own life. The good news is that you have everything you need to begin.

I still have a fondness for my "old Pagan times," and I miss the social side of things sometimes. I will never say never again, but despite all that 2020 threw at me I still don't find my feet wandering back onto the Pagan path. Now I save this document, switch off, and go for a wander in the world.

The Second Half

And what was the first thing I wandered into, but a very relevant book that put my experience into a wider context. The book was *Falling Upward* by Richard Rohr, a Christian monk. It describes the two halves of life and the break between the two—in particular as it applies to the spiritual path in individuals and cultures. Rohr writes:

> Almost all of culture, and even most of religious history, has been invested in the creation and maintenance of first-half-of-life issues: the big three concerns of identity, security, sexuality and gender. They don't just preoccupy us; they totally take over. . . . Most of history has been the forging of structures of security and appropriate loyalty symbols, to announce and defend one's personal identity, one's group, and one's gender issues and

identity. Now we seem to live in a time when more
and more people are asking, 'Is that all there is?'

In our formative years, we are so self-preoccupied
that we are both overly defensive and overly
offensive at the same time, with little time left for
simply living, pure friendship, useless beauty, or
moments of communion with nature or anything.
Yet that kind of ego structuring is exactly what a
young person partly needs to get through the first
twenty years or so, and what tribes need to survive.
So we need boundaries, identity, safety, and some
degree of order and consistency to get started
personally and culturally. We also need to feel
"special"; we need our "narcissistic fix."

He notes that there comes a point where to grow you need to
transcend the rules of the path you are on, while taking them with
you. "People who know how to creatively break the rules also
know why the rules were there in the first place," and "Our first
understanding of law must fail us and disappoint us." He quotes the
Dalai Lama: "Learn and obey the rules very well, so you will know
how to break them properly."

Such discrimination between means and goals is
almost the litmus test of whether you are moving
in the right direction, and all the world religions
at the mature levels will say similar things. For
some reason, religious people tend to confuse the
means with the actual goal. . . . Once your life has
become a constant communion, you know that all
the techniques, formulas, sacraments, and practices
were just a dress rehearsal for the real thing—life
itself—which can actually become a constant
intentional prayer.

Finally, it seems appropriate to end with a story. I will leave you with a classic myth that Rohr explores. It is the second journey of Odysseus, which few know (I certainly didn't); it is also the journey that will happen to all of us. It does not have all the drama and excitement of the first. It may seem just an odd closing chapter of Homer's epic poem. However, it is fully flagged up in the famous first journey, in the prophecy given to Odysseus by Teiresias when in Hades:

> It is often when the ego is most deconstructed
> that we can hear things anew and begin some
> honest reconstruction, even if it is only half heard
> and half hearted. Tiresias holds a golden scepter,
> the symbol of being a divine messenger. . . . an
> authority from without and beyond, unsolicited or
> unsought, and maybe even unwanted by Odysseus
> himself. Often it takes outer authority to send us on
> the path toward our own inner authority.

After returning home to Ithaca at the end of his voyage, he begins a very different journey. He leaves the sea behind and heads into the mainland. Rohr writes: ". . . he is reuniting his small 'island part' with the bigger picture, as it were. He is also reconnecting his outer journey to the 'inland' or his interior world, which is much of the task of the second half of life. What a brilliant metaphor." On his journey, Tiresias instructs him to take an oar, the tool of his first journey, and carry it until he reaches somewhere so far inland that they do not recognize it as an oar and instead think it is a winnowing shovel—a tool used to sort the wheat from the chaff. "The first world of occupation and productivity must now find its full purpose."

There, far from the sea, his journey stops. Odysseus makes a sacrifice to Poseidon, who has been on at him through his earlier journey. "It must have been recognized that to go forward there is always something that has to be let go of, moved beyond, given up, or 'forgiven' to enter the larger picture of the 'gods.'" A sacrifice is made of a wild bull, a breeding boar, and a battering ram—symbols of untrained or immature male energy, of the first half of life. "You cannot walk the second journey with first journey tools. You need a whole new tool kit." On returning home to Ithaca, he makes another sacrifice to all of the gods of heaven. "In human language, he is finally living inside the big and true picture; in Christian language, he is finally connected to the larger 'Kingdom of God.'"

Only when this second journey is complete can Odysseus "live happily with my people around me, until I sink under the comfortable burden of years, and death will come to me gently from the sea." Death is largely a threat to those who have not yet lived their life. Odysseus has lived the journeys of both halves of life, and is ready to freely and finally let go.

Nick Hanks
nick-hanks.co.uk

Sources

- Brian Bates, 1983, *The Way of Wyrd*
- Barbara Brown Taylor, 2009, *An Altar in the World. A Geography of Faith.*
- Ronald L. Grimes, 1982, *Beginnings in Ritual Studies*
- Herrymon Maurer, 1985, *The Way of the Ways*
- John C. Parkin, 2009, *The Way of Fuck It*
- Richard Rohr, 2012, *Falling Upward. A Spirituality for the Two Halves of Life*

Wobbling, but not falling off—Yvonne Aburrow

My spiritual journey

My earliest spiritual experience was probably wanting to be
a witch. At the age of eight, I went to a party at school, which I
thought was fancy dress but turned out not to be, and I asked my
Mum to make me a witch costume. I think I got this idea from
reading *Gobbolino, the Witch's Cat*. Later, I read Cynthia Harnett's
novels and absorbed the idea of the witch as an herbalist and healer
from her book *The Writing on the Hearth*.

As a child, I always loved nature and animals, and wanted to be
able to converse with trees. I also loved Greek and Norse mythology,
Narnia and Middle-Earth. I liked all the Pagan bits in Narnia—the
tree spirits, the talking animals, the river god, the fauns, and the
centaurs. (I did not notice the Christian bits, because I was immersed
in Christianity.)

I was brought up in the exclusive Plymouth Brethren until the
age of nine, but fortunately my parents sheltered me from the worst
effects of this. I used to sit in the meetings and read the gory bits and
the stories in the "Old Testament." One significant thing was that
the Plymouth Brethren did not allow people to have Christmas trees,
but my parents had one anyway, and told us not to mention it at the
meetings. So I asked why we were not supposed to have a Christmas
tree, and my parents said "because it's Pagan." So I asked what a
Pagan was. They said that in the old days, people used to think that
the sun might not come back after the winter solstice, so they would
go up onto hilltops and light fires to make the sun come back. I
thought this sounded lovely and wanted to be a Pagan.

However, I believed in the Christian stuff I had been taught—except
I don't think I ever really believed in the devil. And I don't recall
praying to Jesus, only to God (no idea why). Also, I never believed
in "young earth" creationism. When I learned about the Big Bang
and evolution at school, I asked my Dad how it could be reconciled

with the Bible creation story, and he said that God could have used evolution as his process for making things, and that a day in the creation story was like a million years—because elsewhere in the Bible, it says that a thousand years is like a day to God.

After we left the Plymouth Brethren, my parents attended some other churches, including a charismatic evangelical one, where I learned to "speak in tongues" (also known as glossolalia).

After my parents stopped going to church, I left it for a couple of years and then I went to a United Reformed Church that had a charismatic fellowship group in it.

Around that time, two very significant things happened. I saw the film *Gandhi*, which made me aware that there were very wise and spiritual people in other religions (who, according to the Christians I knew, would not get to heaven). I had always thought it was unfair that people from other religions were supposed to go to hell just because they believed something different.

The other thing was that my best friend, whom I had known since the age of five, and who was a very spiritual and altruistic person, came out to me as gay. I asked my Christian friends about this, and they said that he would go to hell if he persisted in having sex with men. I was pretty sure that he had been born gay, so I thought it was massively unfair that God would create someone gay and then condemn them for it. I was also discovering my own sexuality around this time and wondering why a "try before you buy" approach to marriage was condemned. And I had learned about the Holocaust and concluded that good and evil reside mainly in the human breast, not as some cosmic force or being, and that if God was all powerful, why would he allow such dreadful suffering (free will notwithstanding)?

So at this point I became an atheist.

Coming home to Paganism

I then concluded that there must be some way—political or spiritual—to make the world a better place. I thought about this and decided that consciousness needs raising so that people are more empathetic and compassionate (it turns out that consciousness-raising is about making people aware of their socio-economic or social status, but I did not know that at the time). I thought that one way to help with this was to raise my own consciousness, so I began to look for a spiritual tradition that could help me with that. I rejected any tradition that was against life, sexuality, and the beauty of being embodied in this physical plane, or that seemed more interested in some other reality.

I had read *Puck of Pook's Hill* by Rudyard Kipling, and concluded that Paganism was a good label for my beliefs—that life, sexuality, and nature are sacred, and that there is no all-powerful cosmic creator. I was attracted to Pagan mythology but did not believe in deities literally.

At this point, I thought that I was the only Pagan—I did not know that there were other Pagans. Then, when I went to university, I got involved with battle re-enactment and met other Pagans there, and also at university. In my last year at university, someone started a Pagan society, so I joined it. From that group, someone put me in touch with some Wiccans, and in 1991, after I left university, I was initiated into Wicca. It felt like coming home. The wildness, the connection to nature, the rituals at night in the woods with fire, the honoring of women equally with men—it felt very much like the celebration of life that I was looking for.

I was happy with the coven I was initiated into and stayed in it for three years, until I moved to Scotland. There, it was much harder to find a coven to join, though I tried a couple of different ones. It was very painful, as I missed the closeness of my original coven and the style of the rituals. I got my second degree initiation in 1996, which meant I was then able to initiate others.

Then I moved to Southampton, where there were no existing Wiccan covens. I started an eclectic non-initiatory Pagan group, with a view to initiating them eventually. The various members moved away, and I moved to London to do a post-graduate certificate in education (teaching qualification).

In 2000, I moved to Bristol, and I started a coven with my partner in 2003.

The wobble

After a while, I began to worry about the effects created in the psyche by Wiccan oaths of secrecy (I felt that they created a block). I also wanted a more community-based religion, and I tried Druidry for a while (alongside my existing Wiccan practice). I also started worrying about the very gendered nature of Wiccan deities.

By this time, I had started to believe in deities as something more than archetypes, and I was a member of an online group of polytheists, most of whom were convinced that deities were discrete individual entities, and many of whom were convinced that they had a special relationship with a particular deity. I started to wonder why I had not been chosen by a particular deity.

In 2007, while I was doing an M.A. in contemporary religions and spiritualities, I discovered that Christianity was not as homophobic as I had thought, and that in fact it had a less gendered view of the Divine than I had thought. Traditionally, God was viewed as being without gender. And it was less opposed to the physical plane than I had thought.

I also began to wonder if the problems of the world could ever be solved by human means, since everything is so entangled—capitalism leads to war and oppression and environmental degradation, and if you fix one problem, you're likely to cause another one.

Another problem that I experienced with Paganism around this time was the reburial issue. A number of Pagans were campaigning to have human remains reburied, and I thought this was irrational on several grounds: that archaeology had provided much of the data that enabled the Pagan revival to happen; that there were much more important issues to worry about, such as climate change, social justice issues, and the destruction of the rainforests; and that the best way to treat human remains was to recover their stories so that they can be remembered and honored, and put them safely in museums, which are after all temples to the Muses.

And the other thing was that in 1992, I had performed an exorcism for someone and seen the entity (gray, gangly and with orange eyes) that was doing the haunting with my inner eye. In 2007, someone showed me a photo taken in a cave in the Middle East of something that looked very much like the entity (gray, gangly, and with orange eyes), and you could see the rock through its transparent legs. This freaked me out. I had always assumed that nature spirits were either benign or neutral, and any hostility to humans that they might have would be on environmental grounds. This thing just looked downright nasty.

Also in 2007, I was meditating at the Chalice Well in Glastonbury and had a vision of Jesus. I had no idea what to do with this, as I am a witch. I had been looking for my personal deity, having a crisis about the nature of the cosmos and what to do about the problem of evil, and admiring Christianity for its stance on social justice issues such as poverty. One of my main arguments against Christianity had been removed, and I also discovered that some Christians believed everyone would be saved (so that demolished the other argument).

I had also found that love was a really important transformative factor in healing. Our cat, Harry, was very traumatized when he came to us, and our love drew him out and made him better. I became almost convinced that the idea that "God is love" was actually true.

Prior to this, I'd had a huge reservoir or volcano of anger in my psyche that was directed against Christianity, and which would well up and spill over about almost anything. Now that the anger was removed, there was a locked box underneath it marked "do not open" that contained my fear that the Christian explanation for how the universe works was actually true. Even though I knew in my rational mind that it was not, the idea that it might be true still lurked in some pre-rational area of my mind. The fear caused me actual physical pain in my chest, and at the time, I did not know that this was a symptom of stress.

I could not bear the idea of rejoining an evangelical church, where my involvement with Paganism would almost certainly be seen as demonic, and where my in-depth knowledge of mythology would be in massive conflict with their simplistic worldview. So I thought I would try the Orthodox Church (lots of bells and smells, great ritual, icons, and a church that had done very little persecution of non-Christians), which I did for two months. In many ways, I found their theology helpful and illuminating, as it was very different from Western Christianity on issues like original sin and the meaning of Jesus' death. I did not like their elevation of celibacy to a saintly virtue, nor the fact that they do not have women priests, nor the church's conservative policy on homosexuality.

After two months, I found out that many among the congregation were much more homophobic than I had thought. So I realized I could not bear that, and thought, "Well, I have tried Orthodoxy for two months now, I will try the Unitarians next." So I went to a Unitarian church and there was a woman at the front talking about Zen Buddhism and cats, and there were hymns saying that all religions contain great teachers and offer the possibility of enlightenment. It was wonderful and felt like home.

During this period, I think I went temporarily insane, because I re-enacted 2,000 years of development of religious thought in Europe in the space of six months. I went from polytheism to Christianity, to universalism, back to atheism, and then eventually back to polytheism. It was a theological roller-coaster ride, and I definitely do not recommend taking it so fast.

I am so grateful to the members of the Pagan community who held me steady during this time. One of those people was Cat Chapin-Bishop. The members of my coven at that time were also tremendously supportive, despite it being difficult for them that their new high priestess was having a flirtation with Jesus. The other thing that was really important was Pagans saying that if I was on the right spiritual path for me, that was fine with them. That remains one of the great strengths of Paganism—that we do not believe it is cosmically necessary to be a Pagan and that the same spiritual path may not be right for everyone.

I eventually ended my relationship with Jesus—much to my relief and probably his and everyone else's too.

The nice thing about Unitarianism is that it is inclusive enough to allow its members to be atheists, Buddhists, Wiccans, Pagans, Christians, Hindus, Jews, or just plain Unitarians, because it is about values and social justice and sharing your spiritual insights with others, not about adhering to a specific set of beliefs. You can also change your spiritual focus or mix and match different traditions. It also has really great hymns, and is compatible with reason and science. I made some great friends among the Unitarians, and am glad that I went exploring.

Unitarianism emerged from the anabaptist and humanist movements in the 1500s.[195] Initially the tradition was called Socinianism after one of its founders, Faustus Socinus. The community was persecuted in Northern Italy, so they moved to Poland and founded the town of Rakow, where they set up a printing press. From there, Unitarian ideas were disseminated to England in pamphlets and books. After a century in Rakow, the town was

---

195 Earl Morse Wilbur (1945), *A History of Unitarianism: In Transylvania, England, and America*. Beacon Press.

destroyed by the shock-troops of the Counter-Reformation, and
the community moved to Transylvania, where they were protected
by King John Sigismund I (the only Unitarian king in history).
The Transylvanian Unitarian church still exists. The movement in
England initially could not even call themselves Unitarians because
denying the Trinity was regarded as blasphemous until 1813. After
1813, they were able to identify as Unitarians. Several famous people
became Unitarians, including Joseph Priestley (the discoverer of
oxygen) who moved to America after a Trinitarian mob burned his
house down. During the nineteenth century, Unitarianism became
increasingly liberal, and many Unitarians supported voting rights for
women and the abolition of slavery. The Unitarians were the first in
England to ordain a woman minister, Gertrude von Petzold, in 1904.
The first woman to be ordained in the USA was Olympia Brown,
ordained by the Universalists in 1860. In England, the General
Baptists (who believed in universal salvation) joined the Unitarian
movement during the nineteenth century. In America and Scotland,
Universalist churches developed separately from the Unitarians, but
the two denominations maintained links and exchanged preachers.
In the USA in 1961, the Unitarians and Universalists merged to
form the Unitarian Universalist Association. The movement had
been transformed in the late nineteenth century by the emergence
of Transcendentalism, which was promulgated by Ralph Waldo
Emerson, who had been influenced by reading Rammohun Roy's
translation of the Upanishads.

During the twentieth century, Unitarians supported liberal causes
such as the decriminalization of homosexuality, the ordination of
LGBT+ people, the civil rights movement, same-sex marriage, and
reproductive choice. During the twenty-first century, they have
supported Black Lives Matter and dismantling white supremacy,
among other things.

The structure of Unitarian services is similar to that of other
church services, but the content is radically different and includes

respect for other faiths and an emphasis on social justice. Most Unitarians are also very welcoming and inclusive people, and there is a strong emphasis on reason in the tradition.

I liked Unitarianism so much that I thought I wanted to be a minister. I enjoyed leading services, and I was good at it. (I should think I ought to be after twenty years of writing and facilitating Pagan ritual.) However, several Unitarians asked how it was possible to be a Unitarian and a Wiccan; whereas no Wiccans ever asked me how it was possible to be Wiccan and Unitarian. They were interested in how it worked, but not critical of my choice.

At the end of 2009, I split up with my former partner and moved to Bath. It was an amicable split, and we continued to work together as high priestess and high priest of our coven.

I still liked Unitarianism, but to be a minister I would have had to give up being a Wiccan priestess (not because of any theological conflict, but because one does not have time to be a leader in two religious traditions when one of those commitments is a full-time paid position). I also found that trying to embody the archetype of minister was in conflict with my inner archetype of being a witch. Wicca celebrates the sacredness of the erotic, and (for the most part) Unitarianism does not. So, after one week of being a ministry student—and many, many hints from the Powers that being a Unitarian minister would have been a really, really bad idea for me personally—I quit the training. I am just not interested in mainstream Christian theology, or whether the Hebrew Bible is an accurate account of Israel's history, or whether it is constructed from different texts (Priestly, Elohist, Yahwist and Deuteronomic), or how to do Christology, or any of the other topics covered in the required theology courses. At the time, I was suffering from spiritual burnout. This was partly as a result of events before I joined Unitarianism, but the problem was exacerbated by trying to work as a congregational development worker—which seems to be a role like that of a minister but without the status and respect accorded to a minister.

As I approached the start of my training, I felt depressed, anxious, overworked, overburdened, and conflicted. I thought that this was because I wanted to leave my job, which I did. But once I had left my job, I realized that the feelings were still there. I think that this depression and anxiety was pointing to the deeper issues I had with being in a religious tradition that wasn't right for me, and which wasn't spiritually nourishing for me (although it did heal me in many ways). There seems to be a general lack of clarity on what Unitarianism is. Each Unitarian knows their own mind and their own theology, and I can see a consistency of values across the spectrum, but there does not seem to be a consensus on whether Unitarianism is Christian or not.

A friend commented at the time that my involvement in Unitarianism seemed to be about healing a wound, whereas my involvement in Paganism was like drawing from a well within me.

Shortly after this, I moved to Oxford and made a fresh start, which was really helpful for me.

Coming home to Wicca

I felt such a huge physical sense of relief when I quit the ministerial training. I went to a circle with my coven and felt bits of me that had been clenched and withdrawn reopening like desert flowers gratefully receiving rain. I went to a workshop event with a group of Wiccans and mentioned the experience of sublimated eros in Wiccan ritual, and everyone nodded and smiled (whereas you would have to spend a lot of time explaining this to most people). I knew I was home again, with my beloved community. And strangely, everything in my life started getting better too. I had been unsure how I was going to support myself financially through the training course and where I was going to live; it was a massive period of upheaval in my life.

Eventually, in August 2012, I realized that I couldn't be a Unitarian and a Wiccan. I am a Wiccan and a polytheist, I honor and work with the Pagan deities, I look to the land and Nature for my spiritual nourishment.

I attended a symbel run by two very dear friends and vowed at that point to focus all my energies on Paganism. It was a powerful moment. It was then that I realized that Wicca is my tribe, blood of my blood, heart of my heart.

Also, in 2012, I met my new partner, who has been Wiccan since before he met me. We are very much in love. This helps greatly with feeling positive about life.

I spent most of 2014 writing my book about inclusive Wicca, and clarifying my thoughts about my Craft. During 2015, I worked on the *Pagan Consent Culture* anthology with Christine Hoff Kraemer. During 2016, I worked on my two most recent books: *Dark Mirror: The Inner Work of Witchcraft* and *The Night Journey: Witchcraft as Transformation.*

Wobbling makes you stronger

Sometimes, to truly experience a feeling, you have to go away from it and approach it from a different angle. You have to try to do without your connection to your beloved community to know that they are really your people. Having tested my faith in Paganism, the deities, and the power of Nature, I found that it bent but did not break, it tore but did not disintegrate.

There are numerous spiritual stories where the hero goes past the thing they seek, mistaking it for something else, and then has to double back to find it again by accident. This is especially true of the story of Moses and Al-Khidr. That is often the nature of "spiritual" treasure. It is not immediately obvious that it is treasure.

Many people find that they arrive at a universalist perspective on spirituality, only to find that it is really difficult to sustain the idea that "all is one" (perhaps because your mountain is not the same as my mountain, perhaps because spirituality works better when it has a specific context). They then move once again into their own spiritual perspective and homeland, with a new appreciation of its worth.

So, while having a wobble on your spiritual journey can be really painful and difficult: if you are having one, follow your bliss—whatever that turns out to be. Pay attention to what your body is telling you. Where do you feel most comfortable, most nourished?

Finding My Way to Love: In Search of a Good Life—Calyx

> You do not have to be good…
> You only have to let the soft animal of your body
> love what it loves
>
> from Wild Geese by Mary Oliver (1986)

I have been thinking a great deal about what it means to be good and to live a good life, especially in the context of changing paths—away from a religious framework and an understanding of the world that was chosen for me, and toward one that I have chosen for myself. I have come back to this poem by Mary Oliver again and again, and it has been a guiding force in my life as I have been finding my way to love through a winding path of fundamentalist Christianity, through uncertainty, and finally to Paganism.

You are Not Good

My earliest experience of love was conditional love, as mediated by a fundamentalist Christian sect, from those who had the care of me and who were informed by these beliefs. In this environment, love was entwined with a particular understanding of goodness, and would be withheld if one was bad. This was also the face that God wore, a visage of punishing, incurious, and judgemental terror. The love we expressed to others was based on fear and judgment—I show you I love you only by saving you—and this led to an experience of the world where a sense of otherness was purposely constructed and maintained by fear and where I felt both an inner and outer sense of displacement. The qualities that have made me a good friend and kind human—like curiosity, discomfort in absolutes, and a sense of nuance—did not make me a good fundamentalist. I began to question the certainty that others in the sect seemed to hold about the religious teachings which they unironically called "the Truth," and I asked too many questions and was too unsatisfied with the answers. I was told that I was welcome to do my research on other religions, teachings, and ways, as long as I used the sect's reference materials—which even at a young age I knew was unreasonable. My sense of displacement multiplied as I realized that I was not like those around me, or at least how they portrayed themselves to be. It was as though all along I had been speaking another language and was only mimicking their speech. I knew keenly that who I am as a human was not one that is acceptable in their worldview and I felt a deep sense of loss and a fundamental wounding—how could I love that which is hated? I came to understand that whatever "good" was did not include me. I tried so very hard to fit into the mold as I wanted to be loved, but was never quite able to do so successfully.

This is not what most people experience of Christianity and I am only speaking to my small piece of a greater picture. But I now understand this as spiritual trauma, which caused great harm to me. Eventually, I was quite literally cast out and shunned, and I was left to find a new understanding and belonging of goodness.

What is Good, Anyway?

If you had asked me at this time of uncertainty, I would have said I was agnostic or atheist. However I am very careful to reject the premise that atheism is inherently a reactionary stance or one that grows out of pain. My previous experience of the Divine was a punishing one, and whatever others saw or felt in that relationship was not something that resonated with me. And I had no real theological underpinning to mediate the Divine or come to see the other faces of it. So I closed myself off to any spiritual or religious understandings and placed that part of my life very far from me. Looking back now, I can say that I probably felt an echo of a loss, but it was one that was very distant and only in the periphery of the rest of a very full life.

I found a new narrative of meaning and borrowed the language of poetry to identify my inner experience. A search for what is good led to me finding the numinous in different aspects—particularly in music, and in community, and through my work wherein I supported others. I started moving towards the concept of living a good life versus being good. Therapy of course was and is a big component of this, and of developing self-compassion and deconstructing shame—a never-ending project.

You Do Not Have to Be Good

I cannot say that I had a definitive awareness that I was moving closer to a connection with the Divine, but gradually I felt the echo of the loss resonating within me a bit stronger each day. Eventually I came to recognize it as a call. Mindfulness and meditation were a big component of listening to that inner knowing and recognizing it for what it was, and mindfulness continues to be a regular part of my practice today. I started making circles closer toward a central truth, and, upon reflection, mindful movement and yoga became an easing into a spirituality that felt like coming home. I went back to one of my first loves—rock collecting—and learned about crystals. I was interested in Tarot as an evocative archetypal narrative, and I took workshops to learn this system. I read as widely as I could. I went on silent retreats in the woods. I wanted wildness, to be understood by those who were not tamed, and for the forest to talk back to me; I found the wonder in being recognized by something greater than me who loved me just the same. Eventually, I went in search of the old and wild gods, and I did not want anyone to mediate this experience for me, or to tell me I could only know their version of the world that is hemmed in by fear and judgment. I started learning more about Paganism, witchcraft, and eventually Gardnerian Wicca (in which I had always been interested).

I try to avoid absolute certainty as much as I can, as I have seen how certainty can be shaped into something that harms, but I will say that I have had an experience of the Divine that is difficult to put into words. I know that I was seen and witnessed, and loved in this encounter, and I have come to understand through this that there is no part of me that was ever unlovable or not sacred.

For me, being a Witch and Pagan is not an absolute knowing but more of a gentle wondering—What if you had not fallen and there is nothing from which to be saved? What if you are good and sacred just as you are? How does that impact how you move through the world and in connection with others? In this worldview, knowing and becoming your authentic self and being witnessed by others in love is a sacred act.

My hope for others is that they come to know they too are held in love and to recognize that this is a goodness that is deep and meaningful.

Calyx is a nonbinary Gardnerian Witch and Pagan, living in Ontario, Canada. They are lucky enough to share their space with creatures great and small, and they love all things green and growing, and deep and dark.

My Journey from Judaism to Wicca—Karen Dales

I've always wanted to serve my religious community, even from a young age, though which religious community changed as I grew older.

I was born into an Ashkenazi Jewish home. My parents were first generation Canadians. My grandmother had immigrated from Ukraine/Russia, Bubby[196] from Russia, my grandfather from England, and Zayde[197] from Poland. All arrived in Toronto, Canada in the 1920s—hence they never experienced firsthand the atrocities of the Holocaust. Unfortunately, all of Zayde's family that stayed in Poland were murdered at Auschwitz or Dachau. I still remember the story my mother told me of when the Red Cross came to let Zayde know what had befallen his family.

My parents raised me in a Reform Jewish home, but there were some elements that were clearly Conservative. My mother attempted to keep what I call "Kosher-lite" as we didn't have two kitchens with two sets of appliances, cooking tools, plates, and utensils. Instead, we kept as Kosher as they wanted, observing the High Holidays with large feasts and going to the Shul we were members of. My sister and I were sent to Hebrew School and Saturday School. My father was a member of B'nai Brith, even becoming Canyon Lodge's president, and my mother became a member of Hadassah-WIZO. It was my parents' wish to see both myself and my sister bat mitzvahed.[198] Unfortunately, that was not in the cards.

I love Judaism. I still do. Even as a child growing up in a Jewish home, I studied my religion, attaining one of the highest awards a Jewish child, especially a girl, could achieve within her synagogue. I loved the High Holidays and Shabbat services. Everything about the tradition and religion I loved. Even at a very young age, I

---

196 Bubby or bubbe, Yiddish for grandmother.
197 Zayde or zeyde, Yiddish for grandfather.
198 The female version of Bar Mitzvah

wanted to be a Rabbi, but at that time women were not allowed to be Rabbis. I was also hampered from this dream because no matter how hard I tried, I just could not learn Hebrew, even with the help of a tutor three times a week. Because of that, my parents' wish for me to be Bat Mitzvahed never happened. I was disappointed, but also relieved. It's a lot of preparation and expense to go through that experience.

Because I couldn't become a Rabbi because I am female, I started questioning Judaism—and specifically G-d—around the time I hit puberty. How could a male god create all life when it's a woman that gives birth? That was a question I could never find an answer to at that age. In Reform Judaism, there is no real mystery to discover. I realized I needed answers that Judaism couldn't provide to a teenage girl. Especially after my parents divorced.

I distanced myself from Judaism as I sought answers and direction in my life, though at that time I don't believe I knew the proper terms for that. I floundered during my middle school years. I love Judaism. I love the traditions, the rituals, the food, but what I had experienced thus far in terms of spirituality and answers to my questions left me hollow, spiritually speaking. So I began my search for something that would answer my questions and spiritually fulfill me. Christianity was off the table. It made no sense to me, and the idea of worshiping a 2,000-year-old dead man who died to save me from my sins sounded ridiculous. I didn't want to participate in a religion where I would have to live in fear. As for other religions, I didn't know of any.

One thing that I always loved, even as a child, was Hallowe'en. I also greatly enjoyed movies that were occult horror. Give me Poe, Shelley, anything Gothic, and I devoured it. My favorite shows growing up were The Addams Family and Bewitched. I was probably a Goth before Goth was a thing.

I didn't realize I was searching for Witchcraft and Paganism until I entered High School. There, in my first year, I made a friend whose first question to me was whether I was interested in Witchcraft. Not explicitly sure of what she meant, I said, "Yes." Beth and I became quick friends and she took me to The Occult Shop. It was an eye opening experience. I bought the few books that were available at the time. (It was the early 1980s.)

Everything I read clicked and made sense to me. I finally had an answer to who created everything. In Judaism, G-d is not of this world, but somewhere else. In Christianity, that somewhere else is Heaven. Finally, I found a religion where not only is there a God, but there is also a Goddess, and it takes both of them to create the universe! I was mind-blown! Not only that, but They are found in nature!

The fact that I could connect with deities who reflected my observations of life and nature, including my own budding womanhood, made absolute sense to me. I couldn't connect with the Jewish G-d because He was, well, male. Upon finding a religion that venerated and honored a Goddess, well, that was the bee's knees to me. It made so much more sense, and I delved into studying Wicca, Witchcraft, and Paganism, reading everything and anything I could get my hands on, which was difficult at that time.

I was 15 when I found Paganism, but I had to keep this hidden from my parents, especially my mother. I kept my books hidden. I did my own ceremonies in the privacy of my room. I was alone in my practice and belief since Beth and I had fallen out. No matter, I continued learning and practicing Witchcraft and Paganism on my own. It was lonely. Even so, I still enjoyed the traditions that I grew up with, but I could not reconcile the gender disparity I felt was at the root of my disaffection for the Jewish religion.

It was after I moved out into my own apartment when I went to university that I eventually found people of like spirit. I came "home" to a religious and spiritual community that accepted me for who I was and not who they wanted me to be. I flourished, but I had to keep it secret from my parents until I felt I couldn't keep such an important aspect of who I was becoming from them. My father nary batted an eye. He accepted it. My mother did not. She was furious. It was the start of the ending of my relationship with her.

In university, my newfound Paganism, specifically Wicca, sent me down a rabbit hole of scholastic discovery. I took courses on ancient near eastern religions and cultures, which introduced me to the Gods and Goddesses of the people who eventually became the Jews. I took courses on world religions, where my love of Judaism became a scholastic interest that I delved into further than any synagogue could provide. I took courses on Goddesses and pagan religions from around the world.

During that time, I also took weekly courses and found a teacher with the Wiccan Church of Canada, all the while participating and absolutely loving their weekly open rituals. It was through that community that I eventually found my husband. I eventually moved away from the WCC, as I craved a long-standing tradition, probably because of my Jewish upbringing. I began my search for Gardnerian Wicca, a tradition I was eventually initiated and elevated into.

My desire to serve my religious community came true, but in a different religion and spiritual practice. My husband and I formed a coven and we also created the Toronto Pagan Pub Moot, which is the second longest running Pagan event in Toronto next to the Wiccan Church of Canada.

I have served my Pagan and Wiccan community for almost thirty years, but I have never stopped being Jewish. It's something that many Pagans and Wiccans have difficulty wrapping their heads around. It is a very different culture than the mainstream culture, and I have found that because of this my outlook on certain aspects of the community is different, as well as how we communicate.

Even when my son was born, I had a bris[199] for him as I felt it was important because then he would be Jewish, and if he wished to follow in that religion then he could easily do so. I received a lot of flak from non-Jewish Pagans and Wiccans for deciding to have my son circumcised for religious reasons.

Throughout my experience with the Pagan and Wiccan community, I have experienced anti-Semitism from others, mainly due to their ignorance on what it is to be Jewish. But those instances are far between and few. It's something Jews learn to live with, unfortunately, and thus I always felt that I was going from the frying pan (Judaism) to the fire (Paganism and Wicca) in terms of creating a target on my back for hateful persons.

Now, as I grow older and have learned so much, with so much more to learn, I have rekindled my love of the Jewish religion, especially of the orthodox practices. Now I now know more about the mysteries of Judaism and how they aren't all that different, except for the one thing that stopped me from continuing to be a practicing Jew: my sex. Had I wanted to learn the Torah and the Talmud, I couldn't.

In the end, I received the highest compliment from my husband's Lubavitch Rabbi cousin for my knowledge of Judaism. He said I could have been a Rebbetzin.[200] Instead, I am a High Priestess.

---

199 Bris, from Yiddish ברית (bris), from Hebrew בְּרִית (barit, "covenant"). https://en.wiktionary.org/wiki/bris

200 Rebbetzin, a female rabbi. https://en.wiktionary.org/wiki/rebbetzin

Thanks

Thanks to all the people who supported me through my spiritual wobble in 2007, especially members of my coven, and my high priestess. Thanks also to the commenters on my blog and the various Pagans, Quakers, Quaker Pagans (especially Cat Chapin-Bishop), Orthodox Christians, Unitarians, and other friends with whom I discussed it.

Thanks to the wonderful contributors to this book, Nick Hanks, Heath, Èlia Viader, Calyx, Jasmin, and Karen—for sharing deeply personal experiences.

Thanks to Mark Townsend for writing the foreword, and for being an inspiration.

Thanks to Amy and Risa, the Missing Witches podcast hosts, for having me on the show, being interested in the book, and introducing me to Jasmin.

Thanks to Lucia Moreno Velo of the Writing Spirituality Podcast for talking about including anecdotes in writing, which inspired me to add some at the start of each chapter of this book.

Thanks to Alex for lending me the Griffith and Griffith book, which was helpful in expanding my thinking in a number of areas.

Huge thanks to my wonderful editors and publishers, Victoria Raschke and keifel agostini, for your support and enthusiasm for the book, and for publishing it. Thanks to Jennifer Stevens for proofreading and editing.

Thanks to my lovely husband, Bob, for being you, and my coveners past and present for many wonderful spiritual experiences and friendships.

Thanks to all the people who are out there making religions and spiritual paths safer and more inclusive for marginalized people. And thanks to all those people who have written about their changing spiritual paths, leaving wayfinders for other people in the weird landscape between religions.

Yvonne Aburrow
August 2022

Further reading

In compiling this list of resources, I have tried to avoid books and articles that are trying to persuade people to leave one spiritual tradition in favor of another. I have tried to provide an overview of each tradition, together with accounts of leaving it or becoming disenchanted with it.

All religions

- Daniel Enstedt, Göran Larsson, and Teemu T. Mantsinen, editors (2019), *The Handbook of Leaving Religion.* Brill Handbooks on Contemporary Religion, Volume 18. ISBN: 978-9004331471 (eBook); 978-9004330924 (hardback)
  Available for download: brill.com/view/title/33911

Atheism

- Julian Baggini (2003), *Atheism: A Very Short Introduction.* Oxford University Press, USA.
  ISBN: 978-0192804242.

- Richard Holloway (2000), *Godless Morality: Keeping Religion Out of Ethics.* Canongate Books.
  ISBN: 978-0862419097.

- Martin S Pribble (2013), "Leaving the Tribe: Why I'm no longer part of the online atheism community." *Slate*, 12 December 2013. slate.com/technology/2013/12/why-im-quitting-the-online-atheism-community.html

Buddhism

- Damien Keown (1996, 2000), *Buddhism: A Very Short Introduction.* Oxford University Press.
  ISBN: 978-0192853868.

- John Horgan (2003), "Buddhist Retreat: Why I gave up on finding my religion." *Slate*, 12 February 2003. slate.com/culture/2003/02/why-i-ditched-buddhism.html

Christianity

- Diarmaid MacCulloch (2011), *Christianity: The First Three Thousand Years*. Penguin Publishing Group.
  ISBN: 978-0143118695.

- Kallistos Ware (1995), *The Orthodox Way*. SVS Press.
  ISBN: 978-0913836583.

- Marlene Winell (2006), *Leaving the Fold: A Guide for Former Fundamentalists and Others Leaving Their Religion*. Apocryphile Press.
  ISBN: 978-1933993232.

- Jamie Lee Finch (2019), *You Are Your Own: A Reckoning with the Religious Trauma of Evangelical Christianity.* Independently published.
  ISBN: 978-1075246302.

Cults

- Isaac Bonewits (1979, 2008), "The Advanced Bonewits' Cult Danger Evaluation Frame" (Version 2.7). NeoPagan.net. www.neopagan.net/ABCDEF.html

- RationalWiki (2021), "Cult." RationalWiki. rationalwiki.org/wiki/Cult

- Spiritual Abuse Resources, a program of the International Cultic Studies Association (ICSA) www.spiritualabuseresources.com/

- Amanda Montell (2021), *Cultish: The Language of Fanaticism.* Harper Wave.

Islam

- Karen Armstrong (2000), *Islam: A Short History.* Modern Library.
  ISBN: 978-0679640400.

- Reza Aslan (2011), *No god but God: The Origins, Evolution, and Future of Islam.* Random House.
  ISBN: 978-0812982442.

- Fiyaz Mughal, Aliyah Saleem (Author), *Leaving Faith Behind: The journeys and perspectives of people who have chosen to leave Islam.* Darton Longman & Todd Ltd.
  ISBN: 978-0232533644.

Judaism

- Simon Schama (2014), *The Story of the Jews: Finding the Words 1000 BC-1492 AD.* Ecco.
  ISBN: 978-0060539184.

- Simon Schama (2017), *Belonging: The Story of the Jews 1492-1900.* Allen Lane.
  ISBN: 978-0670068289.

- Schneur Zalman Newfield (2020), *Degrees of Separation: Identity Formation While Leaving Ultra-Orthodox Judaism.* Temple University Press. ISBN: 978-1439918968.

- Ezra Cappell (2020), *Off the Derech: Leaving Orthodox Judaism.* State University of New York Press.
  ISBN: 978-1438477244.

Monotheism—general and comparative

- Karen Armstrong (1994), *A History of God: The 4,000-Year Quest of Judaism, Christianity and Islam.* Ballantine Books.
  ISBN: 978-0345384560.

- Karen Armstrong (2007), *The Bible: The Biography.* Atlantic Books. ISBN: 978-1843543961.

- Reza Aslan (2010), *Beyond Fundamentalism: Confronting Religious Extremism in the Age of Globalization.* Random House. ISBN: 978-0812978308.

- Joseph Campbell (1962), *Oriental Mythology (The Masks of God, Volume 2),* reissued 2021.
  New World Library. ISBN: 978-1608687282.

Paganism

- Prudence Jones (undated), "Introduction to Paganism." *The Pagan Federation.* www.paganfed.org/paganism/
- Patti Wigington (2019), "Intro to Paganism: A 13 Step Study Guide." *Learn Religions.* www.learnreligions.com/intro-to-paganism-step-by-step-study-guide-4006913
- Yvonne Aburrow (2015-2021), "A Beginner's Guide to Paganism" (blog series). *Dowsing for Divinity.* dowsingfordivinity.com/category/a-beginners-guide/
- Carl McColman (2005), "After the Magic." *Beliefnet.* www.beliefnet.com/faiths/2005/09/after-the-magic.aspx
- Carl McColman (2019), "Eight Pagan Books by a Christian Author." *AnamChara.* anamchara.com/eight-pagan-books-by-a-christian-author/

Spirituality

- Paul Heelas and Linda Woodhead (2005), *The Spiritual Revolution: Why Religion is Giving Way to Spirituality.* Wiley.
- Carl McColman (2008), S*pirituality: A Post-Modern and Interfaith Approach to Cultivating a Relationship With God.* ISBN: 978-0979245190.
- David Webster (2012), *Dispirited: How Contemporary Spirituality Makes Us Stupid, Selfish and Unhappy.* Zero Books. ISBN: 978-1846947025.
- Barbara O'Brien (2019), "Spiritual Bypassing: What it is and how to avoid it." *Learn Religions.* www.learnreligions.com/spiritual-bypassing-449505
- Diana Raab (2019), "What Is Spiritual Bypassing?" *Psychology Today.* www.psychologytoday.com/us/blog/the-empowerment-diary/201901/what-is-spiritual-bypassing

Unitarianism / Unitarian Universalism

- Stephen Lingwood, editor (2008), *The Unitarian Life: Voices from the Past and Present.* Lindsey Press. ISBN: 978-0853190769.

- Vernon Marshall (2007), *The Larger View: Unitarians and World Religions.* Lindsey Press. ISBN : 978-0853190745.

- Jerrie Kishpaugh Hildebrand and Shirley Ann Ranck, editors (2017), *Pagan and Earth-Centered Voices in Unitarian Universalism.* Skinner House Books. ISBN: 978-1558967953.

- David Loehr (2005), "Why 'Unitarian Universalism' is Dying." *Journal of Liberal Religion,* Winter 2005. files.meadville.edu/files/resources/why-unitarian-universalism-is-dying.pdf

- Jeanelyse Doran Adams, Earl Koteen, Julia McKay (2006), *"Unitarian Universalism–Staying Alive!"* www.sksm.edu/wp-content/uploads/2014/03/response.pdf

- Anon (2015), "Thinking about leaving UU." *Reddit.* www.reddit.com/r/UUreddit/comments/3fh8bl/thinking_about_leaving_uu/

Getting help with leaving your religion

International resources

- Changing Paths. changingpathsresources.ca
- Faith to Faithless—provides advocacy, public awareness and support for ex-religious people. www.faithtofaithless.com
- International Cultic Studies Association—provides information, education, and help to those adversely affected by or interested in cultic and other high-control groups and relationships. www.icsahome.com
- Recovering from Religion—an international non-profit organization. www.recoveringfromreligion.org
- RfRx Talks, which take place every Monday evening, feature a wide variety of speakers including survivors of religious abuse, and leading experts in religious trauma recovery, relationships, grieving, and more. recoveringfromreligion.org/rfrx
- SNAP (Survivors Network of those Abused by Priests)— support group for people wounded by religious and institutional authorities (priests, ministers, bishops, deacons, nuns, coaches, teachers, and others). www.snapnetwork.org
- Spiritual Abuse Resources (SAR) www.spiritualabuseresources.com
- The Secular Therapy Project will connect you with a therapist who will offer only evidence-based and nonreligious treatment. www.recoveringfromreligion.org/the-secular-therapy
- The Tyler Clementi Foundation: True Faith Doesn't Bully tylerclementi.org/true-faith/
- Beyond Ex-gay Resources. beyondexgay.com

In the USA and Canada

- Footsteps—a non-profit organization which supports people leaving Haredi or Hasidic Jewish communities in the USA. www.footstepsorg.org

- Indian Residential School Survivors Society—a website for Indigenous survivors of residential schools, also known as industrial schools. www.irsss.ca

- What is Spiritual Abuse? [National Domestic Violence Hotline] (US) www.thehotline.org/resources/what-is-spiritual-abuse/

In the UK

- Checklist of cult characteristics— www.icsahome.com/articles/characteristics

- Gillie Jenkinson (2016), Freeing the authentic self: phases of recovery and growth from an abusive cult experience. PhD thesis, University of Nottingham. eprints.nottingham.ac.uk/37507/

- Gillie Jenkinson (2019), Out in the World: Post-Cult Recovery, Therapy Today. www.academia.edu/38689948/ Out_in_the_World_Post-Cult_Recovery

- Gillie Jenkinson (forthcoming), Walking Free from the Trauma of Coercive, Cultic and Spiritual Abuse: A Workbook for Recovery and Growth. Routledge.

- Hope Valley Counselling resources: www.hopevalleycounselling.com/resources

- The House of Survivors—a website for survivors of spiritual abuse and clerical abuse in the Church of England. houseofsurvivors.org

- To Think Again—Reclaiming lives from coercive control and psychological abuse in destructive cults and relationships. www.tothinkagain.co.uk

Bibliography

- *Hávamál: The Words of Odin the High One from the Elder or Poetic Edda* (Sæmund's Edda) translated by Olive Bray and edited by D. L. Ashliman, sites.pitt.edu/~dash/havamal.html
- Catholics for Choice. https://www.catholicsforchoice.org/
- European Academy on Religion and Society (2021), *Breaking the silence: Awareness of spiritual abuse in UK religious communities.* europeanacademyofreligionandsociety. com/news/awareness-of-spiritual-abuse-in-uk-religious-communities/
- Human Rights Campaign: *Stances of Faiths on LGBTQ Issues: Islam–Sunni and Shi'a.* www.hrc.org/resources/stances-of-faiths-on-lgbt-issues-islam
- Jews for Abortion Access. www.jewsforabortionaccess.org/
- Manchester College Oxford Chapel Society (2022), *The Chapel.* https://www.ukunitarians.org.uk/oxford/chapel.htm
- Luke 15:11-32, New Living Translation. Bible Gateway. www.biblegateway.com/passage/?search=Luke%2015%3A11-32&version=NLT
- Pagan and Heathen Symposium (2015), *Pagan and Heathen Symposium Code of Conduct.* pagansymposium.org/code.html
- Point of Pride (2020), *A Trans Day of Visibility Guided Meditation.* www.pointofpride.org/blog/a-trans-day-of-visibility-guided-meditation
- Sharon Presley (2018), "Neither Gods Nor Masters: 19th Century American Women of Freethought, Part 1." *Libertarianism.* www.libertarianism.org/columns/neither-gods-nor-masters-19th-century-american-women-freethought-part-1

- Psalm 91:4, New Living Translation. Bible Gateway. www.biblegateway.com/passage/?search=Psalm+91%3A1-4&version=NLT

- "Quotes on Ritual, Ceremony & Awe." Compiled by Jen at *Ceremonial Musings.* smallcirclesceremonies.com/2021/12/20/quotes-on-ritual-ceremony-awe/

- Religious Coalition for Reproductive Choice rcrc.org/

- Spiritual Abuse Resources (SAR) www.spiritualabuseresources.com

- *Signs of Spiritual Abuse,* by WebMD Editorial Contributors. Medically reviewed by Dan Brennan, M.D., on December 01, 2020. www.webmd.com/mental-health/signs-spiritual-abuse

- The Order of Bards, Ovates, and Druids. druidry.org/

- The Religious Society of Friends (1995-2022), *Quaker faith & practice* (Fifth edition). Chapter 1: "Advices and queries," item 7. qfp.quaker.org.uk/passage/1-02/

- The United Church of Canada—*Gender, Sexuality, and Orientation.* united-church.ca/community-and-faith/being-community/gender-sexuality-and-orientation

- The Final Report of the Truth and Reconciliation Commission of Canada (2015). nctr.ca/records/reports/

- Would Jesus Discriminate? wouldjesusdiscriminate.org/

- Queer Pagan Reading List—*Dowsing for Divinity* dowsingfordivinity.com/queer-pagan-reading-list/

- Yvonne Aburrow (2008), "Do Pagans see their beliefs as compatible with science?" MA thesis, Bath Spa University. hcommons.org/deposits/item/hc:20905

- Yvonne Aburrow (2008), "Theoretical models of Paganism." *The Stroppy Rabbit.* stroppyrabbit.blogspot.com/2008/12/theoretical-models-of-paganism.html

- Yvonne Aburrow (2010), "What is liberal religion?" *The Stroppy Rabbit*. stroppyrabbit.blogspot.com/2010/07/what-is-liberal-religion.html

- Yvonne Aburrow (2011), "A Wiccan perspective on good and evil." *Theologies of Immanence Wiki*. pagantheologies.pbworks.com/w/page/13621957/A%20Wiccan%20perspective%20on%20good%20and%20evil

- Yvonne Aburrow (2011), *Dual-Faith Practice*. hcommons.org/deposits/item/hc:20907

- Yvonne Aburrow (2012), "Fabeness to Gloria in the highest, and on earth peace, bona will toward homies." *Polari Magazine*. www.polarimagazine.com/oralhistory/fabeness-gloria-highest-earth-peace-bona-homies/

- Yvonne Aburrow (2012), *Many Names*. Lulu. www.goodreads.com/book/show/22568443-many-names

- Yvonne Aburrow (2013), "The foundation of Pagan ethics." *Dowsing for Divinity*. dowsingfordivinity.com/2013/04/16/foundation-of-pagan-ethics/

- Yvonne Aburrow (2013), "What is cultural appropriation?" *Dowsing for Divinity*. dowsingfordivinity.com/2013/03/25/cultural-appropriation/

- Yvonne Aburrow (2014), "Pagan leadership." *Dowsing for Divinity*. dowsingfordivinity.com/2014/07/11/pagan-leadership/

- Yvonne Aburrow (2014), "Pagan Prayer." *Dowsing for Divinity*. dowsingfordivinity.com/2014/03/12/pagan-prayer/

- Yvonne Aburrow (2014), "Wiccanate Privilege and Polytheist Wiccans." *Dowsing for Divinity*. dowsingfordivinity.com/2014/03/10/polytheist-wiccans/

- Yvonne Aburrow (2014), "Your mountain is not my mountain and that's just fine." *Dowsing for Divinity*. dowsingfordivinity.com/2014/03/11/mountains/

- Yvonne Aburrow (2014), *All acts of love and pleasure: inclusive Wicca.* Avalonia Books.

- Yvonne Aburrow (2015), "Fraudulent and Unethical Groups." *Gardnerian Wicca.* british-wicca.com/warnings/

- Yvonne Aburrow (2015), "Paganism for Beginners: Finding a Group." *Dowsing for Divinity.* dowsingfordivinity.com/2015/07/30/finding-a-group/

- Yvonne Aburrow (2015), "Paganism for Beginners: Group Dynamics." *Dowsing for Divinity.* dowsingfordivinity.com/2015/09/14/group-dynamics/

- Yvonne Aburrow (2015), "Paganism for Beginners: Values." *Dowsing for Divinity.* dowsingfordivinity.com/2015/06/08/paganism-for-beginners-values/

- Yvonne Aburrow (2015), "Relational Polytheism: Standing Beside the Gods." *Dowsing for Divinity.* dowsingfordivinity.com/2015/08/24/relational-polytheism-standing-beside-the-gods/

- Yvonne Aburrow (2015), "What Color is your Witchcraft?' *Dowsing for Divinity.* dowsingfordivinity.com/2015/07/18/what-colour-is-your-witchcraft/

- Yvonne Aburrow (2015), "Why Pagans Don't Proselytize or Evangelize." *Dowsing for Divinity.* dowsingfordivinity.com/2015/06/19/why-pagans-dont-evangelise/

- Yvonne Aburrow (2016), "Binary Thinking and Dealing with Abuse." *Dowsing for Divinity.* dowsingfordivinity.com/2016/09/16/binary-thinking-and-dealing-with-abuse/

- Yvonne Aburrow (2016), "Grounding and Centering." *Dowsing for Divinity.* dowsingfordivinity.com/2016/01/06/embodied-spirituality-grounding-and-centering/

- Yvonne Aburrow (2016), "The Sit Spot." *Dowsing for Divinity.* dowsingfordivinity.com/2016/01/10/the-sit-spot/

- Yvonne Aburrow (2017), "Triple Goddesses." *Dowsing for Divinity.*
  dowsingfordivinity.com/2017/02/05/triple-goddesses/

- Yvonne Aburrow (2018), "Coming Out: An Act of Truth." *Dowsing for Divinity.* dowsingfordivinity.com/2018/10/26/ coming-out-an-act-of-truth/

- Yvonne Aburrow (2018), "Totalizing Systems." *Dowsing for Divinity.*
  dowsingfordivinity.com/2018/02/25/totalising-systems/

- Yvonne Aburrow (2018), "What Are Ethics Based On?" *Dowsing for Divinity.* dowsingfordivinity.com/2018/10/25/ what-are-ethics-based-on/

- Yvonne Aburrow (2020), *Basics of the Craft.*
  youtu.be/8xJtRX6B0YI

- Yvonne Aburrow (2020), *Dark Mirror: The Inner Work of Witchcraft.* 2nd edition. Published by the Doreen Valiente Foundation in association with the Centre for Pagan Studies.

- Yvonne Aburrow (2020), *The Night Journey: Witchcraft as Transformation.* 2nd edition. Published by the Doreen Valiente Foundation in association with the Centre for Pagan Studies.

- Yvonne Aburrow (2021), "The Threefold Law." *Dowsing for Divinity.* dowsingfordivinity.com/2021/02/14/the-threefold-law/

- Yvonne Aburrow (2021), "The Wiccan Rede." *Dowsing for Divinity.* dowsingfordivinity.com/2021/02/15/the-wiccan-rede/

- Yvonne Aburrow (2021), "Unexamined Baggage." *Dowsing for Divinity.*
  dowsingfordivinity.com/2021/12/29/unexamined-baggage/

- Yvonne Aburrow (2021), "Nature, Tradition, and Ancestors." *Dowsing for Divinity.* dowsingfordivinity. com/2021/11/26/nature-tradition-and-ancestors/

- Herbert Anderson, Edward Foley (2001), *Mighty Stories, Dangerous Rituals: Weaving Together the Human and the Divine.* Jossey-Bass.

- Karen Armstrong (1994), *A History of God: The 4,000-Year Quest of Judaism, Christianity and Islam.* Random House Publishing.

- Richard Attenborough (1982), *Gandhi.* en.wikipedia.org/wiki/Gandhi_(film)

- Kristin Aune (2009), "Between Subordination and Sympathy: Evangelical Christians, Masculinity and Gay Sexuality." *Contemporary Christianity and LGBT Sexualities,* 1st Edition, Routledge.

- John Beckett (2015), "Escaping Fundamentalism." *Under the ancient oaks.* www.patheos.com/blogs/johnbeckett/2015/09/escaping-fundamentalism.html

- John Beckett (2020), "Exorcizing Fundamentalism: The Steps on my Journey." *Under the ancient oaks.* www.patheos.com/blogs/johnbeckett/2020/04/exorcising-fundamentalism-the-steps-on-my-journey.html

- Al Billings (2007), "Religious Faiths as Ex-Girlfriends." *Arcanology.* web.archive.org/web/20070627031106/www.arcanology.com/?p=1521

- Isaac Bonewits, *Advanced Bonewits' Cult Danger Evaluation Frame,* www.neopagan.net/ABCDEF.html

- Erika Bornman (2022), *Mission of Malice: My Exodus from KwaSizaBantu.* Penguin Random House. https://www.litnet.co.za/major-international-award-for-erika-bornman-author-of-mission-of-malice/

- Duane Brayboy (2016), "Two Spirits, One Heart, Five Genders." *Indian Country Today.* indiancountrytoday.com/archive/two-spirits-one-heart-five-genders

- Andrew J Brown (2009), "Another Unorthodox Lecture—Or What On Earth Is the Minister Up To?" *Caute: Making Footprints, not Blueprints.* andrewjbrown.blogspot.com/2009/05/another-unorthodox-lecture-or-what-on.html

- Andrew J Brown (2009), "The Flower Communion—Hard Particularities with Profound Love and Trust." *Caute: Making Footprints, not Blueprints.* andrewjbrown.blogspot.com/2009/06/flower-communion-hard-particularities.html

- Andrew J Brown (2014), "The reflection worth indulging doesn't know where it is going—Leaving behind only footprints and never blueprints." *Caute: Making Footprints, not Blueprints.* andrewjbrown.blogspot.com/2014/07/the-reflection-worth-indulging-doesnt.html

- Bat Bruja (2018), *Godspouse 101: FAQs and My Experiences.* batbruja.wordpress.com/2018/08/17/godspouse-101-faqs-and-my-experiences/

- Christopher Bunn (2013), "The radical evangelical whose support for gay marriage is rocking his field." *The Guardian.* www.theguardian.com/commentisfree/belief/2013/jan/23/evangelical-gay-marriage-steve-chalke

- Star Bustamonte (2019), "Pagans react to new abortion bans." *The Wild Hunt.* https://wildhunt.org/2019/05/pagans-react-to-new-abortion-bans.html

- Jack Chanek (June 2022), "'Traditional' versus 'Reform' Gardnerians." youtu.be/6Y0_s31Dmhk

- Cat Chapin-Bishop (2017), "Quaker and Pagan Means What, Exactly?" *Quaker Pagan Reflections.* quakerpagan.blogspot.com/2017/10/quaker-and-pagan-means-what-exactly.html

- Cat Chapin-Bishop (2007), "Quaker, Pagan, Quakerpagan or Paganquaker: Moving Beyond the Cool Kids' Table." *Quaker Pagan Reflections.* quakerpagan.blogspot. com/2007/05/quaker-pagan-quakerpagan-or-paganquaker. html

- Peter Chapin-Bishop (2007), "Membership and Identity." *Quaker Pagan Reflections.* quakerpagan.blogspot. com/2007/05/on-membership-peter.html

- Adryan Corcione (2022), *The FOLX Transgender Meditation Guide: How to Meditate When You Can't Sit Still.* www.folxhealth.com/library/transgender-meditation

- Edwards, D. N. (2005), "The archaeology of religion." In: Diaz-Andreu, M., Lucy, S., Babić, S., and Edwards, D. N., eds. *The Archaeology of Identity. London and New York: Routledge.* Page 116.

- Gus di Zerega (2012), *Encountering Pagan Deities.* www.patheos.com/pagan/encountering-pagan-deities-gus-dizerega-08-24-2012

- Thora Drakos (2018), "On My Years in CAYA Coven." *Dreams from the West Wind* tadrakos.wordpress. com/2018/03/23/on-my-years-in-caya-coven/ See also https://rabbittestimony.blogspot.com/

- European Academy on Religion and Society. europeanacademyofreligionandsociety.com/news/awareness-of-spiritual-abuse-in-uk-religious-communities/

- Taylor Ellwood and Shauna Aura Knight, editors (2016), *The Pagan Leadership Anthology.* Megalithica Books.

- River Enodian (2018), "Bashing Wicca As A Polytheist or Occultist Doesn't Make You Cool and You Know Nothing About It Besides." *Tea Addicted Witch.* www.patheos.com/ blogs/teaaddictedwitch/2018/06/bashing-wicca-doesnt-make-you-cool/

- Tony Enos (2018), "8 Things You Should Know About Two Spirit People." *Indian Country Today.* indiancountrytoday.com/archive/8-misconceptions-things-know-two-spirit-people

- Nicholas Epley, Benjamin A. Converse, Alexa Delbosc, George A. Monteleone, and John T. Cacioppo (2009), "Believers' estimates of God's beliefs are more egocentric than estimates of other people's beliefs." *PNAS.* www.pnas.org/doi/10.1073/pnas.0908374106

- Harry Emerson Fosdick (1956), *The Living of These Days; An Autobiography.*

- Clarissa Pinkola Estés (1992, 1995), *Women Who Run With the Wolves.* Ballantine Books.

- Ex-Quiverfull life stories, *QF & Abusive Religion Survivor resources.* quiverfullmyblog.wordpress.com/ex-quiverfull-life-stories-survivor-resources/

- Kimberly French (2007), "Carolyn McDade's Spirit of Life: Unitarian Universalism's most beloved song, the woman who wrote it, and the communities that sustain her spirit." *UU World.* www.uuworld.org/articles/carolyn-mcdade-spirit-life

- Rebecca Goldstein (2011), *36 Arguments for the Existence of God: A Work of Fiction.* Vintage.

- Wendy Griffin (2002), "Reviewed Work(s): Earthly Bodies, Magical Selves: Contemporary Pagans and the Search for Community by Sarah M. Pike'. *The Journal of Religion,* 82 (3), Pages 499–501.

- James L. Griffith and Melissa Elliott Griffith (2002), *Encountering the Sacred in Psychotherapy: How to Talk with People about their Spiritual Lives.* New York: Guilford Press.

- Ronald L. Grimes (1982), *Beginnings in Ritual Studies.* University Press of America.

- Diaa Hadid, Abdul Sattar (2019), "Pakistan Wants To Reform Madrassas. Experts Advise Fixing Public Education First." *NPR*. www.npr.org/2019/01/10/682917845/pakistan-wants-to-reform-madrassas-experts-advise-fixing-public-education-first

- Amy Hale (2019), "The Pagan and Occult Fascist Connection and How to Fix It." medium.com/@amyhale93/the-pagan-and-occult-fascist-connection-and-how-to-fix-it-d338c32ee4e6

- Judy Harrow (2002), *Spiritual Mentoring: A Pagan Guide*. Toronto: ECW Press, pages 113-125.

- Judy Harrow (undated), "Prayers from an Earth-Centered Spirituality." *Religious Coalition for Reproductive Choice*. rcrc.org/prayer-from-earth-centered-spirituality/

- Paul Heelas and Linda Woodhead (2005), *The Spiritual Revolution: Why Religion is Giving Way to Spirituality*. Wiley.

- Phil Hine: Queer Magic Interview. youtu.be/rRwIyRKqIKo

- Christine Hoff-Kraemer (2013), "Three Legs on the Pagan Cauldron, or Must Pagans Be Polytheists?" *Dowsing for Divinity*. dowsingfordivinity.com/2013/01/11/must-pagans-be-polytheists/

- Christine Hoff-Kraemer and Yvonne Aburrow, editors (2016), *Pagan Consent Culture. Building Communities of Empathy and Autonomy*. Asphodel Press. www.paganconsentculture.com

- Richard Holloway (2013), *Godless Morality: Keeping Religion Out of Ethics*. Canongate Books.

- Ronald Hutton (1999, 2019), *Triumph of the Moon: A History of Modern Pagan Witchcraft*. Oxford University Press.

- Gillie Jenkinson (2019), "Out in the World: Post-Cult Recovery." *Therapy Today*. www.academia.edu/38689948/Out_in_the_World_Post-Cult_Recovery

- Emma Jones (2017), "Origins, function of modesty in fashion warrant critique." *Miscellany News.* miscellanynews. org/2017/04/12/opinions/origins-function-of-modesty-in-fashion-warrant-critique/

- Kelly (2011), "Quotes and Idioms." *Red Leopard.* www.redleopard.com/2011/05/quotes-and-idioms/

- Mackenzi Kingdon (2017), "Shame and Silence: Recognizing Spiritual Abuse." *Good Therapy.* www.goodtherapy.org/blog/shame-and-silence-recognizing-spiritual-abuse-0201175

- Mackenzi Kingdon, MA, LMH. "Religious Trauma Syndrome and Faith Transitions." *Restoration Counseling.* www.restorationcounselingseattle.com/religious-trauma-transitions

- Michael D. Langone (2015), "Characteristics Associated with Cultic Groups—Revised." *ICSA Today,* Vol. 6, No. 3, 2015, 10. www.icsahome.com/articles/characteristics

- John Lennon, *Imagine.* genius.com/John-lennon-imagine-lyrics

- C.S. Lewis, *Prince Caspian.* www.goodreads.com/work/quotes/3348636-prince-caspian?page=5

- Robert Jay Lifton (1961), *Thought Reform and the Psychology of Totalism: A Study of 'brainwashing' in China.* Norton.

- Jeff Lilly (2008), "The Future of Neopaganism in the West, Part I: Prestige and Stigma." *Druid Journal.* druidjournal. net/2008/03/19/the-future-of-neopaganism-in-the-west-part-i-prestige-and-stigma/

- Jeff Lilly (2008), "The Future of Neopaganism in the West, Part II: Going Organic." *Druid Journal.* druidjournal. net/2008/03/27/the-future-of-neopaganism-in-the-west-part-ii-going-organic/

- Tanya M. Luhrmann (1989, 1991), *Persuasions of the Witch's Craft: Ritual Magic in Contemporary England*. Harvard University Press.

- Diarmaid MacCulloch (2011), *Christianity: The First Three Thousand Years*. Penguin Publishing Group.

- Carolyn McDade (1981), "Song of Community." From the album *Rain Upon Dry Land* (1984). hamiltonsings.ca/wp-content/uploads/2020/09/song-of-community_Carolyn_McDade.pdf

- Hemant Mehta (2022), "A Gen Z shock: Among Zoomers with no religion, women outnumber men." *Only Sky*. onlysky.media/hemant-mehta/a-gen-z-shock-among-zoomers-with-no-religion-women-outnumber-men/

- Nancy Mills (1988), "The Promise of a 'Miracle,' a Tragic Tale of Faith Healing." *Los Angeles Times*. www.latimes.com/archives/la-xpm-1988-05-17-ca-2829-story.html

- Amanda Montell (2021), *Cultish: The Language of Fanaticism*. Harper Wave.

- Charlie Murphy (undated), *Burning Times*. www.christymoore.com/lyrics/burning-times/

- Liz Opp (2007), "Membership and Identity." *The Good Raised Up*. thegoodraisedup.blogspot.com/2007/04/membership-and-identity.html

- Patchwork Crow (2018), *Thinking about personal deities*. patchworkcrow.wordpress.com/2018/11/11/thinking-about-personal-deities

- Porchlight Law (undated), *Co-parenting with Religious Differences*. porchlight.law/co-parenting-with-religious-differences/

- Religion & Ethics News Weekly (2000), *Lewis Rambo Extended Interview,* www.pbs.org/wnet/ religionandethics/2000/11/10/november-10-2000-lewis-rambo-extended-interview/13744/

- RationalWiki: *Cult.* rationalwiki.org/wiki/Cult

- Rabbi Danya Ruttenberg (2022), "My Religion Makes Me Pro-Abortion." *The Atlantic.* www.theatlantic.com/ family/archive/2022/06/judaism-abortion-rights-religious-freedom/661264/

- Harriet Sherwood (2022), "A 'tumultuous journey' from ultra-Orthodox school to physics degree." *The Guardian.* www.theguardian.com/world/2022/jul/22/a-tumultuous-journey-from-ultra-orthodox-school-to-physics-degree

- E. T. Smith, 'Quotes from Beyond the Gender Binary." *The Commons Social Change Library.* commonslibrary.org/quotes-from-beyond-the-gender-binary

- Muriel Strode (1903), "Wind-Wafted Wild Flowers." *The Open Court:* Vol. 1903 : Issue 8, Article 5. Available at: opensiuc.lib.siu.edu/ocj/vol1903/iss8/5

- Detra Thomas (2022), post 1 of 15 on *Humans of New York* @humansofny, Instagram. www.instagram.com/p/Celco-vuteS/

- JRR Tolkien, 'The Road Goes Ever On (song)." *Tolkien Gateway.* tolkiengateway.net/wiki/The_Road_Goes_Ever_On_(song)

- Peterson Toscano (2013), "Ex-Gay Harm—Let Me Count the Ways." *Beyond Ex-Gay.* beyondexgay.com/article/harm1.html and responses to the above: beyondexgay.com/article/harmstories.html

- Peterson Toscano (2017), *The challenges of coming out from conversion therapy.* petersontoscano.com/challenges-coming-conversion-therapy

- Mark Townsend, *Independent Minister*. www.marktownsendministry.co.uk/independent-minister.html

- Polly Toynbee (1983), "Interview with former nun Karen Armstrong." *The Guardian*. www.theguardian.com/world/2015/sep/12/karen-armstrong-nun-interview-polly-toynbee-1983

- Richard Turner (2022), "Identifying abusive cults." *To think again*. www.tothinkagain.co.uk/identifying-a-cult

- Doreen Valiente (1957), *The Charge of the Goddess*. www.doreenvaliente.com/doreen-valiente-Doreen_Valiente_Poetry-11.php

- Laurens van der Post (1978), *A Far-Off Place*. Mariner Books.

- John Walker (2012), "The Bible on Women in Church—An Update." *John Walker's Electronic House*. botherer.org/2012/11/24/the-bible-on-women-in-church-an-update/

- John Walker (2012), "Why the Argument Against Women in Church Leadership Is Theological Rubbish." *John Walker's Electronic House*. botherer.org/2012/11/21/why-the-argument-against-women-in-church-leadership-is-theological-rubbish/

- Carvell Wallace (2018), "Should I Let My Husband Drag My Kids to Church?" *Slate*. slate.com/human-interest/2018/04/parenting-advice-on-a-family-with-one-churchgoing-parent-and-one-who-dislikes-organized-religion.html

- Jason Warick (2022), "Exorcisms, violent discipline and other abuse alleged by former students of private Sask. Christian school." *CBC Investigates*. www.cbc.ca/news/canada/saskatoon/abuse-alleged-former-students-of-private-christian-school-1.6532329

- Patti Wigington (2018), "The Rule of Three: The Law of Threefold Return." *Learn Religions*. www.learnreligions.com/rule-of-three-2562822

- Patti Wigington (2019), "Charge of the Goddess: History and Variations." *Learn Religions.* www.learnreligions.com/charge-of-the-goddess-history-and-variations-4151704

- Patti Wigington (2019), "How Do Pagans and Wiccans Feel About Abortion?' *Learn Religions.* www.learnreligions.com/abortion-in-paganism-and-wicca-2561713

- Wikipedia: *Conversion Therapy: Legal status* en.wikipedia.org/wiki/Conversion_therapy#Legal_status

- Wikipedia: *Exvangelical.* en.wikipedia.org/wiki/Exvangelical

- Wikipedia: *LGBT-affirming religious groups: Shintoism* en.wikipedia.org/wiki/LGBT-affirming_religious_groups#Shintoism

- Wikipedia: *Medical views of conversion therapy,* en.wikipedia.org/wiki/Medical_views_of_conversion_therapy

- Wikipedia: *Purity ring.* en.wikipedia.org/wiki/Purity_ring

- Earl Morse Wilbur (1945), *A History of Unitarianism: In Transylvania, England, and America.* Beacon Press.

- John Wills (2012), "Symbel: The Heathen Drinking Ritual?' *Odroerir*, Vol.2 www.academia.edu/2060520/Symbel_The_Heathen_Drinking_Ritual

- Kim Willsher (2022), "Pupils at Jewish school in France taken into care after abuse allegations." *The Guardian.* www.theguardian.com/world/2022/feb/02/pupils-ultra-orthodox-jewish-beth-yossef-school-france-taken-into-care-after-abuse-allegations

- Woodburne, A.W. (1927), "The Indian Appreciation of Jesus." *The Journal of Religion*, 7 (1)., pp. 43-55. www.journals.uchicago.edu/doi/abs/10.1086/480633

- Michael York (2008), "A Pagan Defence of Theism." *Theologies of Immanence Wiki.* pagantheologies.pbworks.com/w/page/13621955/A%20Pagan%20defence%20of%20theism

Playlist

- Losing My Religion—R.E.M.
- Should I Stay or Should I Go—The Clash
- I Want To Break Free—Queen
- I Wish I Knew How It Would Feel To Be Free—Nina Simone
- Imagine—John Lennon
- Running Up That Hill (A Deal With God)—Kate Bush
- Hallelujah—Leonard Cohen
- Fanfare for the Common Man—Aaron Copland
- Cross Road Blues—Robert Johnson
- Bridge Over Troubled Water—Simon & Garfunkel
- Ashokan Farewell—Jay Ungar
- Burning Times—Charlie Murphy/Christy Moore
- The Christians and the Pagans—Dar Williams
- Blue Boat Home—Peter Mayer
- Mother Spirit, Father Spirit—Norbert Čapek
- All Will Be Well—Meg Barnhouse
- Spirit of Life—Carolyn McDade
- Homeward Bound—Simon & Garfunkel
- Haleluye—Daniel Kahn
- Solsbury Hill—Peter Gabriel
- Hymn to Her—KT Tunstall/The Pretenders
- Nature Boy—Eden Ahbez/Ella Fitzgerald

open.spotify.com/playlist/3tJzhySyepW0l6QMx5EdQQ

Made in the USA
Las Vegas, NV
12 May 2024

89864146R00174